Imprisonment of the Elderly and Death in Custody

Over the past few decades, there has been a sharp increase in the number of elderly prisoners, and hence a rise in the number of prisoners dying in custody. In this book, Khechumyan questions whether respect for human dignity would justify releasing older and seriously ill prisoners. He also examines the normative justifications which could limit the administration of the imprisonment of the elderly and seriously ill.

Khechumyan argues that factors such as a prisoner's age and health could alter the balance between the legitimate goals of punishment, rendering the continued imprisonment 'grossly disproportionate'. To address these issues, Articles 3 and 5 of the European Convention of Human Rights are extensively examined.

This book is a valuable resource for academics, researchers and policy-makers working in the fields of Criminal Justice, Human Rights Law, and Gerontology.

Aleksandr Khechumyan is a researcher at the Max Planck Institute for Foreign and International Criminal Law, Germany. He holds an LL.M. degree in International Human Rights Law from the University of Essex, UK, and Dr.jur. degree from the University of Freiburg, Germany. Khechumyan has extensive practical experience working in both governmental and non-governmental sectors. He has published articles in such journals as *European Human Rights Law Review*, *European Journal on Criminal Policy and Research*, *Policing: An International Journal of Police Strategies and Management*, and *International Journal of Comparative and Applied Criminal Justice*.

Imprisonment of the Elderly and Death in Custody

The Right to Review

Aleksandr Khechumyan

Routledge
Taylor & Francis Group
LONDON AND NEW YORK

First published 2018
by Routledge

2 Park Square, Milton Park, Abingdon, Oxfordshire OX14 4RN
52 Vanderbilt Avenue, New York, NY 10017

Routledge is an imprint of the Taylor & Francis Group, an informa business

First issued in paperback 2020

British Library Cataloguing in Publication Data
A catalogue record for this book is available from the British Library

Library of Congress Cataloging in Publication Data
Names: Khechumyan, Aleksandr, author.
Title: Imprisonment of the elderly and death in custody : the right to review / Aleksandr Khechumyan.
Description: New York, NY : Routledge, 2018. | Includes bibliographical references and index.
Identifiers: LCCN 2017050765| ISBN 9781138554832 | ISBN 9781351371230 (web pdf) | ISBN 9781351371223 (epub) | ISBN 9781351371216 (kindle)
Subjects: LCSH: Older prisoners--United States--Medical care. | Older prisoners--European Union countries--Medical care. | Appellate procedure--United States | Appellate procedure--European Union countries. | Older prisoners--United States--Death. | Older prisoners--European Union countries--Death. | Sentences (Criminal procedure)--United States | Sentences (Criminal procedure)--European Union countries.
Classification: LCC K5519 .K54 2018 | DDC 344.2403/56--dc23
LC record available at https://lccn.loc.gov/2017050765

ISBN: 978-1-138-55483-2 (hbk)
ISBN: 978-0-367-59168-7 (pbk)

Typeset in ITC Galliard by
Servis Filmsetting Ltd, Stockport, Cheshire

To my family

Erstgutachter:	Prof. Dr. Dr. h.c. mult. Hans-Jörg Albrecht
Zweitgutachter:	Prof. Dr. Roland Hefendehl
Tag der Mündliche Prüfung:	31 Januar 2017
Dekan:	Prof. Dr. Boris P. Paal, M.Jur.(Oxford)
Dissertationsort:	Freiburg im Breisgau
Erscheinungsjahr:	2017

Table of Cases

European Court of Human Rights

A and others v United Kingdom [GC] ECHR 2009-II 137
Abdulaziz, Cabales and Balkandali v UK App no 9214/80; 9473/81; 9474/81 (ECtHR, 28 May 1985)
Aleksanyan v Russia no. 46468/06 (ECtHR, 22 December 2008)
Amuur v France ECHR 1996-III 850
Aquilina v Malta [GC] ECHR 1999-III 225
Assenov and Others v Bulgaria ECHR 1998-VIII
Bekos and Koutropoulos v Greece ECHR 2005-XIII 1
Benjamin and Wilson v United Kingdom App no 28212/95 (ECtHR, 26 September 2002)
Bensaid v United Kingdom ECHR 2001-I 303
Bozano v France Series A no 111
Brogan and ors v United Kingdom (1989) Series A no 152-B
Brown v United Kingdom (dec.) App no 968/04 (ECtHR, 26 October 2004)
Brumarescu v Romania ECHR 2001-I 155
Bykov v Russia App no 4378/02 (ECtHR, 10 March 2009).
Cara-Damiani v Italy no 2447/05 (ECtHR, 7 February 2012)
Castravet v Moldova App no 233393/05 (ECtHR, 13 March 2007)
Chahal v United Kingdom (GC) ECHR 1996-V 23
Chaykovskiy v Ukraine App no 2295/06 (ECtHR, 15 October 2009)
Ciulla v Italy (1989) Series A no 148
Clift v United Kingdom [2010] ECHR 11106 (ECtHR)
Conca v Belgium ECHR 2002-I 93
Contrada v Italy (no.2) no. 7509/08 (ECtHR, 11 February 2014)
Corsacov v Moldova App no 18944/02 (ECtHR 4 April 2016)
D.N. v Switzerland [GC] ECHR 2001-III 1.
De Jong, Baljet and Van Den Brink v Netherlands App no 8805/79; 8806/79; 9242/81(ECtHR,22 May 1984).
De Wilde, Ooms and Versyp v Belgium App nos 2832/66; 2835/66; 2899/66 (ECtHR, 18 June 1971).
Denizci and others v Cyprus ECHR 2001-V 225

Dickson v United Kingdom [GC] ECHR 2007-V 99
Dikme v Turkey ECHR 2000-VIII 223
Dougoz v Greece ECHR 2001-II 255.
E v Norway (1990) Series A 181-A
Egmez v Cyprus ECHR 2000-XII 315.
Elci and others v Turkey App nos 23145/93; 25091/94 (ECtHR 13 November 2003).
Enea v Italy [GC] ECHR 2009-IV 163.
Engel v Netherlands App no 5100/71 (ECtHR, 8 June 1976).
Engel v Hungary App no 46857/06 (ECtHR, 20 May 2010).
Farbtuhs v Latvia no. 4672/02 (ECtHR, 2 December 2004).
Farmakopoulos v Belgium (1992) A 235-A
Ganusauskas v Lithuania App no 47922/99 [1999] (unreported) (ECtHR)
Gebura v Poland App no 63131/00 HUDOC *(ECtHR)*
Gladkiy v Russia App no 3242/03 (ECtHR, 21 December 2010)
Grishin v Russia App no 30983/02 (ECtHR, 15 November 2007)
Gusinskiy v Russia ECHR 2004-IV 129
Estelle v Gamble v Turkey no 44084/10 (ECtHR, 5 March 2013)
Handyside v United Kingdom (1976) Series A no 24
Harakchiev and Tolumov v Bulgaria ECHR 2014-III 391.
Henaf v France ECHR 2003-XI 213
Hilal v United Kingdom ECHR 2001-II 293
Holomiov v Moldova App no 30649/05 (ECtHR, 7 November 2006)
Hummatov v Azerbaijan App nos 9852/03 and 13413/04 (ECtHR, 29 November 2007)
Hussain v United Kingdom App no 21928/93 (ECtHR, 21 February 1996)
Hutchinson v United Kingdom [GC] App no 57592/08 (ECtHR, 17 January 2017)
Hutchinson v United Kingdom App no 57592/08 (ECtHR, 3 February 2015)
Hutchison Reid v United Kingdom ECHR 2003-IV 94.
Idalov v Russia [GC] App no 5826/03 (ECtHR, 22 May 2012)
Igdeli v Turkey App no 29256/95 (ECtHR, 20 June 2002)
Ilascu and Others v Moldova and Russia [GC] ECHR 2004-VII 179
Ilhan v Turkey [GC] ECHR 2000-VII 267
Ireland v United Kingdom (1978) Series A no 25167
Jalloh v Germany [GC] ECHR 2006-IX 281
Jecius v Lithuania ECHR 2000-IX 235
Kafkaris v Cyprus (dec.) App no 9644/09 (ECtHR, 21 June 2011)
Kafkaris v Cyprus [GC] ECHR 2008-I 223.
Kalashnikov v Russia ECHR 2001-XI 197.
Khamtokhu and Aksenchik v Russia [GC] App nos 60367/08 and 961/11 (ECtHR 24 January 2017)
Khatayev v Russia App no 56994/09 (ECtHR, 11 October 2011)
Kudla v Poland [GC] ECHR 2000-XI 197
Labita v Italy [GC] ECHR 2000-IV 99

The Greek case (1969) 12 *Yearbook of the European Convention on Human Rights* (Commission Decision)
Chartier v Italy (1982) 33 DR 41
Mansell v United Kingdom 32072/96 (unreported) (European Commission of Human Rights)

England and Wales

AG Reference (No 69 of 2013) (Ian McLoughlin) [2014] EWCA Crim 188
Associated Provincial Picture Houses Ltd v Wednesbury Corporation [1948] 1 KB 223
Attorney General's Ref (No. 77 of 2006) [2006] EWCA Crim 2384
Attorney General's Reference (No.69 of 2013) [2014] 2 Cr App R (S) 40
Attorney General's Reference (No.73 of 2006) [2006] EWCA Crim 2508
Attorney General's Reference (No.38 of 2013) [2014] Cr App R (S) 61
Attorney-General's Reference (No. 07) [2005] EWCA 1056
Bata (Setting of Minimum Term) [2006] EWCA 468
Begum v Denbigh High School Governors [2006] UKHL 15
Bugdaycay v Secretary of State for the Home Department [1987] 1 AC 514
Council of Civil Service Unions v Minister for the Civil Service [1985] AC 374
Ghaidan v Godin-Mendoza [2004] UKHL 30
Huang v Secretary of State for the Home Department [2007] UKHL 11
International Transport Roth Gmbh v Secretary of State for the Home Department [2003] QB 728
Pretty v DPP [2002] 1 AC 800
Pro-Life Alliance v British Broadcasting Corporation [2004] 1 AC 185
Queen (on the application of A.S) v The Secretary of State for Justice [2009] EWHC (Admin) 1315
Queen (on the application of I R) v Dr G Shetty [2003] EWHC (Admin) 3022
Queen (on the application of Limbuela) v Home Secretary [2004] EWHC 219 (Admin)
Queen on the application of A v Governor of HMYOI Huntercombe (2006) CO/8038/2006 [2006] EWHC 2544 (Admin)
R. *(Anderson) v Secretary of State for the Home Department* [2002] UKHL 46
R.*(Black) v Secretary of State for Justice* [2008] EWCA Civ 359
R. *(Black) v Secretary of State for Justice* [2009] 2 WLR 282
R. *(Bloggs 61) v Home Secretary* [2003] 1 WLR 2724
R. *(Brooke and another) v Parole Board* [2008] EWCA Civ 29
R. *(Clift) v Secretary of State for the Home Department* [2007] 1 AC 484
R. *(Daly) v Secretary of State for the Home Department* [2001] 2 AC 532
R. *(Giles) v Parole Board and Another* [2004] 1 AC 1
R. *(Johnson) v Secretary of State for the Home Department* [2007] 1 WLR 1990
R. *(Limbuela) v Secretary of State* [2005] UKHL 66
R. *(Limbuela) v Secretary of State for the Home Department* [2004] QB 1440
R. *(N) v M* [2002] EWCA Civ 1789

R. (O'Connell) v Parole Board [2009] EWCA Civ 867
R. (O'Connell) v Parole Board [2007] EWHC 2591 (Admin)
R. (on the application of Foley) v Parole Board for England and Wales [2012] EWHC 2184 (Admin)
R. (on the Application of Graham, Allen) v Secretary of State for Justice [2007] 6608/2007; [2008] 29 ACD
R. (on the application of Spinks) v Secretary of State for the Home Department [2004] EWHC 2916 (Admin)
R. (P&Q) v Home Secretary [2001] EWCA 1151
R. (Sim) v Parole Board [2004] QB 1288
R. (Smith and West) v Parole Board [2005] 1 WLR 350
R. (Smith) v Parole Board [2003] EWCA 1269.
R. (Spinks) v Secretary of State for the Home Department [2005] EWCA Civ 275
R. (Turgut) v Secretary of State for the Home Department [2000] HRLR 337
R. (West) v the Parole Board [2003] 70 Prison LR
R. (Wilkinson) v Broadmoor Special Hospital Authority and others [2002] 1 WLR 419
R. (Wilkinson) v IRC [2005] UKHL 30
R. v A (No 2) [2001] UKHL 25
R. v A (No 2) [2002] 1 AC 45
R. v Anderson [1999] 1 Cr App R (S) 273
R. v Aramah (John Uzu) [1983] 76 Cr App R (S) 190
R. v Archer [2007] 71 Cr App R (S)
R. v Arshad [2015] 54 Cr App R (S) 391
R. v Ashford [2005] EWCA Crim 1056
R. v Bernard (Basil Mortimer) [1997] 1 Cr App R (S) 135
R. v Bieber [2009] 1 WLR 223
R. v Blackshaw [2012] 1 Cr App R (S) 679
R. v Brian Gregory Cunningham [1993] 14 Cr App R (S) 444
R. v Cahill (Stephen) [2009] EWCA Crim 420
R. v Davenport (Edward) [2014] EWCA Crim 835
R. v Director of Public Prosecutions, ex p. Kebilene [2000] 2 AC 326
R. v Dittman and Anderson [2013] 1 Cr App R (S) 21
R. v Douglas Gary Vinter [2009] 1949602 WL
R. v Edwards (Noel George) [2015] 814 EWCA Crim
R. v Edwards (Noel George) [2015] 814 EWCA Crim
R. v Fontes [2006] 1 Cr App R (S) 76
R. v Governor of Brockhill Prison ex p Evans (No 2) [2001] 1 AC 19
R. v Green (Paul Palmerston) [1992] 13 Cr App R (S) 613
R. v Hall (Daniel Patrick) [2013] 2 Cr App R (S) 68
R. v Harold S. [1998] 1 Cr App R (S) 261
R. v John Francis C. [1993] 14 Cr App R (S) 562
R. v Kolawole [2005] 2 Cr App R (S) 14
R. v Lambert [2001] UKHL 37
R. v Leatherbarrow (Thomas) [1992] 13 Cr App R (S) 632

Acknowledgments

This book draws upon research supported by the Max Planck International Research Network on Aging (MaxNetAging) and Max Planck Institute for Foreign and International Criminal Law. Without their generous financial and administrative assistance this book would not have been possible. I would like to thank Professor Hans-Jörg Albrecht, Professor Roland Hefendehl, Dr Natalie Mann, Dr Elina Steinerte and this book's anonymous reviewers whose constructive criticism have considerably improved the final piece. Special thanks are due to Alison Kirk and Chloe James, my editors at Routledge, for their patience and support during the process of preparing the manuscript for publication.

A special tribute is due to Professor Dirk van Zyl Smit for his illuminating insights into the topic and for his encouragement. Mary Angela Murphy and Dr Elaine Dewhurst, also deserve a special mention for supporting me when it was most needed.

I would also like to express my profound gratitude to a number of people who have provided me with unstinting support. Firstly, I would like to thank my late parents Razmik and Taguhi, for their constant encouragement and love. I would also like to say a special thank you to my late uncle, David, who would have been so pleased to see this book published.

Last, but not least, I would like to say a special thank you to my children, Elizabeth and Daniel, and my beloved wife Meri for their love, patience and support.

Aleksandr Khechumyan
23 October 2017

Foreword

Even in our "enlightened age" there are some issues that we would rather not think about. One of these is the fate of prisoners whose sentences are so long that they are condemned to die in prison.

I was first confronted by the sheer horror of this fate in 1997, when I visited a specialist medical geriatric facility in a prison near Huntsville in Texas. The sympathetic chief warden told me that it cost more to keep a prisoner there than in the finest clinic in Dallas. Given the excellent medical facilities, I believed him. He also told me that he allowed these prisoners to associate freely with one another. I could see this with my own eyes, for the communal rooms were filled with drooling old men, sitting together but staring vacantly into the distance. The warden explained that when these prisoners became seriously ill he moved them into a frail care section and, when they were "about to expire", he put them in the cardiac section so as not to distress the other prisoners. Would I like to see that too? the warden enquired solicitously. I demurred. It was more than I could bear. Twenty years later I remain haunted by the memory of these old and dying men with no prospect of release. Do lives have to end like this?

Aleksandr Khechumyan's new book, *Imprisonment of the Elderly and Death in Custody: The Right to Review*, addresses my heart-rending question. He does so by using the tools of the comparative lawyer. What human rights standards should apply to these forgotten prisoners? At the very least, the universal right to human dignity that all human beings share, comes the reply. But this is only part of his answer.

This book is not an abstract lamentation for unrecognised rights. At its core it is a critical legal analysis of the powers states have to put different people in prison until they die there. The scholarship ranges widely, focusing on the law in the USA, Germany, and England and Wales in particular, as well as on the national apex courts and regional human rights courts that seek to restrict abuse of the power to punish.

Part of the book addresses the power to imprison until death. The imposition of life sentences is of course part of this, for they are the primary source of death-in-prison sentences. The book considers why such sentences are regarded as acceptable at all and closely analyses attempts by the German Federal Constitutional Court and the European Court of Human Rights to ensure that the imposition of life sentences is always accompanied by a power to release. It notes that in the USA, life sentences from which release is effectively impossible have been accepted uncritically by the Supreme Court. Even there, however, such sentences have gradually come to be regarded as too harsh to impose on juveniles.

Life imprisonment is not the only sentence that may result in death in prison. A very long fixed term sentence can lead inexorably to the same outcome if it would stretch far beyond human life expectancy – as 99-year sentences do in Alaska, which has no formal provision for life imprisonment. This book analyses such sentences and also addresses the related question of long sentences imposed on elderly offenders, which have the same effect of extending their prison terms beyond their ordinary life expectancy.

The other side of the equation is the possibility of release from all these different kinds of death-in-prison sentences. This book deals thoroughly with this question. It points out that sound release procedures can offer a partial solution to the problem of growing numbers of ill or simply elderly prisoners otherwise destined to end their lives in prison. This pragmatic response deserves the careful attention it gets here, for the underlying issues are complex. How and by whom should release decisions be made? What substantive and procedural standards should such decisions meet? How can one ensure that individuals who are dying are not simply pushed out of prison in their last days to die a lonely death in the community?

In assembling the answers that different jurisdictions give to these questions, this book makes a contribution to penological knowledge. Its most valuable contribution, however, is to show that – provided the appropriate release provisions are in place – careful, human rights-based lawyering can provide ways of dealing with the problem of mass incarceration of the elderly and dying.

Nottingham, 31 October 2017

Dirk van Zyl Smit
Professor of Comparative and International Penal Law
University for Nottingham

Introduction

Abstract
The ageing of the world population is having a profound effect on many institutions, including prisons. In the past few decades the number of prisoners aged 50 and over has risen significantly in many jurisdictions. With reference to jurisdictions such as England and Wales and the US this chapter outlines the mismatch between the needs of elderly prisoners and the prisons' capacity to meet these needs. This outline demonstrates that among elderly prisoners there many who die in prison or are seriously ill. Although imprisonment for a crime is a legitimate deprivation of the right to liberty, human rights place certain limits on the administration of imprisonment. Against this backdrop this chapter sets the stage for exploring the human rights limits on continued imprisonment of those elderly prisoners who are seriously ill or are serving sentences with mandatory custodial terms longer than their life expectancy.

The UN Report on World Population Ageing projects that by 2050, for the first time in the history of humanity, the number of people aged 60 and over will exceed the number of younger people.[1] The proportion of elderly people in society is higher in developed countries and is projected to rise further.[2] This ageing of the population is having a profound effect on many institutions, including prisons. In the past few decades, in many jurisdictions, the number of prisoners aged 50 and over[3] has increased significantly. In recent years much research has been done on elderly prisoners from the perspectives of criminology, social work and law. Some studies have adopted a holistic approach in researching the prison

1 United Nations Population Division, 'World Population Ageing 1950–2050: Executive Summary' (New York 2001), http://www.un.org/esa/population/publications/worldageing19502050/pdf/62executivesummary_english.pdf, accessed 15 November 2017.

2 United Nations Population Division, 'World Population Ageing 2015' (New York, 2015) 3, available at http://www.un.org/en/development/desa/population/publications/pdf/ageing/WPA2015_Report.pdf, accessed 5 November 2017

3 The 50-year-old benchmark is the most commonly utilised to refer to ageing, elderly or older offenders. It is argued that the ageing process is accelerated by as much as 10 years in a prison setting. See e.g. John J Kerbs and Jennifer M Jolley (eds), *Senior citizens behind bars: Challenges for the criminal justice system* (Lynne Reinner, 2014), 6.

experience of the elderly, while others have focused on specific aspects of the experience of elderly prisoners, or of various subcategories of elderly prisoners such as elderly women,[4] those with chronic illnesses and disabilities,[5] and elderly terminally ill prisoners.[6] Much of the debate focused on solutions to problems associated with the rise of the elderly prison population. In this context, the issue of early compassionate release of dying and seriously ill elderly prisoners was also discussed.[7] The majority of existing studies on this topic concentrate on the criteria, benefits or the various barriers hindering the early release of elderly prisoners. This book does not attempt to add another dimension to this debate. By contrast, the aim of this book is to explore the human rights limits of the continued imprisonment of elderly prisoners.

Elderly prisoners

In 2016 prisoners aged 50 and over constituted only 15% of the entire prison population in England and Wales. However, they are the fastest-growing age group in the prison estate and have increased by 169% between 2002 and 2016.[8] A similar trend can also be observed across the Atlantic. In 2013 in the US the number of prisoners aged 55 or older under the jurisdiction of State

4 Azrini Wahidin, *Older women in the criminal justice system: Running out of time* (Kingsley, London, 2004).

5 Elizabeth C Dretsch, 'Chronically Ill Inmates' in Lior Gideon (ed), *Special Needs Offenders in Correctional Institutions*, 1st edn, (SAGE Publications, 2013).

6 John F Linder, 'Palliative Care for Prison Inmates "Don't Let Me Die in Prison"' (2007) 298(8) *Journal of American Medical Assosiation* 894; John F Linder and Frederick J Meyers, 'Palliative and End-of-Life Care in Correctional Settings' (2009) 5(1–2) *Journal of Social Work in End-Of-Life & Palliative Care* 7.

7 William EJ Adams, 'Incarceration of Older Criminals: Balancing Safety, Cost, and Humanitarian Concerns' (1995) 19(2) *Nova Law Review* 465; Jaye B Anno and others, *Correctional Heath Care: Addressing the Needs of Elderly, Chronically Ill and Terminally Ill Inmates* (Washington, DC, Department of Justice, 2004).; Molly F James, 'The Sentencing of Elderly Criminals' (1992) 29(3) Am Crim L Rev 1025; John J Kerbs, 'Arguments and strategies for the selective decarceration of older prisoners' in Max B Rothman, Burton D Dunlop and Pamela Entzel (eds), *Elders, crime, and the criminal justice system: Myth, perceptions, and reality in the 21st century* (Springer series on life styles and issues in aging, Springer,2000); Susan Lundstrom, 'Dying to Get out a Study on Necessity, Importance, and Effectiveness of Prison Early Release Programs for Elderly Inmates Suffering from HIV Disease and Other Terminal-Centered Illnesses' (1994) 9(1) BYU Journal of Public Law 155; Eva Steiner, 'Early Release for Seriously Ill and Elderly Prisoners: Should French Practice be Followed?' (2003) 50(3) *Probation Journal* 267; Ashley L Demyan, 'What's Compassion Got to Do with It? An Empirical Examination of Medical Release in California Prisons' (PhD Dissertation, University of California, Irvine 2013); William W Berry, III, 'Extraordinary and Compelling: A Re-examination of the Justifications for Compassionate Release' (2009) 68(4) *Maryland Law Review* 850; Brie A Williams, 'Balancing Punishment and Compassion for Seriously Ill' (2011) 155(2) Ann Intern Med 122; V Handtke and others, 'The collision of care and punishment: Ageing prisoners view on compassionate release' [2016] *Punishment & Society*.

8 Grahame Allen and Chirs Watson, 'UK Prison Population Statistics' (London 2017). Briefing Paper 12.

correctional authorities constituted 10% of the total State prison population, an increase of 400% from 1993.[9] The number of Federal prisoners age 50 or older increased from 9,000 in 1994 to 30,000 in 2011. This makes up 17% of the total prison population under Federal jurisdiction – a 330% increase.[10] In Canada 23.5% of the population in federal custody was aged 50 and over in 2015.[11] The proportion of the inmate population aged 50 years and older has grown considerably in the last 15 years; in 2000, this age cohort represented only 12% of the inmate population.[12] There has been also a rise in the number of elderly prisoners in other Western European countries such as Germany,[13] France[14] and Italy.[15]

The growth of this section of the prison population is due both to an increase in the number of prisoners growing old in prison because of longer sentences and to an increase in the number of people sentenced to immediate prison terms in old age.[16] In England and Wales the pursuance of offences, especially of a sexual nature, committed decades ago, has contributed to the increase of the number of older people sentenced to prison terms.[17] This seems to be part of a general trend of greater intolerance towards sexual offending[18] and 'greater readiness and technical capacity ... to pursue and secure convictions against sex offenders, including cases of "historic" offences'.[19]

Indeed, in this jurisdiction sexual offenders make up by far the biggest group

9 E Ann Carson and William J Sabol, 'Aging of the State Prison Population, 1993–2013' (2016) 1, www.bjs.gov/content/pub/pdf/aspp9313.pdf accessed 15 November 2017.

10 Kim KiDeuk and Bryce Peterson, 'Aging Behind Bars: Trends and Implications of Graying Prisoners in the Federal Prison System' (2014) 3, www.urban.org/research/publication/ accessed 19 June 2017.

11 Public Safety Canada, 'Corrections and Conditoinal Release: Statistical Overview 2015' (Ottawa 2016) 47, accessed 5 October 2017.

12 The Office of the Correctional Investigator, 'Annual Report of the Office of the Correctional Investigator 2014–2015' (Ottawa 2015) 11, www.oci-bec.gc.ca/cnt/rpt/index-eng.aspx, accessed 5 October 2017

13 Klaus Laubenthal, 'Strafvollzug an älteren Menschen', in Franziska Kunz and Hermann-Josef Gertz (eds), *Straffälligkeit älterer Menschen: Interdisziplinäre Beiträge aus Forschung und Praxis* (Springer Berlin, Heidelberg, 2015) 132.

14 Marcelo F Aebi and Natalia Delgrande, 'Council of Europe Annual Penal Statistics: SPACE I – Prison Populations Survey 2013' (Strasbourg, 2015) 70; See also publications of the same series from 2007 to 2012.

15 ibid.

16 House of Commons Justice Committee, 'Older prisoners: Fifth Report of Session 2013–2014' (Vol.I: Report, together with formal minutes, oral and written evidence, London 2013) 7.

17 Elaine Crawley and Richard Sparks, 'Hidden Injuries? Researching the Experiences of Older Men in English Prisons' (2005) 44(4) *The Howard Journal* 345, 348; House of Commons Justice Committee, 'Older prisoners' (n.16) 7; Prisons & Probation Ombudsman, 'Learning from PPO Investigations – Thematic Review: Older Prisoners' (2017) 10.

18 Amanda Matravers and Gareth V Hughes, 'Unprincipled sentencing? The policy approach to dangerous sex offenders' in Michael H Tonry (ed), *Confronting crime: Crime control policy under New Labour* (Willan, Cullompton, 2003).

19 Crawley and Sparks, 'Hidden Injuries? Researching the Experiences of Older Men in English Prisons' (n.17) 348; House of Commons Justice Committee, 'Older prisoners' (n.16) 7.

among prisoners aged 50 and over.[20] However, the elderly prison population is far from being homogeneous in terms of type of offence. The crimes for which prisoners aged 50 and over serve their punishments include a wide variety of offences ranging from property crimes to drugs and violence against the person.[21]

There is a wide variety among elderly prisoners not only in terms of crimes committed and sentences served but also in terms of needs. Prisoners, like their counterparts in communities, age differently; there are variations in terms of physical and mental capabilities within the cohort of elderly people.[22] These variations are made vivid in the studies on elderly prisoners.[23] One such study depicted this variety in the following terms:[24]

> On our visits to HMP Dartmoor and HMP Isle of Wight, we met prisoners who were near to or older than 70 who were active, mobile and articulate; we also met prisoners who were much younger but had very limited mobility and reported severe health needs that would not have been typical for their age group in the community.

Despite differences in terms of needs, ageing is characterised by general decline, and by increased incidence of morbidity and infirmity.[25] Empirical studies have demonstrated that prisoners aged 50–59 and those aged 60 and over have a physical and mental health status which is significantly worse than that of prisoners aged 18–49.[26] A UK Ministry of Justice study reported that 59% of prisoners aged 50 and over had a longstanding illness or disability, compared to 27% of younger prisoners.[27] Similarly, according to a study by the US Bureau of Justice Statistics, prisoners aged 50 or more were about three times more likely than younger prisoners to report chronic diseases. These conditions include cancer, high blood pressure or hypertension, stroke-related problems, diabetes

20 Natalie Mann, *Doing harder time? The experiences of an ageing male prison population in England and Wales* (Farnham UK, Ashgate 2012) 5.

21 ibid.

22 George L Maddox, 'Aging Differently' (1987) 27(5) *The Gerontologist* 557.

23 House of Commons Justice Committee, 'Older Prisoners: Fifth Report of Session 2013–2014' (Vol.II Additional written evidence, London 2013). Justice Committee Reports, written submission from Dr Elaine Crawley.

24 House of Commons Justice Committee, 'Older prisoners' (n.16) 12.

25 Maddox (n.22) 558; Kristina Larsson and Mats Thorslund, 'Chapter 8: Old people's health' (2006) 34(67 suppl) *Scandinavian Journal of Public Health* 185, 186; Adrian J Hayes and others, 'The health and social needs of older male prisoners' (2012) 27(11) *International Journal of Geriatric Psychiatry* 1155.

26 Hayes and others (n.25) 1159–1161

27 Samuel Omolade, 'The needs and characteristics of older prisoners: Results from the Surveying Prisoner Crime Reduction (SPCR) survey' (London, 2014). Analytical Summary 5–6, https://insidetime.org/download/research_&_reports/ministry_of_justice/needs-older-prisoners-spcr-survey_2014_Oct14.pdf, accessed 15 November 2017

or high blood sugar, heart-related problems, kidney-related problems, arthritis or rheumatism, asthma, and cirrhosis of the liver.[28]

Researchers have also revealed that mental illness is prevalent among elderly prisoners. A study by Fazel and colleagues which assessed psychiatric morbidity of men prisoners aged 60 and over in 15 prisons in England and Wales revealed that 53% of the sample had a major psychiatric illness. Thirty per cent of these prisoners suffered from a depressive disorder. This was estimated to be significantly higher than the prevalence of mental disorders among younger prisoners and among older adults in the community.[29] A more recent study by Hayes and colleagues demonstrated that the prevalence of mental disorders among prisoners aged 50–59 was even higher than that of prisoners aged 60 and over. Despite the difference between the two age groups in regard to the prevalence of mental disorders, a comparative analysis demonstrated that in terms of mental and physical health these two age groups had rather similar needs which were significantly different from those of younger prisoners.[30] The US studies depict a similar picture, demonstrating a significantly higher prevalence of psychiatric conditions among elderly prisoners compared to their counterparts in the community.[31]

Furthermore, cognitive impairments such as dementia, Alzheimer's or Parkinson's disease, which are more likely to be associated with elderly people, are assumed to affect approximately 5% of prisoners age 55 and over in England and Wales.[32] In the US, one study estimated the number of prisoners with dementia based on the prevalence of this disease in the general population. Taking this rate as a baseline, this study calculated that in 2010 there were 41,740 prisoners with dementia. This number is projected to rise to 127,130 by 2050.[33]

Given the fact that chronic diseases are progressive, many elderly prisoners experience increasing levels of functional impairment and an increasing number of older inmates with chronic diseases reach a terminal stage and die in prison.[34] The data on the number of terminally ill prisoners are either unavailable or difficult to obtain.[35] However, the mortality statistics give some idea of the extent of the problem; death from natural causes is prevalent among prisoners age 50 and

28 Laura Maruschak, Marcus Berzofsky and Jennifer Unangst, 'Medical Problems of State and Federal Prisoners and Jail Inmates, 2011–12' (Washington, DC, US Dept of Justice, 2016) 5.

29 Seena Fazel and others, 'Hidden psychiatric morbidity in elderly prisoners' (2001) 179(6) *The British Journal of Psychiatry* 535, 537–538.

30 Hayes and others (n.25), 1158–1161.

31 See e.g. H Koenig and others, 'Depression and anxiety disorder among older male inmates at a federal correctional facility' (1995) 46(4) *Psychiatric Services* 399.

32 Prison Reform Trust, 'Bromley Briefings Prison Factfile' (London, Autumn 2014), Bromley Briefings Prison Factfile 51, www.thebromleytrust.org.uk/files/bromleybriefingsautumn2014.pdf, accessed 15 November 2017.

33 J Willson and S Barboza, 'The looming chanllange of dementia in corrections' (2010) 24(2) *Correct Care* 12.

34 Anita N Blowers, Jennifer M Jolley and John J Kerbs, 'The Age-Segregation Debate' in John J Kerbs and Jennifer M Jolley (eds), *Senior citizens behind bars: Challenges for the criminal justice system* (Lynne Reinner, 2014) 137.

35 Ministry of Justice to Aleksandr Khechumyan (10 October 2014).

over.[36] From 2004 to 2014 in England and Wales, 823 prisoners aged 50 and over died in prison from natural causes, representing more than 68% of the total number of deaths by natural causes in prison for that time period.[37]

In the US, from 1999 to 2008, there were 3,354 deaths of prisoners under Federal jurisdiction. Of these cases 2,902 were deaths from illnesses, excluding those from AIDS.[38] Between 2000 and 2011, 32,414 State prisoners died from illnesses other than AIDS.[39] Between 2000 and 2011, 14,953 of the State prisoners who died from illnesses other than AIDS were aged 55 and older.[40] Moreover, these data show that prisoners aged 55 and older died from cancer, heart and respiratory diseases at a rate at least at five times higher than prisoners in any other age group. Apart from highlighting the extent of terminal illness in State and Federal prisons, these data demonstrate a strong correlation between the age of inmates and the cause of death.[41]

Management of elderly prisoners

Empirical research has demonstrated that the needs of elderly prisoners are different from those of younger prisoners.[42] Traditionally, prisons have been designed to accommodate young, able-bodied male inmates, and therefore neither physical set-up of prisons nor the services are set to cater for the special needs of elderly prisoners.[43] As Crawley and Sparks report:

> Their [prison's] very fabric (the stairs and steps and walkaways, the distances, the gates, the football pitches and gymnasia; the serveries and queues; the communal showers; the incessant background noise) is, in general, constructed in blithe unconsciousness of the needs and sensibilities of the old.[44]

36 Ministry of Justice, 'Safety in Custody statistics: December 2014' (London 2015). Safety in Custody Statistics, 7.

37 Ministry of Justice, 'Deaths in Prison Custody: England and Wales' (update by December 2014, London 2015). Safety in Custody.

38 Bureau of Justice Statistics, US Department of Justice, 'Deaths of prisoners under federal jursidiction, by cause of death, 1999–2008' (2009), www.bjs.gov/index.cfm?ty=tp&tid=194, accessed 15 November 2017.

39 Margaret Noonan and Scott Ginder, 'Mortality in Local Jails and State Prisons, 2000–2011: Statistical Tables' (2013) Table 14, p.1, www.bjs.gov/index.cfm?ty=pbdetail&iid=4757, accessed 15 November 2017.

40 ibid, Table 21, p.22.

41 ibid, 3.

42 Margaret E Leigey, 'Bio-Psycho-Social Needs' in John J Kerbs and Jennifer M Jolley (eds), *Senior citizens behind bars: Challenges for the criminal justice system*; Elaine Crawley and Richard Sparks, *Age of imprisonment: Work, life and death among older men in British prisons* (Willan, Cullompton, 2013); Mann (n.20); Wahidin, *Older women in the criminal justice system* (n.4).

43 Elaine Crawley, 'Institutional Thoughtlessness in Prisons and Its Impacts on the Day-to-Day Prison Lives of Elderly Men' (2005) 21(4) *Journal of Contemporary Criminal Justice* 350, 351–352; Mann (n.20) 41 Ron H Aday, *Aging prisoners: Crisis in American corrections* (Praeger, 2002).

44 Crawley and Sparks, 'Hidden Injuries? Researching the Experiences of Older Men in English Prisons' (n.17) 350.

Since the early 1970s, the US Federal Bureau of Prisons recognised 'the need for special programming' for elderly prisoners.[45] As reported in the literature, the US is the first country to systematically segregate the elderly from the mainstream prison population.[46] Both at Federal and State levels many segregated prisons or prison wings have been developed to house elderly prisoners in order to protect them from victimisation, to provide them with age-specific training and education programmes, and to better meet their health care and mobility needs.[47]

In other countries segregated prison facilities for elderly prisoners are not widely available. For instance, in Germany there are segregated wings for elderly prisoners in some prisons and only one segregated facility with a capacity to accommodate 240 inmates.[48] In England and Wales there were some isolated attempts to provide age-segregated prison units. In 1997, HMP Kingston opened one such unit. However, according to reports, the conditions in this unit were even worse than in the prison generally, and it was therefore forced to close in 2005.[49] The only segregated unit for elderly prisoners which is currently operating is the 20-bed wing at HMP Norwich for elderly lifers requiring nursing care and assistance with activities of daily living.[50] In addition to this small unit for elderly prisoners, there has been a variety of local initiatives introducing special schemes, programmes and accommodation for elderly prisoners.[51]

The UK Ministry of Justice refuses to develop a special policy on elderly prisoners. Despite calls to put in place such a policy,[52] the Ministry of Justice remains reluctant to develop and implement a common approach, because it does not view elderly prisoners as a uniform group for which it is possible to have a 'sensible set of criteria'.[53] According to the Ministry of Justice, distinguishing a group of adult prisoners from the mainstream prison population and establishing for them a national strategy for older prisoners is not the best way of proceeding, because it is not possible to generalise on what their needs are.[54] The Ministry's

45 P C Kratcoski and G A Pownall, 'Federal Bureau of Prisons Programming for Older Inmates' (1989) 53(2) *Federal Probation* 28, 35.

46 Mann (n.20) 6.

47 Adams (n.7); Aday (n.43) 153.

48 Laubenthal (n.13) 138.

49 Mann (n.20) 7.

50 House of Commons Justice Committee, 'Older Prisoners' (n.23) 29.

51 See e.g. Francesca Cooney and Julia Barggins, 'DoingTime: Good practice with older people in prison – the views of prison staff' (London 2010), available at www.prisonreformtrust.org.uk/uploads/documents/doingtimegoodpractice.pdf, accessed 15 November 2017; Mann (n.20) Appendix 1.

52 See e.g. Department of Health, 'A pathway to care for older offenders: A toolkit for good practice' (London 2007), webarchive.nationalarchives.gov.uk/20130123192716/http://www.dh.gov.uk/en/Publicationsandstatistics/Publications/PublicationsPolicyAndGuidance/DH_079928 accessed 15 November 2017; HM Chief Inspector of Prisons, 'No problems old and quiet: Older prisoners in England and Wales: A thematic review by HM Chief Inspector of Prisons' (2004) www.justiceinspectorates.gov.uk/hmiprisons/wp-content/uploads/sites/4/2014/08/OlderPrisoners-2004.pdf, accessed 15 November 2014.

53 House of Commons Justice Committee, 'Older prisoners' (n.16) 14.

54 ibid, 50.

priority is to treat each prisoner individually. This priority is addressed by the Prison Service Instruction 32/2011, which prescribes rules to ensure equality in the prison estate, including rules on identifying and meeting particular needs of individual prisoners.[55]

Although local initiatives have been praised as positive developments,[56] the lack of a national strategy has been criticised by prison reform charities and researchers, who argue that this approach results in the further marginalisation of old people in prisons.[57] Many prison officers have often been reluctant to recognise the specific needs of elderly prisoners, justifying their approach by the 'sameness' principle to ensure that prisoners receive their entitlements without particular distinction.[58] The negative effects of applying this principle are mitigated to some extent by the resistance and disobedience of younger prisoners, which require officers to use the principle with more flexibility.[59] In the case of elderly prisoners, who are a more obedient and passive group, the sameness principle is more easily enforceable, often leading to arbitrary denial of benefits and imposition of burdens.[60]

Crawley and Sparks coined the expression 'institutional thoughtlessness' to describe acts which result from enforcing the principle of 'sameness' by individual prison officers in relation to elderly prisoners, such as not allowing enough time to complete certain tasks without taking into account the age and difficulties with mobility.[61] Like other prisoners in the 'weakest positions in institutional hierarchies', elderly prisoners are in need of such 'privileges'[62] because they are not able effectively to defend their position.[63] Elderly prisoners are a powerless group 'peripheral to policy, advocacy, and, to some extent, to prison theory and research'.[64] In this situation, not having a dedicated national strategy deepens their marginalisation and vulnerability, making them dependent on local initiatives which are not available in every prison.[65]

55 Prison Service Instruction 32/2011 14 April 2011, PSI 32/2011 (National Offender Managment Service).
56 Mann (n.20) 7–8; Crawley and Sparks, 'Hidden Injuries? Researching the Experiences of Older Men in English Prisons' (n.17) 354; Azrini Wahidin (ed), *Ageing, crime and society* (Willan 2006).
57 Crawley (n.43) 360.
58 ibid, 355–356.
59 Richard Sparks, Anthony E Bottoms and Will Hay, *Prisons and the problem of order* (Clarendon studies in criminology, Clarendon, Oxford 1996).
60 Crawley and Sparks, 'Hidden Injuries? Researching the Experiences of Older Men in English Prisons' (n.17), 352.
61 Crawley (n.43), 352.
62 Crawley and Sparks, 'Hidden Injuries? Researching the Experiences of Older Men in English Prisons' (n.17), 354.
63 Thomas Mathiesen, *The defences of the weak: A sociological study of a Norwegian correctional institution* (Reprint of 1972 London edn, Routledge 1965).
64 Crawley (n.43), 360.
65 House of Commons Justice Committee, 'Older prisoners' (n.16), 30.

Prisons' capacity to ensure provision of care meeting needs of elderly prisoners

In the US, prisons are obliged to provide prisoners with medical care of a 'quality acceptable within prudent professional standards', which is roughly equal to the care widely available in the community, but falls short of the care available in the best civilian clinics.[66] The 'deliberate indifference' to medical needs of prisoners constitutes a violation of the prohibition of cruel and unusual punishment under the Eighth Amendment of the US Constitution.[67] Within these standards elderly prisoners in the US are entitled to receive medical services meeting their needs. Furthermore, the Americans with Disabilities Act 1990, which partially applies to prisoners, prohibits discrimination on the basis of a physical or mental impairment against qualified individuals in relation to services provided by or on behalf of a public entity.[68] However, it is widely reported in the literature that, despite legal requirements, only a few exemplary prisons are able to provide adequate medical and mental health care to elderly, chronically and terminally ill prisoners.[69]

Historically, prisons in England and Wales had their own health service independent of the National Health Service. However, following reports criticising the quality of health care services in prisons, which was below the quality available to the general public, the Department of Health and the Home Office agreed to transfer prison health care to the NHS.[70]

In 2001 the Department of Health published the 'National Service Framework for Older People', which emphasised provision of person-centred care for older people whether in their homes or in residential settings. It articulated the importance of providing integrated health and social care services to older people, requiring the coordinated efforts of health care and local authorities.[71] Following publication of the Framework, the Prison Service issued 'Prison Service Instruction 2001/021', confirming the applicability of the Department of Health standards for health and social care of older people in prisons.[72]

Furthermore, in 2007 Department of Health published a 'toolkit' for good practice for the care of older prisoners which strongly emphasised the need for

66 See e.g. *Estelle v Gamble*, 429 U.S. 97, 102 (1976).

67 ibid.

68 John J Kerbs, Jennifer M Jolley and Naoki Kanaboshi, 'The interplay between law and social science in the age-segregation debate' (2015) 38(1) *Journal of Crime and Justice* 77, 3

69 Aday (n.43); Anno and others (n.7); Timothy Curtin, 'The Continuing Problem of America's Aging Prison Population and the Search for a Cost-Effective and Socially Acceptable Means of Addressing It' (2007) 15 Elder LJ 473.

70 Ken Howse, 'Growing Old in Prison: A scoping study on older prisoners' (London 2003) 4, www.prisonreformtrust.org.uk/uploads/documents/Growing.Old.Book_-_small.pdf, accessed 15 November 2017.

71 Department of Health, 'National Service Framework for Older People' (2001), www.gov.uk/government/publications/quality-standards-for-care-services-for-older-people, accessed 15 November 2017.

72 National service framework for older people 2001, Prison Service Order 21/2001 (Her Majesty's Prison Service).

continued assessment of the physical and mental health and social care needs of elderly prisoners.[73] The toolkit made a number of recommendations, including identifying, training and supporting older prisoners lead in prison healthcare units, fostering a culture of respect for older prisoners, providing special accommodation for frail older prisoners, selecting and training prisoners for a prisoners' helper scheme under the supervision of social services.[74] In addition to these guidelines, the Care Act 2014 determined the eligibility criteria for qualifying for social care and clarified that the responsibility for care and support of the needs of prisoners lies with the local authority of the area where the prison is situated.[75]

Since April 2006, the NHS has been responsible for the provision of health care in most of the prisons in England.[76] It is assumed that prisoners are provided with a quality of health care equal to that available to the general public.[77] When possible, primary and secondary health care services are provided within the prison by prison nursing staff and local general practitioners covering the prison area. However, prisoners are also escorted to outside hospitals for clinical referrals.[78]

A further law which is highly relevant to elderly prisoners is the Equality Act 2010, which replaced the Disability Discrimination Act.[79] This Act prohibits discrimination, i.e. treating a person less favourably than others because of characteristics specified in the law, including age and disability.[80] Furthermore, the Act imposes a duty on providers of public services to make adjustments to their policies, practices and estate in order to eliminate any disadvantages that individuals may experience because of the protected characteristics.[81]

In recent years a law and policy framework has been put in place in England and Wales requiring provision of prison conditions and health and social care suitable for the needs of prisoners, including the elderly.[82] However, the legal requirements are not universally met. According to various reports, the requirement to make prison environments physically accessible for infirm and disabled prisoners is often not implemented in practice and in some cases cannot be

73 Department of Health, 'A pathway to care for older offenders' (n.52) 11.

74 ibid, 14.

75 Care Act 2014, s.76.

76 Prisons and Probation Ombudsman for England and Wales, 'End of Life Care' (2013). Learning from PPO Investigations 10, available at www.ppo.gov.uk/app/uploads/2014/07/Learning_from_PPO_investigations_-_End_of_life_care_final_web.pdf, accessed 15 November 2017.

77 Department of Health, 'National Service Framework for Older People' (n.71) 4.

78 Prison Service Order 3050 Continuity of Health Care for Prisoners 2006, PSO 3050 (Her Majesty's Prison Service).

79 Equality Act 2010, s.28.

80 ibid, s.13.

81 ibid, s/20.

82 Department of Health, 'National Service Framework for Older People' (n.71); National service framework for older people (n.72); Department of Health, 'A pathway to care for older offenders' (n.52); Prison Service Order 3050 Continuity of Health Care for Prisoners (n.78); Equality Act (n.79) ss 13, 20, 26, 27, 28; Prison Service Instruction 2011/32 Ensuring Equality 2011 (Her Majesty's Prison Service); Care Act (n.75).

implemented.[83] Access to specialised health care is problematic[84] and is often disrupted because of security considerations,[85] while social care according to the UK House of Commons Justice Committee is 'spare, variable and in some cases non-existing'.[86]

Dying in prison and compassionate release

One of the consequences of the ageing of the prison population is the increased number of deaths in prisons from natural causes. This issue presents a special challenge to prison administrations because, in the past, foreseeable deaths in prisons were rare. The review of literature demonstrates that in the US prisoners who die in prison are provided with the end-of-life care at prison hospices. It is reported that since introduction of the first prison hospice in 1987, the number of prison hospices in the US has grown rapidly. These programmes largely follow the structures and practices of similar community programmes.[87] However, some authors emphasise that prison hospices have limited capacity to accommodate the rapidly rising numbers of dying prisoners.[88] Furthermore, the literature identifies a number of challenges faced by prison hospices, centred around the collision between the idea of end-of-life care and prison polices, trust between prison staff and prisoners, and the stigmatisation of prisoners by prison staff.[89]

According to the National Hospice and Palliative Care Organisation, palliative care is an intensive programme to enhance choice, comfort and promote quality of life for individuals approaching the end of life, and their families.[90] End-of-life care aims to ensure a comfortable death, which includes aggressive pain control using narcotic drugs, presence of family members, and an adequate environment.[91] It was identified that prison hospices take a rather conservative approach when prescribing narcotics because of the risk that prescribed drugs

83 House of Commons Justice Committee, 'Older prisoners' (n.16) 18.

84 House of Commons Justice Committee, 'Older prisoners' (n.16) 8; Wahidin, *Older women in the criminal justice system* (n.4) 130–140; Mann (n.20) 46–49.

85 House of Commons Justice Committee, 'Older prisoners' (n.16) 8; Wahidin, *Older women in the criminal justice system* (n.4) 130–140; Mann (n.20) 46–49.

86 House of Commons Justice Committee, 'Older prisoners' (n.16) 29.

87 K Stone, I Papadopoulos and D Kelly, 'Establishing hospice care for prison populations: An integrative review assessing the UK and USA perspective' (2012) 26(8) *Palliative Medicine* 969, 970.

88 Stone, Papadopoulos and Kelly (n.87) 970; HC Hoffman and GE Dickinson, 'Characteristics of Prison Hospice Programs in the United States' (2011) 28(4) *American Journal of Hospice and Palliative Medicine* 245.

89 See e.g. Nancy N Dubler, 'The Collision of Confinement and Care: End-of-Life Care in Prisons and Jails' (1998) 26(2) *The Journal of Law, Medicine & Ethics* 149; Barbara L Granse, 'Why should We Even Care? Hospice Social Work Practice in a Prison Setting' (2003) 73(3) *Swith College Studies in Social Work* 359; Anno and others (n.7).

90 National Hospice and Palliative Care Organisation, 'Hospice Standards for Practice of Hospice Programs' (2000), www.nhpco.org/ethical-and-position-statements/preamble-and-philosophy, accessed 15 November 2017.

91 Anno and others (n.7) 52.

will be smuggled into the general prison.[92] Moreover, giving family members an unlimited access to dying inmates and ensuring an adequate environment has been also identified as a problem in prison hospices.[93]

The lack of trust between dying inmates and their care-givers appears to be a further obstacle to the provision of effective end-of-life care in prisons. It was articulated that a prerequisite for decent end-of-life care in any setting is a trusting relationship between the patient and the care-givers. Such relationships are especially difficult to establish in a prison environment. Prisoners treat correctional medical personnel as part of the prison staff and, perhaps fairly, transfer the attitude of mistrust to them.[94] Even if the medical staff and care-givers are not part of the prison staff, access to health care is controlled by security staff. This makes it difficult to distinguish between denial of care or treatment to the prisoner and a refusal by the prisoner to undergo it.[95]

Yet another obstacle to making a dignified death possible in prison is the stigmatisation of prisoners by prison staff. The popular belief that prisoners deserve suffering is most often shared by prison officers and medical staff.[96] Reports from hospice practitioners confirm the existence of such attitudes among prison nurses[97] and even success stories of prison hospices reported negative attitudes and resistance from prison staff to compassionate care.[98] For all these reasons, many commentators have questioned the capability of prison hospices to provide inmates with effective end-of-life care and death with dignity.[99]

Death in prison may, indeed, be avoided when it is foreseeable. In the US, both the Federal and the vast majority of State jurisdictions have provisions allowing early release of seriously or terminally ill prisoners; 46 states and the Federal jurisdiction have developed polices allowing medical release of prisoners. Although these policies differ in terms of eligibility criteria and procedure, the Federal jurisdiction and the vast majority of states include terminal illness as a criterion for release.[100]

Despite the availability of mechanisms to allow terminally ill prisoners to die at home or at a community hospice surrounded by family and friends, only a few

92 S Yampolskaya and N Winston, 'Hospice care in prison: General principles and outcomes' (2003) 20(4) *American Journal of Hospice and Palliative Medicine* 290, 291.

93 RH Aday, 'Aging prisoners' concerns toward dying in prison' (2005) 52(3) Omega-Death Dying (*Omega-Journal of Death and Dying*) 199 213; Granse (n.89), 366; Dubler (n.89), 152.

94 Granse (n.89), 363.

95 Dubler (n.89), 152.

96 Felicia Cohn, 'The Ethics of End-of-Life Care for Prison Inmates' (1999) 27(3) *The Journal of Law, Medicine & Ethics* 252, 256–257, http://journals.sagepub.com/doi/abs/10.1111/j.1748-720X.1999.tb01459.x, accessed 15 November 2017.

97 Granse (n.89), 370.

98 Carol Evans, 'The Louisiana State Penitentiary: Angola Prison Hospice' (2002) 5(4) *Journal of Palliative Medicine* 553, 554.

99 See e.g. Dubler (n.89); Granse (n.89); Anno and others (n.7); Human Rights Watch, 'Old Behind Bars: The Aging Prison Population in the United States' (24 January 2012) 86.

100 Demyan (n.7) 6–8.

terminally ill prisoners are released each year.[101] For instance, there were only 25 motions to courts for release of terminally ill prisoners by the Federal Bureau of Prisons in 2011, and 37 motions on combined medical grounds as of November 2012.[102] The situation is not much different in state jurisdictions. From 1999 to 2008 New Mexico released only 35 prisoners, with Missouri releasing 236 from 1998 to 2008 under combined geriatric and terminal illness grounds.[103] In the period from 1995 to 2011 California released 276 terminally ill and permanently incapacitated prisoners.[104]

Several studies have attempted to reveal the reasons behind the gap between the law and practice of medical release in different jurisdictions, identifying various grounds for the low impact of medical release laws. Although in the studied jurisdictions these laws were not similar, the literature identified some common grounds responsible for the low impact of these laws. These were political and public opinion considerations, narrow eligibility criteria and procedural flaws in legal regulations.[105]

Similarly, prisons in England and Wales are required to provide end-of-life care to prisoners or send them somewhere where such care can be provided.[106] The end-of-life care in prisons should be in line with the standards of the National Institute for Health and Care Excellence (NICE). These standards suggest that end-of-life care facilities should meet particular requirements. They need to have an appropriately trained staff, a procedure for identification and assessment of those approaching the end of life, to be able to give holistic support to the individuals, and to continue providing support to the family after the death of the patient.[107]

In the period from 2013 to 2017, the Prison and Probation Ombudsman of England and Wales released two thematic reports concerning the end-of-life care in prisons. These reports are based on the investigations of natural deaths of prisoners in England and Wales that occurred between 2007 and 2015. Prisoners aged 50 and over constituted 80% of all deaths occurring between 2007 and 2012,[108] while the report covering the period between 2013 and 2015 was based on the sample consisting only of prisoners aged 50 and over.[109] Compared to the ratio of distribution of the general prison population in the prison estate, a disproportionate percentage of prisoners dying from natural causes were in high

101 Tina Chiu, 'It's About Time: Ageing Prisoners, Increasing Costs, and Geriatric Release' (2010); Human Rights Watch, 'The Answer is No: Too Little Compassionate Release in US Federal Prisons' (2012).

102 Human Rights Watch (n.101) 2.

103 Chiu (n.101) 6–7.

104 Demyan (n.7) 53.

105 Demyan (n.7) 149–150; Human Rights Watch (n 101) 61–62; Chiu (n.101) 8–10

106 Prisons & Probation Ombudsman (n.17) 19.

107 ibid.

108 Prisons and Probation Ombudsman for England and Wales, 'End of Life Care' (n.76) 15.

109 Prisons & Probation Ombudsman (n.17) 11–12.

security prisons serving sentences for sexual and other serious offences.[110] This reflects the fact that prisoners aged 50 and over are more likely to be found in high security prisons. They made up 20% of the population of high security prisons, while making up only 12% of the total prison population.[111]

The reports demonstrate that between 2007 and 2013, 30% of prisoners who died of natural causes did so in prison, while the other 54% and 15% respectively died in a hospital or a hospice.[112] A small number of prisons in the sample adapted the dying prisoners' cells on the wing in order to provide palliative care, while others established palliative care suites designed to provide such care in their health care wings.[113] Furthermore, in 65% of cases in the sample the prison had accommodated the special care needs of prisoners. This included providing a special bed or mattress, installing an alarm cord, or moving the prisoner to the ground floor in order to enable better accessibility of facilities.[114]

At the same time the Ombudsman expressed concern with regard to a number of aspects of the organisation of end-of-life care of prisoners. The areas of concern are appropriate accommodation for dying prisoners, palliative care plans, involvement of family members, use of restraints for dying prisoners, and the early release process. In many cases investigated by the Ombudsman prisoners died in their cells, where it was not possible to fit necessary medical equipment to facilitate the end-of-life care. According to the report this is a situation which concerns many prisons, because many of them are situated in old buildings which were built with young and able-bodied prisoners in mind and without taking into account the specificities of the end-of-life care. Therefore, it will be difficult to find appropriate rooms to fit the large equipment necessary to facilitate the end-of-life care of dying prisoners.[115]

Furthermore, the standards for end-of-life care require putting in place an effective care plan which concerns issues of pain relief, psychological and emotional support, and involvement of the prisoner's family where appropriate. The reports highlighted that often there were no such plans in place which might ensure more effective and coordinated care.[116] In addition, in many cases no Family Liaison Officer was appointed to ensure involvement of family members in the end-of-life care of dying prisoners.[117] As a result, in many cases family members were informed about the situation of a dying prisoner shortly before the death.[118]

Inappropriate use of restraints for terminally ill and dying prisoners is an overreaching theme of many reports of the Prisons and Probation Ombudsmen.

110 ibid.

111 ibid 17.

112 Prisons and Probation Ombudsman for England and Wales, 'End of Life Care' (n.76) 17.

113 ibid.

114 ibid.

115 Prisons & Probation Ombudsman (n.17) 19.

116 Prisons & Probation Ombudsman (n.17) 19–20; Prisons and Probation Ombudsman for England and Wales, 'End of Life Care' (n.76) 18.

117 Prisons and Probation Ombudsman for England and Wales, 'End of Life Care' (n.76) 23–24

118 Prisons & Probation Ombudsman (n.17) 21–22.

Between January and October 2012, the Prisons and Probation Ombudsman of England and Wales published 23 reports of the natural death of prisoners in which the use of restraints had been inappropriate.[119] This issue was also under the spotlight in the thematic reports on end-of-life care[120] and older prisoners.[121]

According to the respective regulation, the decision on whether to restrain a prisoner during an outside hospital visit depends on the risk assessment of a prisoner, which includes risk of harm to others in the case of escape and the probability of escape. For the risk assessment in the cases of outside hospital escorts and bedwatch, the medical opinion regarding the prisoner's ability to escape must be considered.[122] Furthermore, the concordat on 'Prisoners Escort and Bedwatch Function', which was signed between the National Offender Management Service (NOMS) and the NHS, notes that it is inhumane to use restraints on terminally or seriously ill patients save in cases when the use of such measures is justified by security considerations.[123] However, as the reports demonstrate, prisons often either do not carry out any risk assessments for the use of restraints or the category of risk assigned to the prisoner does not correctly reflect the actual risk posed.[124] Even in cases where death was expected, the majority of prisoners in the cases investigated by the Prisons and Probation Ombudsman remained restrained.[125]

Apart from the issues specific to the provision of the end-of-life care in prisons, the Prisons and Probation Ombudsman identified early release as one of the problematic aspects of organisation of the end-of-life care in prisons. The Secretary of State can grant compassionate release to terminally ill prisoners who are likely to die soon and those who are bedridden or severely incapacitated irrespective of the type of the sentence and the time served. [126] Although no imperative life expectancy period is specified as an eligibility requirement for terminally ill inmates, three months is recommended as an appropriate period.[127] Apart from the requirements related to the illness of a prisoner, the respective policy documents established other restrictive requirements mainly related to risk of reoffending by the prisoner. [128]

Furthermore, prison governors can release prisoners on temporary licence (ROTL) for precisely defined activities which cannot be provided in the prison.[129]

119 Prisons and Probation Ombudsman for England and Wales, 'Fatal incidents investigation: restraints' (2013). Learning lessons bulletin 2, 2 accessed 9 October 2015.

120 Prisons and Probation Ombudsman for England and Wales, 'End of Life Care' (n.76) 19–21

121 Prisons & Probation Ombudsman (n.17) 16–18.

122 Prisons and Probation Ombudsman for England and Wales, 'Fatal incidents investigation: restraints' (n.119) 2.

123 Prisons and Probation Ombudsman for England and Wales, 'End of Life Care' (n.76) 13.

124 ibid, 19.

125 Prisons and Probation Ombudsman for England and Wales, 'Fatal incidents investigation: restraints' (n.119) 2; Prisons and Probation Ombudsman for England and Wales, 'End of Life Care' (n.76) 19–20; Prisons & Probation Ombudsman (n.17) 16.

126 Prison Service Order 6000, 31 March 2005: PSO 6000 (Her Majesty's Prison Service) 12.

127 ibid.

128 ibid, 12.

129 Prison Service Order 6300: Release on temporary licence 2005 (HM Prison Service).

The ROTL is usually used for moving dying prisoners to community hospices shortly before death, allowing relatives to have unlimited access to their loved ones.[130] In contrast to the compassionate release, ROTL excludes from consideration Category A prisoners, those identified as high risk of escape and prisoners who have been convicted but not yet sentenced.[131]

In the period 2004–2013, only 92 prisoners both determinate (fixed-length) and indeterminate were released on compassionate grounds.[132] Furthermore, it is very likely that there were no cases in which a bedridden or similarly incapacitated prisoner was released on compassionate grounds. Such prisoners, however, are also eligible for compassionate release.[133] It is not possible to find out how many prisoners formally met the eligibility criteria for compassionate release, nor how many compassionate release applications were rejected: such data are not collected by the Ministry of Justice.[134] However, the Prisons and Probation Ombudsman's reports demonstrate that both compassionate release and ROTL are considered only in a minority of cases of natural deaths in prisons. In the period 2007–2012, the ROTL was considered in 58 and granted only in 30 out of 214 cases reviewed by the Prisons and Probation Ombudsman.[135] In the same sample 78 prisoners were considered for compassionate release, which was granted in only 13 cases and 26 were still awaiting a decision on their application at the time of death.[136] In the period 2013–2015 only 36% of a sample of 314 prisoners who died in prison were considered for compassionate release. In 43% of these cases no decision had been made at the time of the death.[137]

In 2013 the Minister for Prisons and Probation, while giving evidence to the House of Commons Justice Committee, stated that the reasons behind the infrequent use of the power of compassionate release are public opinion, considerations of victims' interests, the impossibility of precisely determining remaining life expectancy and the wish of some prisoners to die in prison.[138] The Minister conceded that he faced difficult decisions regarding compassionate release of terminally ill prisoners because he needed to meet public expectations of compassion in allowing terminally ill prisoners to go home, effectively to die, but at the same time he had to be careful not to release a prisoner too early.[139]

Despite the fact that the Minister specifies some grand reasons for the infrequent use of compassionate release, the Ombudsman's review revealed deficiencies in the process of both compassionate release and ROTL. The first deficiency relates to the process of the application. According to the Ombudsman the

130 Prisons and Probation Ombudsman for England and Wales, 'End of Life Care' (n.76) 22.
131 Prison Service Order 6300: Release on temporary licence (n.129).
132 Ministry of Justice (n.35).
133 House of Commons Justice Committee, 'Older prisoners' (n.16) 11.
134 Ministry of Justice (n.35).
135 Prisons and Probation Ombudsman for England and Wales, 'End of Life Care' (n.76) 22.
136 ibid.
137 Prisons and Probation Ombudsman (n.17) 24.
138 House of Commons Justice Committee, 'Older Prisoners' (n.23) 32–33.
139 ibid.

process is often disorganised and there is a lack of clarity as to who is responsible for initiating the process and taking the application forward.[140] This results in delays in initiating the applications and leads to situations where applications are still pending by the time of the prisoner's death.[141] The second is in regard to the assessment of a prisoner's risk of reoffending. According to the Prisons and Probation Ombudsman (PPO) the risk assessments for the purposes of compassionate release and ROTL are frequently treated as box-ticking exercises without taking into account the effect of the medical condition of the prisoner on the actual risk of reoffending, 'but rather based on the risk the offender would have posed when healthy'.[142] Consequently, applications are evaluated on an incorrect assessment of risk. Taking into account the fundamental role of the level of risk posed by a prisoner for making decisions on compassionate release and ROTL applications, the decisions made on incorrect assessment of the risk potentially result in the denial of early release in cases where it could have been granted.

Conclusion

The rise in the elderly prison population is a growing issue in many countries. These countries include, but are not limited to, the UK,[143] Germany,[144] France,[145] Italy,[146] the US[147] and Canada.[148] Traditionally, prisons were designed to hold young deviant men rather than elderly, frail, seriously ill and dying inmates.[149] In recent years a law and policy framework has been developed in various jurisdictions to meet the needs of these prisoners.[150] However, it is widely reported that, despite legal requirements, only a few exemplary prisons are able to provide adequate prison conditions, and medical and mental health care to elderly, chronically and terminally ill prisoners.[151] Furthermore, legal mechanisms for the early release of very old, terminally or otherwise seriously ill prisoners have not had much impact on the situation of these prisoners.[152]

140 Prisons and Probation Ombudsman (n.17) 23.
141 ibid, 23–24.
142 ibid, 23.
143 See e.g. Allen and Watson (n.8).
144 E.g. Laubenthal (n.13).
145 Aebi and Delgrande (n.14) 70; See also publications of the same series from 2007 to 2012.
146 ibid.
147 Carson and Sabol (n 9); KiDeuk and Peterson (n.10).
148 Public Safety Canada (n.11) 47.
149 Crawley (n.43), 351–352; Mann (n.20) 41; Aday (n.43).
150 See e.g. Department of Health, 'National Service Framework for Older People' (n.71); National service framework for older people (n.72); Department of Health, 'A pathway to care for older offenders' (n.52); Prison Service Order 3050 Continuity of Health Care for Prisoners (n.78); Equality Act (n.79) ss.13, 20, 26, 27, 28; Prison Service Instruction 2011/32 Ensuring Equality (n 82); Care Act (n.75); Kerbs and Jolley (eds) (n.3).
151 Aday (n.43); Anno and others (n.7); Curtin (n.69).
152 See e.g. Chiu (n.101); Human Rights Watch (n.101); Demyan (n.7); Ministry of Justice (n.35).

The prison population aged 50 or over is a diverse group in terms of crimes committed, length and type of sentences served, and health status. In this population there are many determinate and indeterminate prisoners, including various types of lifer, whose sentences are longer than the life expectancy of their cohorts in their respective countries. They could be released automatically or be considered for discretional release only if they are lucky enough not to suffer from a fatal illness and if, against all the odds, they manage to live longer than the life expectancy for their cohorts. Moreover, some elderly prisoners are seriously or terminally ill. This may make their experience of imprisonment more onerous or in some case the imprisonment may impact the course of illness, speeding up the deterioration of their health.

Imprisonment for a crime after conviction by a competent court is a lawful deprivation of an individual's right to liberty. Such deprivation of this right is explicitly authorised in many international and regional human rights treaties and national Constitutions.[153] Elderly people are not exempted from imprisonment as punishment for a crime. However, cruel, inhuman, degrading or unusual punishment is almost universally prohibited.[154] Despite differences of legal frameworks and different judicial tests used for assessment of similar situations, jurisdictions with large and growing elderly prison populations, such as England and Germany, the US and Canada, recognise that deprivation of the right to liberty for a crime should not undermine human dignity. The protection of human dignity in the context of administration of sentences is realised through different legal concepts which are applicable to distinct situations. This requirement includes prohibition of grossly disproportionate punishments, which means that the means of achieving the aims of the punishment should not undermine the right to human dignity.[155] However, this standard was articulated to apply only on rare and unique occasions.[156]

Furthermore, it is widely accepted that criminal punishment is not intended

153 International Covenant on Civil and Political Rights adopted 16 December 1966,entered into force 23 March 1976 (United Nations General Assembly) Art.9(1); European Convention on Human Rights 1950, ECHR (Council of Europe) Art.5(1)(a); American Convention on Human Rights 1969 (Organisation of American States) Art.7(2)(3); Constitution 17 September 1787 (United States of America) XIV Amendment; Grundgesetz 1949, GG (Bundesrepublik Deutschland) Art.2. Abs.2; Human Rights Act 1998, Sch.1 Part 1.

154 Universal Declaration of Human Rights 1948 (United Nations General Assembly) Art.5; International Covenant on Civil and Political Rights (n.1) Art.7; European Convention on Human Rights (n.1) Art.3; American Convention on Human Rights (n.1) Art.5(2); African Charter on Human and Peoples' Rights 1981 (Assembly of the Organisation of African Unity) Art.5; M. Cherif Bassiouni, 'Human Rights in the Context of Criminal Justice: Identifying International Procedural Protections and Equivalent Protections in National Constitutions' (1993) 3 *Duke Journal of Comparative and International Law* 235.

155 *Solem v Helm* 463 US 277 (1983) 297–300; *R v Smith* [1987] 1 SCR 1045, 1073; *Vinter and others v United Kingdom* (2012) App no. 66069/09 and 130/10 and 3896/10 (ECtHR, 17 January 2012), para.89; *Vinter and others v United Kingdom* [GC] ECHR 2013-III 317, para.102.

156 See e.g. *Lockyer v Andrade* 538 U.S. 63 (2003); *Vinter v United Kingdom* (n.155) paras 88–89; *Vinter v United Kingdom* [GC] (n.155), para.102.

to inflict physical or mental suffering or humiliation which goes beyond what would be considered as justified by the practical demands of a penal system.[157] Punishment which causes suffering beyond the threshold marking the limit of the practical demands of a penal system offends against human dignity.[158] There is already case law from the European Court of Human Rights (ECtHR) which explicitly states that in certain circumstances the detention of an elderly person over a lengthy period may be degrading in violation of Article 3 of the European Convention on Human Rights (ECHR).[159] Furthermore, the ECtHR articulated that, in exceptional circumstances, when the health of a prisoner is absolutely incompatible with detention, Article 3 ECHR may require the detainee to be released.[160] In this regard the Court emphasised the important role of a domestic legal mechanism for protection of Article 3 rights of seriously ill prisoners.[161]

Finally, even if the aims of retribution and deterrence justify deprivation of the right to liberty for life, respect for human dignity forbids depriving a human being of hope to atone for her/his crime and regain the right to liberty at some point. This requirement implies a legal obligation to have in place a procedure in order to check whether, after the passage of a certain length of time, continued imprisonment of life prisoners still serves a legitimate purpose. The respect for human dignity requires release of a prisoner serving a life sentence if the review demonstrates that continued imprisonment is not justified by the legitimate aims of punishment.

In recent times the right to review in the context of life sentences has received legal recognition both in the US[162] and in Europe.[163] However, in the US the Supreme Court has so far recognised this right only in relation to juveniles. Moreover, the Court excluded from the scope of that right those juveniles whose sentence of life imprisonment for homicide-related offences was non-mandatory. The Supreme Court also left untouched the issue of the content of the right and due process safeguards attached to it.[164]

By contrast, in Europe, the scope of the right to review of life sentences is broader. In recent case law the ECtHR has recognised that a possibility of review and a prospect of release should be given to all prisoners, even to lifers.[165] This recognition on the part of the ECtHR imposes a legal obligation on its 47 Member States[166] to have in place a review procedure equipped with adequate

157 See e.g. Nigel S Rodley, *The treatment of prisoners under international law* (3rd edn, Oxford University Press 2009) ch.9.

158 ibid.

159 *Sawoniuk v United Kingdom (dec.)* no. 63716/00 ECHR 2001-VI 375; *Papon v France (no. 1) (dec.)* ECHR 2001-VI 459.

160 See e.g. *Chaykovskiy v Ukraine* App no. 2295/06 (ECtHR, 15 October 2009), para.55; *Grishin v Russia* App no. 30983/02 (ECtHR, 15 November 2007), para.71.

161 *Gülay Cetin v Turkey* no. 44084/10 paras 131–132 (ECtHR, 5 March 2013).

162 See e.g. *Graham v Florida* 130 SCt 2011 2023 (2010); *Miller v Alabama* 132 S Ct 2455 (2012).

163 See e.g. *Vinter v United Kingdom* [GC] (n.155).

164 See e.g. *Graham v Florida* (n.162); *Miller v Alabama* (n.162).

165 See e.g. *Kafkaris v Cyprus* [GC] ECHR 2008-I 223.

166 David J Harris, Michael O'Boyle and Colin Warbrick, *Law of the European Convention on Human Rights*, 2nd edn (Oxford University Press, 2009) 2, 23–28.

procedural safeguards in order to check whether, after the passage of a certain time, generally 25 years, continued imprisonment is still justified by the legitimate aims of punishment.[167] The requirement of review also applies directly to those elderly prisoners who are serving life sentences. However, among elderly prisoners there are many life or indeterminate and fixed-term prisoners whose mandatory custodial term is longer than the life expectancy of their cohorts in their respective countries. Moreover, some elderly prisoners are seriously or terminally ill.

As mentioned above, prohibition of torture or cruel, inhuman or degrading treatment or punishment places certain limits on the administration of imprisonment after conviction by a court of law. Without much elaboration, the ECtHR articulated that detention of an elderly person for a lengthy period may raise an issue under Article 3.

In the case of seriously ill prisoners it went further, interpreting Article 3 as to require the release of lawfully detained prisoners whose health is absolutely incompatible with detention. The Court emphasised the importance of specific legal procedures for complying with Article 3. This interpretation of Article 3 already offers a weighty safeguard to elderly and seriously ill prisoners in Council of Europe (CoE) countries. This requirement, however, comes into effect only when it is already determined that the continued imprisonment is absolutely incompatible with detention. In order to determine whether continued imprisonment is absolutely incompatible with detention, a review of the situation is required. Although the Court emphasised the importance of specific procedures for the release of seriously ill prisoners, it did not state that such procedures are required by the ECHR. In fact, currently the process of review of compatibility of continued imprisonment with the health of seriously ill detainees is left outside the scope of the ECHR. As a result, review of the compatibility of health of a detainee with continued deprivation of liberty is often conducted under loose executive powers which lack adequate safeguards against arbitrariness.

In this regard, the right to review under Article 3 has a broader scope. As the analysis in the substantive part of this book will show, the requirement of review under Article 3 has a preventative function.[168] In the context of life sentences it aims to review whether or not continued imprisonment is still compatible with the ECHR. A life prisoner is not made to wait until the violation of the Convention has taken place. The preventative aspect of Article 3 comes into effect automatically at the point in time when it is assumed that further detention may be in violation of the Convention covering the process of review. The right to review provides a weighty guarantee for protection of Article 3 rights of life prisoners. It has a much broader scope than the exceptional requirement of release of ill prisoners which in any case do not cover relatively healthy elderly prisoners whose sentences are longer than their actuarial life expectancy. Therefore, this book

167 See e.g. *Vinter v United Kingdom* [GC] (n.155); *Murray v the Netherlands* [GC] App no 10511/10 (ECtHR, 26 April 2016).

168 *Vinter v United Kingdom* [GC] (n.155) per Judge Mahoney.

explores the issue of applicability of the right to review under Article 3 of the ECHR to prisoners who serve fixed-term or indeterminate sentences with longer mandatory custodial terms than their actuarial life expectancies, and those who are terminally or otherwise seriously ill.

At present only the ECtHR has interpreted the prohibition of torture or inhuman or degrading treatment or punishment to include a requirement of review of life sentences without any exception on the ground of the gravity of the offence or the age at the time the crime was committed. Therefore, as the point of departure, this book takes the ECtHR's position on the right to review under Article 3, which means that the arguments on the applicability of the right to review would be directly relevant only to elderly and seriously ill prisoners in CoE countries. However, the book also outlines the position of the Supreme Courts of the US and Canada in regard to the protection of human dignity in the context of sentencing and administration of sentences. This outline, indeed, highlights some similarities in the development of the case law in regard to this issue in all reviewed jurisdictions. This demonstrates that the legal arguments developed in this book could also have some relevance to these jurisdictions.

Likewise, the majority of the case law examples which are used to support the arguments advanced in this book come from the ECtHR and English courts. Moreover, the book turns to the power of compassionate release in England and Wales as an example of executive power which would not meet the Article 3 requirement of review of continued imprisonment of elderly and seriously ill prisoners. However, the model it proposes is abstract and could be adapted to other relevant jurisdictions.

This book aims to fill the gap in our understanding of the impact of old age and serious illness on the severity of punishment by subjecting the law in this area to a rigorous and innovative analysis. It makes contributions to the fields of penology, human rights law and jurisprudence by engaging in debates on measurement of penal severity, 'gross disproportionality' and the role of procedural safeguards in keeping imprisonment within human rights limits. By examining the issue of equal impact of punishment, the book also contributes to debates on equal/unequal treatment of elderly people more commonly found in the literature on the law relating to the elderly.[169] This book goes some way to demonstrating the importance of giving a fair chance to seriously ill and dying prisoners to regain their freedom by proving that they have atoned for their crimes and can be safely released from prison.

With the continued rise in the population of elderly prisoners, the number of those suffering from serious illnesses or dying in prison can be expected to

169 See in general Israel Doron (ed), *Theories on law and ageing: The jurisprudence of elder law* (Springer 2009); MI Hall, 'Equity Theory: Responding to the Material Exploitation of the Vulnerable but Capable' in Israel Doron (ed), *Theories on law and ageing: The jurisprudence of elder law* (Springer 2009); Helen Meenan, 'Age Discrimination and the Future Development of Elder Rights in the European Union: Walking Side by Side or Hand in Hand?' in Israel Doron (ed), *Beyond elder law: New directions in law and aging* (Springer 2012).

rise further.[170] Prisons are not the places to treat the seriously ill or to provide comfort for the dying; continued imprisonment of these prisoners comes at enormous human and financial cost. Judging by the prevalence of sexual and other serious offenders among those who die in prison, the cost of keeping them may seem to be justified.[171] However, the report of the Prisons and Probation Ombudsman of England and Wales and other studies demonstrate that in many cases the category of risk assigned to prisoners does not correctly reflect the actual risk posed.[172] These findings emphasise the importance of a release mechanism to provide seriously ill and dying prisoners with a fair chance of demonstrating their atonement and regaining their freedom before they die. Even if they are not released, having in place a fair procedure for determining the lawfulness of continued imprisonment is necessary for showing the respect for the human being significantly affected by the decision and upholding the rule of law.

170 See e.g. Prisons and Probation Ombudsman (n.17) 10.

171 ibid, 11.

172 Prisons and Probation Ombudsman for England and Wales, 'End of Life Care' (n.76) 19.

1 Human rights limits on continued imprisonment

Abstract

Deprivation of the right to liberty after conviction by a court of law is explicitly authorised in many international and regional human rights treaties and national Constitutions. Elderly people are not exempted from imprisonment as a punishment for a crime. However, cruel, inhuman, degrading or unusual punishment is almost universally prohibited. Although imprisonment after conviction by a competent court per se *is not regarded as cruel, inhuman, degrading or unusual punishment, courts at both international and national levels have interpreted respective provisions as imposing some limits on administration of imprisonment. Different courts and tribunals have interpreted the prohibition of cruel, inhuman or degrading punishment as putting limits on the method and manner of administration of imprisonment. Furthermore, the same provision has been interpreted as putting limits on prison sentences of excessive length and requiring rigorous procedural safeguards in order to ensure compatibility of ultimate sentences, such as life imprisonment, with human rights. This chapter explores the above outlined human rights limits of imprisonment with reference to the jurisprudence of some national and supranational courts. It aims to highlight the relevant principles in order to explore their applicability to continued imprisonment of elderly and seriously ill prisoners.*

Restricting the method and manner of the administration of imprisonment

The various approaches of different courts in interpreting the prohibition of cruel, inhuman, degrading or unusual punishment as putting limits on the method and manner of administration of imprisonment have been well researched and discussed in the literature.[1] What follows is a short outline of the approach of the European Court of Human Rights (ECtHR) and the US Supreme Court.

1 For the approaches of the International Covenant on Civil and Political Rights (CCPR), the European Court of Human Rights (ECtHR) and the Inter-American Court of Human Rights (IACHR) see Nigel S Rodley, *The treatment of prisoners under international law* (3rd edn, Oxford

The European approach

The ECtHR, in particular, recognises that the forcible, but lawful, subjection of individuals to the demands of penal systems in most, if not in all, cases contains elements of humiliation. However, this inevitable element of humiliation is justified by the practical demands of the penal system and the nature of judicial punishment.[2] The ECtHR held that, in order for judicial punishment to be regarded as 'degrading' within the meaning of Article 3 of the European Convention on Human Rights (ECHR), 'the humiliation or debasement must attain a particular level and in any event must be other than usual element of humiliation' which is generally inherent in judicial punishment.[3] The threshold of the level of humiliation or debasement that is required in being judicial in the scope of Article 3 is relative, depending 'on all the circumstances of the case and, in particular, on the nature and context of the punishment itself and the manner and method of its execution'.[4]

With the development of case law on Article 3, the ECtHR has articulated particular situations which might push lawfully imposed punishment and treatment associated with it beyond the inevitable element of humiliation justified by the practical demands of the penal system and the nature of judicial punishment.[5] In particular, the ECtHR has articulated that not securing proper conditions of detention, failing to secure the health and wellbeing of prisoners and subjecting them to distress or hardship beyond the practical demands of imprisonment would push the level of humiliation and debasement inherent in judicial punishment beyond its inevitable level.[6] As a rule, the question whether or not in a particular case the situation went beyond the inevitable element of humiliation is assessed on the basis of specific incidents that occurred during deprivation of liberty or the cumulative effect of different conditions of imprisonment.[7]

Furthermore, in this regard the Court also discussed the subjective component of treatment or conditions to which the inmate was subjected. It held that:[8]

> although the question whether the purpose of the treatment was to humiliate or debase the victim is a factor to be taken into account, the absence

University Press 2009); David J Harris, Michael O'Boyle and Colin Warbrick, *Law of the European Convention on Human Rights* (2nd edn, Oxford University Press 2009) ch.3.

2 *Tyrer v United Kingdom* (1978) Series A no 26 para.30.

3 ibid.

4 ibid.

5 On the point of replacing evaluative assessment of the meaning of torture, inhuman, degrading treatment or punishment with using precedent cases see Jeremy Waldron, 'Inhuman and Degrading Treatment: The Words Themselves' (2010) 23(2) Can JL & Jurisprudence 269.

6 See e.g. *Kudla v Poland* [GC] ECHR 2000-XI 197 paras 92–94; *Kalashnikov v Russia* ECHR 2001-XI 197 para.95.

7 *Ireland v United Kingdom* (1978) Series A no 25 167; *Peers v Greece* ECHR 2001-III 275 28–34; *Dougoz v Greece* ECHR 2001-II 255 46; *Price v United Kingdom* ECHR 2001-VII 153 30; *Henaf v France* ECHR 2003-XI 213 13.

8 *V. v United Kingdom* [GC] [1999] IX ECHR 111 para.71; *Peers v Greece* (n.7) para.74.

of any such purpose cannot conclusively rule out a finding of violation of Article 3.

There have been several cases before the ECtHR arguing that the continued imprisonment of applicants is degrading or inhuman in violation of Article 3 of the ECHR because of the impact of very old age or a serious medical condition on the prison experience.[9] The ECtHR explicitly stated that the Convention contains no prohibition against the imprisonment of elderly persons, but also noted that 'under certain circumstances the detention of an elderly person over a lengthy period might raise an issue under Article 3'.[10] Subsequent case law on the subject demonstrates that this approach has become one of the general principles which ECtHR uses to assess relevant claims.[11] The Court pointed out that 'regard is to be had to the particular circumstances of each specific case'.[12]

By contrast, the ECtHR has developed detailed rules for the assessment of compatibility with the continued imprisonment in cases of fatally or otherwise seriously ill prisoners. As the case law demonstrates, in both categories the ECtHR generally applies the same standard regardless of whether the illness is fatal in the short term or otherwise serious. The starting position of the ECtHR is that Article 3 of the ECHR cannot be interpreted as laying down a general obligation to release prisoners on the ground of ill-health.[13] However, it imposes an obligation on the State to protect the health and wellbeing of prisoners by, *inter alia*, providing them with the necessary medical assistance.[14] Moreover, it requires the State to ensure that conditions of detention are compatible with human dignity and that 'the manner and method of execution of the measures imposed do not subject her/him to distress or hardship of an intensity exceeding the unavoidable level of suffering inherent in detention'.[15]

Further development of the case law on the subject has brought the recognition on the part of the ECtHR that the health of a detainee is 'among the factors to be taken into account in determining how a custodial sentence is to be served'.[16] The ECtHR clearly stated that 'Article 3 may require the release of a detainee only in exceptional cases and under certain conditions, where his or her

9 See e.g. *Priebke v Italy* (dec.) no.48799/99 (ECtHR, 5 April 2001); *Sawoniuk v United Kingdom* (dec.) no. 63716/00 ECHR 2001-VI 375; *Papon v France (no. 1)* (dec) ECHR 2001-VI 459.

10 *Sawoniuk v United Kingdom* (n.9); *Papon v France (no. 1)* (n.9).

11 *Mouisel v France* ECHR 2002-IX 219 38; *Matencio v France* no. 58749/00 76 (ECtHR, 15 January 2004); *Sakkopoulos v Greece* no. 61828/00 39 (ECtHR, 15 January 2004); *Farbtuhs v Latvia* no. 4672/02 53 (ECtHR, 2 December 2004).

12 *Papon v France (no. 1)* (n.9); *Priebke v Italy* (n.9); *Sawoniuk v United Kingdom* (n.9).

13 See e.g. *Kudla v Poland* [GC] (n.8) para.93-94; *Mouisel v France* (n.13) para.40; *Sakkopoulos v Greece* (n.13) para.38; *Holomiov v Moldova* App.no. 30649/05 (ECtHR, 7 November 2006) para.112; *Grishin v Russia* App no. 30983/02 (ECtHR, 15 November 2007) para.71; *Enea v Italy* [GC] ECHR 2009-IV 163 para.58; *Chaykovskiy v Ukraine* App no. 2295/06 (ECtHR, 15 October 2009) para.54.

14 See e.g. *Kudla v Poland* [GC] (n.6) paras 92–94; *Kalashnikov v Russia* (n.6) para.95.

15 See e.g. *Kudla v Poland* [GC] (n.6) para.94; *Mouisel v France* (n.11) para.40.

16 See e.g. *Mouisel v France* (n.11) paras 43–44; *Matencio v France* (n.11) para.76; *Sakkopoulos v*

health is absolutely incompatible with detention'.[17] In cases where a prisoner suffers from a serious illness, the provision of necessary care is not enough to satisfy the requirements of Article 3. The authorities also need to consider, in view of the applicant's state of health, whether or not she/he should continue to be detained.[18] The ECtHR emphasised the importance of domestic legal mechanisms designated specifically to review the continued deprivation of liberty in view of serious illness for the protection of rights under Article 3.[19]

The approach of the US Supreme Court

In the US, the Supreme Court has also developed a considerable jurisprudence on the applicability of the Eighth Amendment (prohibition of cruel and unusual punishment) of the US Constitution in the context of imprisonment. In the case of *Estelle v Gamble*, Justice Marshall, writing for the majority, stated that the Eighth Amendment prohibition of cruel and unusual punishment also embodied 'broad and idealistic concepts of dignity, civilized standards, humanity, and decency'.[20] According to the majority, punishments 'which are incompatible with the evolving standards of decency that mark the progress of maturing society or involve unnecessary and wanton infliction of pain' do not meet these standards and therefore violate the Eighth Amendment.[21] Denial of appropriate medical care to prisoners could result in needless pain and suffering which is inconsistent with contemporary standards of decency and thus constitutes unnecessary and wanton infliction of pain prohibited by the Eighth Amendment. However, not all cases of medical mistreatment of prisoners would constitute a violation of the Eighth Amendment, but only those where mistreatment involved deliberate indifference to serious medical needs.[22]

Apart from the medical mistreatment of prisoners, the Eighth Amendment litigation before the US Supreme Court involved cases concerning prison conditions. In the case *Rhodes v Chapman*,[23] relying on the doctrine of 'evolving standards of decency that mark the progress of maturing society', the Court held that conditions that result in 'unquestioned and serous deprivation of basic human needs' or 'deprive inmates of the minimal civilized measure of life's necessities' may be infliction of unnecessary and wanton pain in violation of the Eighth

Greece (n.11) para.38; *Farbtuhs v Latvia* (n.11) para.52; *Gülay Cetin v Turkey* no. 44084/10 para.103 (ECtHR, 5 March 2013).

17 See e.g. *Chaykovskiy v Ukraine* (n.13) para.55; *Grishin v Russia* (n.13) para.71.

18 *Farbtuhs v Latvia* (n.11); *Scoppola v Italy* no. 50550/06 (ECtHR, 10 June 2008); *Cara-Damiani v Italy* no. 2447/05 (ECtHR, 7 February 2012); *Contrada v Italy (no.2)* no. 7509/08 (ECtHR, 11 February 2014).

19 *Gülay Cetin v Turkey* (n.16) paras 131–132.

20 *Estelle v Gamble*, 429 U.S. 97, 102 (1976).

21 ibid, 102–103.

22 ibid, 103–106.

23 *Rhodes v Chapman*, 452 U.S. 337 (1981).

Amendment.[24] In this case the Court found that the claimants were not able to demonstrate that the conditions, e.g. double celling, were so bad as not to be able to meet their basic human needs.[25] Therefore, it did not discuss whether in cases relating to prison conditions, apart from establishing the objective component, i.e. deprivation of basic human needs, any proof of a subjective component is also required.[26]

In the subsequent judgments the Supreme Court clarified that, in order to demonstrate a violation of the Eighth Amendment in the context of enforcement of prison sentence, the inmate is required to prove both an objective component, i.e. 'was the deprivation sufficiently serious?', and a subjective component, i.e. 'did the officials act with a sufficiently culpable state of mind?'.[27] Depending on the context the subjective component test might involve demonstrating only 'deliberate indifference' to the basic needs of prisoners or 'malicious and sadistic use of force for the very purpose of causing harm'.[28]

Furthermore, as with the standard of proof of the subjective component of the treatment prohibited by the Eighth Amendment, the Court clarified that the standard of proof for the objective component also depends on the context. In some cases it might be required to demonstrate that as a result of the treatment the victim sustained a significant injury. However, this is not required in cases of physical abuse. In these cases the objective component is *per se* satisfied.[29]

Outlawing excessive prison sentences

Various national and international courts have interpreted the prohibition of cruel, inhuman or degrading treatment or punishment as not only serving as a check on the method and manner of administration of imprisonment, but also outlawing 'grossly' disproportionate punishments, including prison sentences of excessive length.[30] In legal scholarship there has been much consideration of the issue of 'grossly' disproportionate prison terms as human rights violations.[31] Dirk

24 ibid, 347.
25 ibid, 352.
26 *Wilson v Seiter*, 501 U.S. 294 (1991) 298.
27 ibid, 304.
28 ibid, 302.
29 *Hudson v McMillian*, 112 S. Ct. 995, (1992) 1000.
30 Dirk van Zyl Smit and Andrew Ashworth, 'Disproportionate Sentences as Human Rights Violations' (2004) 67(4) *Modern Law Review* 541.
31 For a general discussion on 'grossly' disproportionate sentences as human rights violations see van Zyl Smit and Ashworth (n.30); Richard S Frase, 'Excessive Prison Sentences, Punishment Goals, and the Eighth Amendment: "Proportionality" Relative to What?' (2005) 89 Minn L Rev 571; van Zyl Smit, 'Constitutional Jurisprudence and Proportionality in Sentencing' (1995) 3(4) *European Journal of Crime, Criminal Law and Criminal Justice* 369; Richard A Bierschbach, 'Proportionality and Parole' (2012) 160 *University of Pennsylvania Law Review* 1745; Steven Grossman, 'Proportionality in Non-Capital Sentencing: The Supreme Court's Tortured Approach to Cruel and Unusual Punishment' (1996) 84(1) *Kentucky Law Journal* 107; William W Berry III, 'Eighth Amendment Differentness' (2013) 78(4) *Missouri Law Review* 1053; Deborah A

van Zyl Smit and Andrew Ashworth have argued that 'grossly' disproportionate sentences should be outlawed because:[32]

> 'Firstly, punishment, particularly imprisonment, constitutes a prima facie violation of an individual's right to liberty; secondly that in principle such a measure can be justified only where a person has been convicted of a serious offence; thirdly that respect for rights, and limitation on the arbitrary use of state power, requires that substantial deprivations of an offender's liberty should only be permissible if the offender has committed a very serious offence; and finally that to allow states to impose substantial restrictions or deprivations of liberty where the offence was not serious would be to condone the use of individuals merely as a means to an end, which is inconsistent with fundamental respect for the dignity of each human being.'

They have also convincingly demonstrated that the right not to be subjected to 'grossly' disproportionate punishment has been recognised and practised by many national and supranational courts.[33]

However, the opponents of interpreting the prohibition of cruel, inhuman or degrading treatment or punishment as also outlawing excessive prison terms have criticised such development.[34] One of the most outspoken critics of such interpretation, the late Justice Scalia, Associate Justice of the US Supreme Court, in his concurring opinion in the case of *Ewing v California*,[35] argued that the Eighth Amendment of the US Constitution does not require proportionality of prison sentences because in this context proportionality of punishment 'is inherently a concept tied to the penological goal of retribution'.[36] The principle of proportionality requires proportionality between the severity of the crime (the harm caused or intended and the degree of culpability as determined by the degree of intent, motives, role in the offence and mental illness or other diminished capacity)[37] and punishment. In the view of Justice Scalia, non-retributive purposes of punishment, including deterrence, public protection and rehabilita-

Schwartz and J Wishingrad, 'Eighth Amendment, Beccaria, and the Enlightenment: An Historical Justification for the Weems v. United States Excessive Punishment Doctrine' (1975) 24(3) Buff L Rev 783; Margaret R Gibbs, 'Eighth Amendment. Narrow Proportionality Requirement Preserves Deference to Legislative Judgment' (1992) 82(4) *Journal of Criminal Law & Criminology* 955; John E Gibbs, 'Jurisprudential Juxtaposition: Application of Graham v. Florida to Adult Sentences' (2010–2011) 38 Florida St U Law Review 957; Youngjae Lee, 'Why Proportionality Matters' (2012) 160(6) *University of Pennsylvania Law Review* 1835.

32 van Zyl Smit and Ashworth (n.30), 542.

33 ibid.

34 See e.g. John D Castiglione, 'Qualitative and Quantitative Proportionality: A Specific Critique of Retributivism' (2010) 71(1) *Ohio State Law Journal* 71.

35 *Ewing v California* 538 U.S. 11 (2003).

36 ibid, 31.

37 Michael S Moore, *Placing Blame: A Theory of the Criminal Law* (Oxford University Press 2010) 300.

tion, are alien to the concept of proportionality.[38] In this case only one more Justice agreed with Scalia's approach. However, in the next case on the same issue the two sceptics of proportionality combined with those Justices, who accept only a very narrow proportionality requirement for imprisonment, producing a majority judgment which some commentators regard as a 'virtual abolition of the disproportionality principle in the US Constitution'.[39]

The argument of Justice Scalia, that the Eighth Amendment of the US Constitution does not require adopting a particular penal policy, seems also to be relevant to other jurisdictions. The ECtHR, for instance, has also articulated that apart from the penological goal of retribution (punishment),[40] the Contracting States are also free to pursue utilitarian goals, including deterrence,[41] incapacitation[42] and rehabilitation.[43] However, this reservation to the principle of 'gross disproportionality' of punishment could be sidestepped. In this context, this principle should be seen putting constraints on the permissible limitations of human rights, rather than as a retributive principle requiring the severity of the sentence to be commensurate with the seriousness of the offence. As a principle constraining permissible restrictions on human rights in general, proportionality is widely practised by national and international courts.[44] Although the particularities of the judicial tests used by various courts differ, the core of the test looks to balance the ends (the objective of the restriction itself) and means (the measure designed to meet the objective) of the restriction with the value of the fundamental right itself.[45]

Such tests are usually used by courts in relation to the rights which have an explicit limitation clause inserted into the text of the norm prescribing the right. However, on the example of the case law of the EctHR, it has been successfully argued that for the rights that have no limitation clause, the Court considered the ends and means proportionality of prima facie limitation in the process of determining the scope of the right itself.[46] According to Kavanagh, despite differences in the structure of the rights, the process of determining the scope of the rights is not fundamentally different. In relation to 'qualified' rights, courts tend to adopt a two-stage process of determining the scope of a right: the first stage

38 *Ewing v California* (n.35) 32.

39 van Zyl Smit and Ashworth (n.30), 545.

40 *Sawoniuk v United Kingdom* (n.9); *V. v the United Kingdom* [GC] ECHR 1999-IX 111.

41 *M.C. v Bulgaria* ECHR 2003-XII 1.

42 *Weeks v United Kingdom* Series A no 114.

43 *Dickson v United Kingdom* [GC] ECHR 2007-V 99; *Vinter v the United Kingdom* [GC] ECHR 2013-III 317 para.111.

44 See e.g. Alec Stone Sweet and Jud Mathews, 'Proportionality Balancing and Global Constitutionalism' (2008) 47 *Columbia Journal of Transnational Law* 73, 75

45 See e.g. *Regina (Daly) v Secretary of State for the Home Department* [2001] 2 AC 532 (House of Lords), 547; Jeremy McBride, 'Proportionality and the European Convention on Human Rights' in Evelyn Ellis (ed), *The Principle of Proportionality in the Laws of Europe* (Hart, Oxford 1999)

46 Simon Atrill, 'Keeping the executive in the picture: a reply to Professor Leigh' [2003] *Public Law* 41; Aileen Kavanagh, *Constitutional review under the UK Human Rights Act* (1st edn, Cambridge University Press 2009).

involves establishing whether there has been a prima facie violation of the right, whereas the second stage is the assessment of whether or not the interference was proportionate. The latter is a balancing exercise between the importance of a Convention right on the one hand and the severity of interference plus the aim which a particular measure attempted to achieve on the other.

While there are no similar stages of adjudication in 'unqualified' rights cases, the problem of 'assessment of whether the right has been contravened is presented in the form of a delineation of the scope of the right'.[47] For instance, Article 3 of the ECHR prohibits torture or inhuman or degrading treatment or punishment in absolute terms. However, the ECtHR has established that in order to be in breach of Article 3, legitimate imprisonment (which in general inevitably involves some degree of suffering and humiliation) must inflict suffering and humiliation which in any event 'go beyond that inevitable element of suffering or humiliation connected with a given form of legitimate treatment or punishment'.[48] Similarly, the ECtHR tends to say that ill-treatment must attain a minimum level of severity, which depends on all the circumstances of the case.[49] Thus, determining whether the ill-treatment attained the minimum level of severity, or in other words determining the scope of the right under Article 3, inevitably involves a degree of balancing. In this context, the legitimate requirements of a custodial sentence (public interest) are weighted against the rights of an individual. This is crudely similar to the balancing exercised during the adjudication of 'qualified' rights.

Indeed, jurisprudence of courts in different jurisdictions demonstrates that, while considering the issue of excessiveness of a prison term, the principle of proportionality is used not in a narrow sense as a retributive principle, but rather as a principle constraining permissible restrictions on human rights. Indeed, evidence supporting the above articulated position can be found in the case law of courts in the US and Canada as well as in Europe.

The approach of the US

The late Justice Scalia argued that, in the context of the appropriateness of a prison sentence, proportionality could only be understood as a retributive principle requiring that the imposed punishment is commensurate with the seriousness of the crime. However, the case law of the Supreme Court on this matter demonstrates that this is not the approach of the majority of the Supreme Court Justices.

In the recent history of the US Supreme Court there was only one case where the Court found that a prison term was in violation of the Eighth Amendment because of its excessiveness.[50] While the Court did not find a violation of the Eighth Amendment in the rest of the cases on this issue, these cases demonstrate

47 Kavanagh (n.46).
48 *Kalashnikov v Russia* (n.6) para.95.
49 *Kudla v Poland* [GC] (n.6) para.91.
50 *Solem v Helm* 463 US 277 (1983).

that the Court approves a 'broad and basic proportionality principle that takes into account all of the justifications for penal sanctions'.[51]

In *Solem v Helm*,[52] the Supreme Court articulated the following test to measure the proportionality of the sentence. Justice Powell, writing for the majority of the Court, stated that the assessment of proportionality 'should be guided by objective factors'.[53] Three such factors were identified based on the review of previous case law on the issue.

The first pillar in the proportionality review is the comparison of the gravity of the offence with the severity of the sentence.[54] According to Justice Powell, this could be considered as an objective factor because courts are competent in assessing both elements and are required to conduct similar assessments in different contexts.[55] He stated that the gravity of the offence should be measured based on the harm caused or threatened and the offender's culpability, including her/his intent and motives.[56]

Second, if this comparison indicates that the sentence is 'grossly disproportionate', the Court turns to comparing the sentences imposed on other criminals in the same jurisdiction. Powell stated that 'if more serious crimes are subject to the same penalty, or to less serious penalties, that is some indication that the punishment at issue may be excessive'.[57]

Finally, the sentence imposed on the defendant in a material case should be compared to sentences imposed in other state jurisdictions for the same crime.[58] A violation of the Eighth Amendment would be found if the defendant in the material case is sentenced to a more severe sentence than in any other state.[59]

Justice Powell accepted that it is legitimate for states to impose harsher penalties on repeat offenders in order to incapacitate them. As a habitual offender, Helm was sentenced to life without parole for issuing a 'no account' cheque to the value of $100. However, after considering Helm's criminal history, Justice Powell concluded that the sentence was:[60]

> unlikely to advance the goals of our criminal justice system in any substantial way. Neither Helm nor the State will have an incentive to pursue clearly needed treatment for his alcohol problem, or any other program of rehabilitation.

51 *Ewing v California* (n.36) 33–35; *Harmelin v Michigan* 501 US 957 (1991).
52 *Solem v Helm* (n.50).
53 ibid 290–291.
54 ibid 290–292.
55 ibid 292.
56 ibid 293–294.
57 ibid 291.
58 ibid 292.
59 ibid 300.
60 ibid 297 n.22.

In the leading Canadian case on this issue the Supreme Court Justice Lamer defined a gross disproportionality test :[61]

> In assessing whether a sentence is grossly disproportionate, the court must first consider the gravity of the offence, the personal characteristics of the offender and the particular circumstances of the case in order to determine what range of sentences would have been appropriate to punish, rehabilitate or deter this particular offender or to protect the public from this particular offender.

Furthermore, in the same case Justice McIntyre articulated three characteristics which, in combination with one another or alone, indicate 'gross disproportionality' of punishment. This is the case when:[62]

> (1) the punishment is of such character or duration as to outrage the public conscience or be degrading to human dignity;
> (2) the punishment goes beyond what is necessary for the achievement of a valid social aim, having regard to the legitimate purposes of punishment and the adequacy of possible alternatives; or
> (3) the punishment is arbitrarily imposed in the sense that it is not applied on a rational basis in accordance with ascertained or ascertainable standards.

In this case the Court held that the statutory provision prescribing a minimum mandatory term of seven years for importing narcotics breached the prohibition of the 'cruel and unusual' clause of the Canadian Charter of Rights and Freedoms. The holding of the Court was based on 'certainty' that 'there would be cases in which, in the light of the circumstances of the offender and the offence' the seven years' minimum term would be grossly disproportionate.[63]

The reasoning of the respective Justices in this case clearly indicates that outlawing a minimum mandatory prison term because of gross disproportionality was not based exclusively on the retributive concept of proportionality. The Court clearly points out that prison terms which are imposed based on other punishment purposes can also be constrained by a general constitutional principle of proportionality. Moreover, the Court in this case went on to assess explicitly whether the seven-year mandatory minimum prison term for importing narcotics can be justified under the Section 1 of the Charter of Rights and Freedoms. This provision provides that a Charter right may be subject to such 'reasonable limits as may be demonstrably justified in a free and democratic society'.[64] It found that while the deterrence of importation and trafficking of hard drugs was an objective 'of sufficient importance to warrant overriding a constitutionally protected right

61 *R v Smith* [1987] 1 SCR 1045, 1073.

62 ibid 1097–1098.

63 Don Stuart, *Charter justice in Canadian criminal law* (6th edn, Carswell 2014) 531.

64 'Canadian Charter of Rights and Freedoms', Part I of the Constitution Act 1982.

or freedom', the means employed to achieve this objective were disproportionate: general deterrence did not require all those who imported narcotics to be sentenced to a minimum of seven years imprisonment regardless of the circumstances of a particular case.[65]

The European approach

The jurisprudence of the German Federal Constitutional Court demonstrates that the Court uses the very same legal term both in adjudication of human rights with limitation clauses and claims of excessiveness of punishment adjudicated under the human dignity clause. Unlike English legal language, where the term 'proportionality' is used to define both the retributive principle of sentencing and the principle which puts constraints on the permissible limitations of human rights, in Germany two different terms are used. These are respectively '*Tatproportionalität*'[66] and '*Verhältnismäßigkeitsgrundsatz*'.[67]

The leading German case on the proportionality of a prison term is the case on life imprisonment decided by the Federal Constitutional Court in 1977.[68] This case originated from the submission of a State Court which, in a case of an aggravated homicide, was obliged to impose a mandatory sentence of life imprisonment. The State Court decided that a mandatory sentence of life imprisonment is incompatible with several clauses of the German Federal Constitution. Therefore, it referred the case to the Federal Constitutional Court, putting forward questions covering the whole range of issues concerning constitutionality of life imprisonment. Among other arguments the State Court also maintained that life imprisonment is incompatible with the aims of deterrence and reform, as well as atonement and retribution, which have been recognised by the Constitutional Court as legitimate aims of punishment. Furthermore, the State Court argued that the mandatory nature of the punishment of life imprisonment for all cases of aggravated homicide is unconstitutional, because the rule of law principle requires the proposed punishment to be in a just relationship with the seriousness of the crime and the culpability of the offender.[69]

The judgment of the Federal Constitutional Court in this case endorsed the proportionality principle as a valid principle limiting State punishment. The Court stated that although the state is entitled to deprive an individual from her/his right to liberty, in doing so the state is constrained by number of constitutional

65 *R v Smith* (n.61) 1079–1081.

66 See e.g. Tatjana Hörnle, *Tatproportionale Strafzumessung* (Zugl.: München, Univ. Diss. 1998. Strafrechtliche Abhandlungen N.F. 123, Duncker & Humblot 1999); Wolfgang Frisch and Hans-Jörg Albrecht (eds), *Tatproportionalität: Normative und empirische Aspekte einer tatproportionalen Strafzumessung; Buchenbach-Symposium 1999* (CF Müller Wissenschaft, 2003).

67 See e.g. Gertrude Lübbe-Wolff, 'The Principle of Proportionality in the Case- Law of the German Federal Constitutional Court' (2014) 34 *Human Rights Law Journal* 12; Johannes Saurer, 'Die Globalisierung des Verhältnismäßigkeitsgrundsatzes' (2012) 51(1) *Der Staat* 3.

68 *45 BVerfGE 187*, 21 June 1977.

69 ibid 190–196.

principles, including the constitutional principle of proportionality. The Court particularly stressed that:[70]

> … in line with Article 2(II) of the Constitution the right to liberty can be limited by a law. However, in designing such limitations the legislature is constrained by the Constitution in number of ways. It must observe both the inviolability of human dignity (Art. 1(I)), the highest principle of the constitutional order, and other constitutional norms, specifically the principle of equality (Art.3(I)), the requirements of the rule of law and the social state (Art.20(I)). Since the liberty of an individual is already such an important legal interest that it could only be limited based on weighty grounds, the lifelong deprivation of this right requires a specifically strict check against the standard of *Verhältnismaßigkeitsgrundsatz.*

It is remarkable that the Constitutional Court used the term '*Verhältnismaßigkeitsgrundsatz*' rather than '*Tatproportionalität*' in order to describe the principle which should be used to check whether a term of imprisonment, in this case imprisonment for life, would fit within the constitutionally permissible limitations of human right to liberty.

This ground-breaking judgment offers yet more evidence demonstrating that the constitutional principle of proportionality of punishment (*Verhältnismaßigkeitsgrundsatz)* is different from the retributive proportionality and serves as a limiting principle even in cases where sentences pursue other than retributive aims. First of all, this is evident from the reasoning of the Court concerning proportionality of the mandatory life imprisonment in cases of aggravated homicide. In this regard, the Court articulated that, as a mandatory punishment, life imprisonment is available only for aggravated homicide and genocide. In other cases the criminal code allows judges to decide, in accordance with the sentencing principles prescribed in Article 46 of the Criminal Code, which particular punishment to impose within the range prescribed in the law.[71] Indeed, this Article identifies culpability of the offender as the basis of imposition of the punishment, but at the same time requires judges to take into account the expected effects of the punishment on the future life of the offender in society.[72] Taking such effects into account definitely goes beyond the retributive principle of proportionality.

Furthermore, in responding to the State Court's submission concerning the incompatibility of life imprisonment with the legitimate aims of punishment, the Constitutional Court reaffirmed that deterrence, reform, atonement and retribution are legitimate aims of punishment. The Court stated that the theories of punishment are not a primary Constitutional concern. However, it recognised that German criminal law theory and practice broadly follow the Unifying

70 ibid 223.

71 ibid , 260.

72 German Criminal Code 15 May 1871, StGB (Bundestag) §46 (1).

Theory (*Vereinigungstheorie*) which – albeit with a different emphasis – attempts to keep the aims of punishment in a balanced relationship. After assessing life imprisonment in the light of the purposes of punishment, the Constitutional Court concluded that the punishment of life imprisonment is compatible with those aims. According to the Court, for the crime of aggravated homicide, which infringes upon the highest value protected by the criminal law, it is justified to prescribe the heaviest penalty, even if it cannot be empirically demonstrated that such punishment has a general preventative effect. Moreover, life imprisonment for aggravated homicide matches the perception of justice in society and does not exclude the possibility of the reform of the offender.[73]

The fact that the Constitutional Court stressed that theories of punishment were largely irrelevant for determining whether a right-limiting measure complies with the Constitution, demonstrates that the proportionality principle (*Verhältnismaßigkeitsgrundsatz*), is not part of any particular punishment rationale. It is, rather, a general Constitutional principle with which any rights-limiting legal measures, including deprivation of liberty as a punishment for a crime, should comply. The Court stressed that punishment which breaches the constitutional principle of proportionality cannot be a part of constitutionally compliant order.[74]

In this judgment the Constitutional Court also endorsed principles generally associated with the retributive rationale of punishment. It particularly stated that the protection of human dignity prohibits the State from turning a human being into a mere object of crime prevention in violation of her/his constitutionally protected social worth and respect.[75] According to the Court, several constitutional norms and the principle of rule of law endorse the principle of culpability which is the basis of imposition of punishment. It requires imposition of a punishment that fits the seriousness of the crime and the culpability of the offender; the imposed punishment should not surpass the culpability of the offender.[76]

These statements, however, should not be regarded as evidence of equating the constitutional principle of proportionality (as applied in the context of punishment) with the retributive proportionality principle: such assumption would be contrary to the substance and the findings of the judgment. First of all, accepting the principle of culpability as a basis of imposition of punishment does not mean endorsement of a retributive punishment rationale. Furthermore, the judgment explicitly states that deprivation of liberty of a prisoner sentenced to life can be continued indefinitely based solely on the aim of protecting the public, if the prisoner remains dangerous despite serving a long term in prison.[77]

On the contrary, the statements regarding culpability and impermissibility of turning an individual into a mere object of crime prevention should be seen as

73 *45 BVerfGE 187*, 21 June 1977 (n.70) , 254–259.
74 ibid 259.
75 ibid 228.
76 ibid 259.
77 ibid 242.

part of the Court's arguments substantiating its main finding in this case. This is the holding that, even if the crime committed is the most serious one, the State cannot forcefully deprive an individual of her/his freedom without at least giving her/him a chance to atone for her/his deeds and regain freedom.[78] This finding of the Court will be discussed in more detail in the subsequent section. At this point it is important to demonstrate that, despite some seemingly confusing statements, the Court confirmed that the prohibition of 'grossly' disproportionate prison sentences exists independently of a particular punishment rationale which is a basis of a State's penal policy in the particular period.

There is also some evidence coming from English case law demonstrating that the principle of proportionality is accepted as a valid principle outlawing prison sentences of excessive length. This issue was discussed in the context of the relationship between Article 5 of the ECHR and domestic law. In the case of *Governor of Brockhill Prison, ex p. Evans (No. 2)* Lord Hope articulated that 'assuming that the detention is lawful under domestic law, it is nevertheless open to criticism on the ground that it is arbitrary because, for example, it was resorted to in bad faith or was not proportionate'.[79] The idea was further developed by Lord Woolf CJ in a case concerning compatibility with the ECHR of the legislation prescribing an automatic life sentence for a second serious sexual or violent offence. In this case Lord Woolf articulated:[80]

> … we recognise that there have been, and will be, cases where section 2 of the 1997 Act has, and will, operate in a proportionate manner. However, as the section has hitherto been interpreted, it can clearly operate in a disproportionate manner. It is easy to find examples of situations where two offences could be committed which were categorised as serious by the section but where it would be wholly disproportionate to impose a life sentence to protect the public. Whenever a person is convicted of an offence, there is always some risk that he or she may offend again. Equally, there are a significant number of cases in which two serious offences will have been committed where the risk is not of a degree which can justify a life sentence. We refer again to the very wide span of manslaughter, which is a serious offence within the Act. An unjustified push can result in someone falling, hitting his head and suffering fatal injuries. The offence is manslaughter. The offender may have committed another serious offence when a young man. A life sentence in such circumstances may well be arbitrary and disproportionate and contravene Article 5. It could also be a punishment which contravenes Article 3.

This passage clearly demonstrates that proportionality is regarded as a principle limiting excessive prison sentences. It also demonstrates that this principle would

78 ibid 228.

79 *R v Governor of Brockhill Prison ex p Evans (No 2)* [2001] 1 AC 19, 858.

80 *R v Offen* [2001] 1 WLR 253 (Court of Appeal), 277.

be regarded as a valid limitation of punishment not only in cases where the sentences pursue the aim of retribution, but also in cases where the aim of the prison term is, for instance, incapacitation of a dangerous offender.

Finally, it should be mentioned that the ECtHR articulated on many occasions that 'an arbitrary or disproportionately lengthy sentence might in some circumstances raise issues under the Convention'.[81] In the case of *Vinter and Others v the United Kingdom* after considering comparative materials before it, the Fourth Section of the Court noted that:[82]

> gross disproportionality is a widely accepted and applied test for determining when a sentence will amount to inhuman or degrading punishment, or equivalent constitutional norms.

Furthermore, both the Chamber and the Grand Chamber of the ECtHR accepted that a 'grossly disproportionate sentence could amount to ill-treatment contrary to Article 3 at the moment of its imposition'.[83] However, both Chambers came to the conclusion that the test to satisfy the substantive requirement of gross disproportionality (measuring proportion between the severity of punishment in a particular case and its purposes) is very strict. The Court in fact indicated that it would interfere on this issue only on 'rare and unique' occasions.[84] In line with its long-standing case law, the ECtHR refused to interpret the ECHR as setting strict limits on Contracting States in matters of 'choice of a specific criminal justice system'.[85] According to the Grand Chamber:[86]

> issues relating to just and proportionate punishment are the subject of rational debate and civilised disagreement. Accordingly, Contracting States must be allowed a margin of appreciation in deciding on the appropriate length of prison sentences for particular crimes. As the Court has stated, it is not its role to decide what is the appropriate term of detention applicable to a particular offence or to pronounce on the appropriate length of detention or other sentence which should be served by a person after conviction by a competent court.

Although the Grand Chamber refused to interpret Article 3 of the ECHR as imposing strict limits on Contracting States in matters of sentencing, it agreed with the Chamber that any 'grossly disproportionate' punishment would violate

81 *V. v United Kingdom* [GC] (n.40) , paras 97–101; *Sawoniuk v United Kingdom* (n.9).

82 *Vinter v United Kingdom* (2012) App no. 66069/09 and 130/10 and 3896/10 (ECtHR, 17 January 2012) para.88.

83 *Vinter v United Kingdom* (n.82) para.89; *Vinter and v United Kingdom* [GC] (n.43) para.102.

84 *Vinter v United Kingdom* (n.82) paras 88–89; *Vinter v United Kingdom* [GC] (n.43) para.102.

85 *Vinter v United Kingdom* [GC] (n.43) para.104; *Kafkaris v Cyprus* [GC] ECHR 2008-I 223 para.99; *T. v United Kindgom* [GC] App no 24724/94 (ECtHR, 16 December 1999) para.117; *V. v United Kingdom* [GC] (n.42) para.118; *Sawoniuk v United Kingdom* (n.9).

86 *Vinter v United Kingdom* [GC] (n.43) para.105.

Article 3. This sets an absolute bar on the severity of punishment that Contracting States are allowed to impose in the pursuit of the aims of punishment which, as both Chambers agreed, include retribution/punishment, deterrence, public protection or rehabilitation.[87] In this judgment, apart from explicitly stating that Article 3 of the ECHR prohibits 'grossly disproportionate sentences', it also recognised that this limitation is relevant not only to sentences which pursue the aim of retribution/punishment, but also to those which pursue other aims, such as deterrence, public protection or rehabilitation.

Life imprisonment and human dignity

As demonstrated in the preceding section, many national and international courts have recognised that the power of the State to determine the length of deprivation of the right to liberty for a crime is not unlimited. This power is limited by the principle of proportionality. However, according to the US Supreme Court, lengthy prison sentences such as 25 years to life for the theft of goods worth $1,197 committed by a recidivist,[88] or a 50-year minimum sentence for the third-time property offence (two counts of shoplifting of videotapes worth about $150)[89] did not to violate the constitutional requirement of proportionality of punishment. This requirement was not violated even by imposing the most severe punishment available in the State of Michigan, a mandatory life imprisonment without parole, for possession of 672 grams of cocaine.[90]

Furthermore, the German Federal Constitutional Court disagreed with the submission of the State Court that life imprisonment for an aggravated homicide is a purposeless and disproportionate punishment.[91] The ECtHR came to a similar conclusion, stating that a non-mandatory whole-life sentence which is imposed by a judge after considering all circumstances of the case is not *per se* grossly disproportionate.[92]

As it stands, the proportionality requirement does not outlaw even life imprisonment, the ultimate punishment in the majority of the jurisdictions across the world.[93] However, legal developments in Europe and to some degree in the US demonstrate that to be compatible with human rights such sentences should not deprive the prisoner of the hope of being able to achieve release from prison at some time in the future.

87 ibid para.111.
88 *Ewing v California* (n.35).
89 *Lockyer v Andrade* 538 U.S. 63 (2003)
90 *Harmelin v Michigan* (n.51).
91 *45 BVerfGE 187,* 21 June 1977 (n.68) 267.
92 *Vinter v United Kingdom* (n.82) para. 92; *Vinter v United Kingdom* [GC] (n.43) para.106
93 Catherine Appleton and Dirk van Zyl Smit, 'A Summary Report on Life Imprisonment Worldwide' (Nottingham, September 2017) 3.

Developments in Europe

In the German life imprisonment case discussed in the preceding section, the State Court, referring to research findings, argued in its submission to the Constitutional Court that life imprisonment violates human dignity by permanently excluding the offender from society and causing irreparable damage to the personality of the incarcerated person.[94] Furthermore, according to the State Court, even the fact that the vast majority of life prisoners were granted pardon could not make the life sentence constitutional, because it is inherently unconstitutional.[95]

After examining the large number of studies and hearing expert testimonies regarding the negative effects of long-term imprisonment, the Federal Constitutional Court concluded that life imprisonment as implemented in the Federal Republic of Germany does not violate human dignity. This conclusion was based on the following three findings of the Court. First, the Court found that, based on the current state of research, the suggestion that long-term imprisonment causes irreparable physical or psychological damage to prisoners cannot be generalised. Second, the German Prison Act 1976 (StVollzG) prescribed resocialisation as the aim of the implementation of all prison sentences, including life sentences, which meant that even lifers must be prepared for future reintegration into society and this will prevent irreparable physical or psychological damage to prisoners.[96] Finally, as the data demonstrated, only a few life-sentenced prisoners actually served their whole life in prison. The vast majority were released through pardon after serving in the region of 15 to 25 years, depending on the Federal State.[97]

The fact that the newly-adopted Prison Act prescribed resocialisation as the aim of implementation of prison sentences, including life imprisonment was essential for 'saving' life imprisonment from being found unconstitutional, because the Court found that resocialisation of life-sentenced prisoners is a constitutional requirement. The Court deduced this requirement from the constitutional recognition of human dignity and the principle of the social state (*socialstaatsprinzip*). According to the Court the constitutional recognition of human dignity is based on the idea of humans as creatures with inherent morality who are entitled to develop their personality freely within society and not to be made mere objects for the aims of the State. The fundamental prerequisites for the individual and social existence of humans must be preserved. Therefore, it would be incompatible to deprive a human being of his/her liberty without at least a chance of regaining freedom.[98]

The Court argued that the resocialisation of prisoners, including lifers, is constitutionally required in any community that regards human dignity as the most

94 *45 BVerfGE 187*, 21 June 1977 (n.68) 192.
95 ibid 195.
96 ibid 238–240.
97 ibid 241.
98 ibid 228–229.

important value and commits itself to the principles of social justice. In such a community it is the obligation of the State to take all reasonable steps available within the legal framework to achieve the resocialisation of prisoners.[99] However, human dignity would not be violated if the life prisoner were not released because he/she remained dangerous, despite the efforts of the State to resocialise him/her. From the point of view of the Constitution, it is irrelevant whether the enforcement of life imprisonment on the ground of dangerousness is carried out as a punishment for a crime or as a preventative measure. It is the obligation of the State to protect society from dangerous offenders through depriving them of their right to liberty. Nevertheless, when determining the issue of dangerousness, the constitutional principle of proportionality must be observed. Furthermore, even in such exceptional cases, the aim of resocialising the prisoner should remain in place.[100]

Given the fact that the vast majority of lifers were released through pardon, the Court was satisfied that the obligation of the State to give a chance to life prisoners to achieve release existed not only in theory but was also fulfilled in practice.[101] However, the Court discussed in detail the issue of suitability of pardon as a mechanism for implementing the right to resocialisation. The Court's assessment of the constitutionality of life imprisonment in the light of the right to human dignity and the rule of law principle demonstrated that the enforcement of life imprisonment compatible with human dignity is possible only when a prisoner has a concrete and viable chance of regaining her/his freedom. If the prisoner, notwithstanding the changes in her/his personality, had to abandon any hope of ever regaining her/his freedom, human dignity would be degraded. Based on the thorough analysis of the power of pardon in the light of the constitutional requirement to enable lifers to regain their freedom, the Court concluded that the institution of the pardon alone is not sufficient.[102] The principle of the rule of law requires a dedicated legislative mechanism of the review of life sentences in all cases after prisoners have already served the minimum term prescribed by law.[103]

In coming to this conclusion, the Court discussed in detail the pros and cons of the pardon and of an ordinary review mechanism prescribed in the legislation. In the category of disadvantages of pardon the Court considered the unfettered discretion of the authority. The power of pardon is a prerogative of various elected officials in different Federal States and is exercised at their total discretion, resulting in large differences in the time served by offenders sentenced to life imprisonment for murder. Moreover, as the jurisprudence of the Constitutional Court demonstrates, the lawfulness of the pardon decisions are not subject to review by the courts.[104] The existing procedure deterred prisoners even from

99 ibid 238–239.
100 ibid 242.
101 ibid 241–242.
102 ibid 245.
103 ibid 242–243.
104 ibid.

applying for pardon on their own initiative, because rejection of the application resulted in an ineligibility period for consideration of pardon.[105]

Furthermore, pardon decisions could not be regarded as impartial, because they were made by politicians and therefore were heavily influenced by public opinion. The pardon, as practised in cases of life prisoners, has gone beyond its original purpose, taking over a judicial function; in cases of life prisoners, decisions mostly depended on the prognosis of dangerousness, which is by no means a function that can fit within the nature of pardon. Moreover, this assessment is conducted as part of an internal process which lacks any guarantees of fairness and impartiality; the decisions rejecting pardon neither state the reasons for rejection nor disclose evidence on which the decision is based. According to the Court the current praxis of pardon does not allow a consistent practice of review of life imprisonment to develop, creating a state of uncertainty for the prisoner and impairing her/his resocialisation.[106]

The Constitutional Court also considered the arguments against the introduction of a dedicated mechanism for the review of life sentences. Some experts opposed such review, because it contradicts the nature of life imprisonment which is being imposed as a punishment appropriate to the severity of crime and the culpability of the offender. Such a move changes the aim of punishment midway in the sentence, turning it into a preventative detention justified by the dangerousness of the offender. It will also damage the deterrent effect of life imprisonment, negatively affecting the security feelings of people and creating the impression that life imprisonment is abolished through the 'back door'.[107] Furthermore, the creation of an ordinary review mechanism will blur the distinction between the life and fixed-term imprisonment, leading to the erosion of the institution of punishment and undermining of victims' interests. Finally, designing the conditions of release and supervision of released lifers will also be problematic.[108]

After considering the cons of both approaches, the Constitutional Court articulated that, although the establishment of a dedicated legislative mechanism for the review of continued enforcement of life imprisonment is not unproblematic, the problems do not outweigh the advantages of such a solution over pardon.[109] According to the Court, the tensions between the punishment that is proportionate to the seriousness of the crime and early release are not unique to life imprisonment. This is also relevant to early release from a fixed prison term. Moreover, such tensions exist even in the case of pardon. The tensions between retribution and resocialisation may be eased through establishing release criteria which will not only look at the dangerousness of the offender, but will also take into account

105 ibid 219.
106 ibid 219–220.
107 ibid 244.
108 ibid.
109 ibid 246.

the further need for punishment and deterrence.[110] As to the aim of deterrence of crimes which carry life imprisonment, this would not suffer either, because the possibility of release through pardon already exists. Finally, the complexity of issues connected with conditions of release and supervision cannot be decisive for the necessity of such regulation. Moreover, such issues also exist for release through pardon.[111]

The Constitutional Court reiterated that life imprisonment is the most severe punishment available in the law and should remain so, because it is necessary for the protection of the public from the most serious crimes. As long as the protection of the public requires life imprisonment, it should not only be imposed, but also enforced for the whole life of the prisoner. However, experience demonstrates that protection of the public does not always require that life imprisonment be enforced until the end of life. There is a sufficient number of life prisoners who run no serious risk of reoffending. In such cases it is not possible to justify the enforcement of life imprisonment in full. The fact that many lifers pose little danger to the public, together with the finding that lifelong deprivation of liberty could lead to irreparable damage of personality, strongly supports giving a possibility of release to life prisoners.[112] This could not be achieved through reforming the power of pardon, because the nature of the power of pardon is such as not to allow tying it to particular legal regulations. The rule of law principle and the substantive justice require that the conditions and the procedure of review of life imprisonment be regulated by law, because this is an existential issue for affected individuals. It follows that it is the Constitutional obligation of the legislature to design and adopt a law allowing areview of life imprisonment which is compatible with the above requirements. However, within the contours of the Constitutionm the law-maker should be given freedom to design such a mechanism.[113]

This judgment of the German Federal Constitutional Court seems to have inspired the Grand Chamber of the ECtHR in the case of *Vinter*[114] to come out with a similar interpretation of human dignity, which is the core value protected under the ECHR.[115] This case originated from separate applications by three prisoners serving whole life sentences in England. The applicants argued before the ECtHR that imposition of life sentences that are irreducible *de jure* and *de facto* violate Article 3 of the ECHR 'because of the imposition of hopelessness that came with such a sentence'.[116]

According to the Fourth Chamber of the ECtHR, whole life sentences are normally imposed for very serious crimes which, even if they do not attract a life sentence in some jurisdictions, would normally carry very long sentences of up to several decades of imprisonment. Therefore, anyone convicted of such offences,

110 ibid 251.
111 ibid 252.
112 ibid 249–250.
113 ibid 252.
114 *Vinter v United Kingdom* [GC] (n.43)
115 ibid para.113.
116 *Vinter v United Kingdom* (n.82) para.78.

whether sentenced to imprisonment for life or for a determinate term, shall expect to serve a long prison term 'before he can realistically have any hope of release'.[117] For these reasons, according to the Chamber, an Article 3 issue could arise only if it could be shown that:[118]

> (i) that the applicant's continued imprisonment can no longer be justified on any legitimate penological grounds (such as punishment, deterrence, public protection or rehabilitation); and (ii) ... the sentence is irreducible de facto and de iure.

The Chamber expressed doubts that in the material case the sentences are *de facto* reducible; in line with the Secretary of State's written policy of compassionate release – the only available release mechanism for such sentences – even if there were no legitimate penological goals for continued imprisonment, whole life prisoners would remain in prison as long as they did not become terminally ill or bedridden. However, in the material case the Fourth Section of the Court found no violation of Article 3, because, according to the Court, it could not be said that in the case of any of the applicants the continued imprisonment could no longer be justified on any legitimate penological grounds.[119]

The applicants disagreed with the findings of the Chamber and took the case to the Grand Chamber, arguing that the Chamber erred in finding that no issue under Article 3 would arise until such time as all the legitimate penological grounds that justified the imposition of the punishment ceased to exist. According to the applicants, such an approach was flawed: it failed to address the issue that applicants' whole life sentences in themselves constituted a violation of a requirement of review of Article 3. Such a requirement should 'be built into a whole life sentence to ensure there was no breach of Article 3'.[120] They accepted that no issue under Article 3 would arise if a life prisoner spent her/his whole life in prison in case s/he remained risk to society. However, they argued that:

> a whole life order which was imposed purely for the purposes of punishment directly undermined human dignity, destroyed the human spirit and ignored the capacity for countervailing justifications for conditional release which could arise in the future. The justifications for detention included, as the Chamber had found, punishment, deterrence, public protection and rehabilitation. But the balance of these factors could change over time. An unreviewable whole life order meant that a prisoner would remain incarcerated until death irrespective of whatever changes in these factors might take place in the course of his or her sentence.[121]

117 ibid para.92.
118 ibid.
119 ibid para.95.
120 *Vinter v United Kingdom* [GC] (n.43) para.98.
121 ibid para.99.

The Grand Chamber found a violation of Article 3 in this case. It came to the conclusion that life imprisonment which is *de jure* and *de facto* irreducible is incompatible with Article 3 of the ECHR.[122] According to the Grand Chamber, a life sentence would be considered irreducible where national law does not afford any possibility of review 'with a view to its commutation, remission, termination or the conditional release of the prisoners'.[123] It is also not sufficient to meet the requirements of reducibility if the release mechanism allows for the release solely for those who are infirm or close to death.[124] However, the life sentence cannot be regarded as irreducible if in fact the prisoner remains in prison indefinitely because release was refused on the basis that continued imprisonment was necessary for public protection. The fact that the prisoner has served a very long sentence does not weaken the State's positive obligation to protect the public by continuing to imprison life prisoners 'as long as they remain dangerous'.[125]

According to the Grand Chamber, an irreducible life sentence is in violation of Article 3 because, as the review of international and comparative law materials has demonstrated, retribution cannot be regarded as a static aim justifying imprisonment until death. Such a review shows clear support for the idea that, even in cases where the aims of punishment attract a sentence of life imprisonment at the time of sentencing, human dignity requires that an offender be given a chance to rehabilitate her/himself and regain her/his freedom one day. The Grand Chamber came to the conclusion that a possibility of rehabilitation and the prospect of release based on the goal of rehabilitation being achieved should be offered to all prisoners, including lifers.[126] It stated that:[127]

> while punishment remains one of the aims of imprisonment, the emphasis in European penal policy is now on the rehabilitative aim of imprisonment, particularly towards the end of a long prison sentence.

Furthermore, the ECtHR articulated that in order for a life sentence to remain compatible with Article 3, it is necessary to have a possibility of review with a prospect of release. Such a review mechanism is necessary because the purposes of punishment, which could justify sentencing an offender to life imprisonment, are not necessarily static: many will be present at the time of the imposition of life sentence, but the balance between them may shift in the course of the sentence.[128] According to the Court:[129]

122 ibid 121.
123 ibid para.109.
124 ibid para.113, 127.
125 ibid para.108.
126 ibid para.114.
127 ibid para.115.
128 ibid 111.
129 ibid para.111.

> what may be the primary justification for detention at the start of the sentence may not be so after a lengthy period into the service of the sentence. It is only by carrying out a review of the justification for continued detention at an appropriate point in the sentence that these factors or shifts can be properly evaluated.

In this case the Court declined to state when the review of a whole life imprisonment should be carried out and did not prescribe whether the form of review should be judicial or executive. It limited itself to stating that there is clear support in international and comparative law for a 'dedicated mechanism guaranteeing a review no later than 25 years after the imposition of a life sentence, with further periodic reviews thereafter'.[130] However, the Grand Chamber disagreed with the finding of the Chamber that in this context Article 3 would come into play only if it could be demonstrated that in the particular case the continued imprisonment was not justified by any of the stated purposes of punishment. The Grand Chamber stated that:[131]

> Although the requisite review is a prospective event necessarily subsequent to the passing of the sentence, a whole life prisoner should not be obliged to wait and serve an indeterminate number of years of his sentence before he can raise the complaint that the legal conditions attaching to his sentence fail to comply with the requirements of Article 3 in this regard. This would be contrary both to legal certainty and to the general principles on victim status within the meaning of that term in Article 34 of the Convention. Furthermore, in cases where the sentence, on imposition, is irreducible under domestic law, it would be capricious to expect the prisoner to work towards his own rehabilitation without knowing whether, at an unspecified, future date, a mechanism might be introduced which would allow him, on the basis of that rehabilitation, to be considered for release. A whole life prisoner is entitled to know, at the outset of his sentence, what he must do to be considered for release and under what conditions, including when a review of his sentence will take place or may be sought. Consequently, where domestic law does not provide any mechanism or possibility for review of a whole life sentence, the incompatibility with Article 3 on this ground already arises at the moment of the imposition of the whole life sentence and not at a later stage of incarceration.

In the next judgment on the issue of reducibility of life imprisonment the Grand Chamber provided more details on the meaning of *de facto* reducibility. In the case of *Murray v the Netherlands*[132] the applicant raised several independent but interrelated complaints under Article 3 of the ECHR. First, he submitted

130 ibid para.120.
131 ibid para.122.
132 *Murray v the Netherlands* App no 47940/99 (ECtHR, 10 December 2013).

that the only possibility of release from his life sentence was pardon which, however, was 'inadequate and ineffective' offering no hope of release, either *de facto* or *de jure*.[133] Furthermore, the applicant also complained that, despite being diagnosed with mental illness at sentencing, he had never received treatment which would help to improve his mental health.[134]

After the submission of the application, but before it was heard by the ECtHR, the Government adopted new legislation allowing review of life sentences after 20 years minimum term with the possibility of periodic reviews every five years thereafter. A domestic court was authorised to review life sentences and grant release if life imprisonment in a particular case no longer served any reasonable purpose. The legislation indicated that, while assessing whether continued life imprisonment serves any reasonable purpose, the Court will take into account the position of a victim and the risk of recidivism. The decision of the Court cannot be appealed, but if release is refused the situation must be reviewed after a further five years.[135]

The Third Section of the ECtHR had no difficulties in finding that the newly adopted legislative arrangements in the respective jurisdiction offered both a possibility of review and a prospect of release from life imprisonment. Therefore, the continued life imprisonment of the applicant met the reducibility requirement of Article 3.[136] The Court did not assess whether the existence of pardon – the only possibility of release for the applicant before the introduction of the new legislative review mechanism – was enough to meet the reducibility requirement of Article 3.[137]

A decisive factor in the ECtHR's finding of no violation of Article 3 was the fact that after the submission of the application to the ECtHR the domestic court reviewed the applicant's life imprisonment and found that, although he had already spent 33 years in prison, imprisonment still served a reasonable purpose. In coming to this conclusion the Court took into account psychiatric reports, which stated that the applicant was suffering from an antisocial personality disorder, his attitude towards his crime and the position of the relatives of the victim.[138]

Furthermore, the ECtHR observed that, although the applicant was never treated for his mental illness, he still received some psychiatric help for his personality disorder. The psychiatric help was interrupted when the applicant, upon his own request, was transferred to another prison where at the time of his arrival such help was not available, but had become available by the time of the review. Furthermore, the applicant provided information neither on seeking psychiatric treatment himself nor on the adequacy of these services to his needs. Therefore,

133 ibid, para.47.
134 ibid para.63.
135 ibid para.42.
136 ibid para.59.
137 ibid para.58.
138 ibid paras 28–35.

the Court found that the information provided by the applicant was not sufficient to find a violation of Article 3 in regard to not providing him with the treatment required by his mental condition.[139]

The applicant requested referral to the Grand Chamber and further argued that while after introduction of new legislation his sentence was *de jure* reducible, it remained *de facto* irreducible, because he was never provided with psychiatric treatment to reduce his risk of reoffending, and therefore it would 'continue to be considered too high'.[140] In contrast to the Chamber, the Grand Chamber considered indivisible the questions of the availability of psychiatric treatment to the applicant during his incarceration and reducibility of his life sentence.[141] The Grand Chamber observed that life prisoners with mental health problems may not be sufficiently aware of their conditions and the need for treatment, and therefore it is the responsibility of the government to assess prisoners' need of psychiatric treatment with the view of facilitating their rehabilitation. Such assessment should be conducted regardless of whether or not a request for treatment has been made by a prisoner. Furthermore, the government must provide life prisoners in need of psychiatric treatment with measures or treatment capable of enabling the prisoner to improve her/his condition and rehabilitate him/herself. This obligation is fulfilled by the mere fact of providing the requisite treatment, regardless of whether the prisoner will take her/his chance. In summary, life prisoners with mental health problems must be detained under such conditions and provided with such treatment as would be capable of giving them a chance to rehabilitate themselves in order to have a hope of release.[142]

In regard to the applicant's life imprisonment, the Grand Chamber concluded that the reason for refusing his release both on pardon and after a review by a domestic court was the risk of recidivism. Despite the recommendation either to place him in a specialised psychiatric institution for lengthy treatment or to provide treatment in a prison setting in order to avoid recidivism, the applicant received no specialised psychiatric treatment, but only some 'sort of psychiatric help'. Therefore, the applicant found himself in a situation where his release was refused, because he presented a high risk of reoffending owing to his mental condition for which he received no assessment of treatment needs and no specific treatment. In this situation neither the availability of pardon nor review by a court could have led to the release of the applicant. Therefore, 'the applicant's life sentence was not *de facto* reducible as required by Article 3'.[143]

139 ibid paras 72–73

140 *Murray v the Netherlands* [GC] App no 10511/10, para.3 (ECtHR, 26 April 2016).

141 ibid para.116.

142 ibid paras 108–112.

143 ibid para.123.

Due process guarantees derived from ECtHR case law on reducibility of whole life sentences

In the case of *Vinter v UK* the Grand Chamber neither prescribed a specific form of review, nor specified any due process guarantees which should be observed during such reviews. Furthermore, the Grand Chamber declared inadmissible the submission that the absence of a review mechanism in domestic legislation was also a violation of Article 5(4) of the ECHR. In this regard the jurisdiction of the Grand Chamber was restricted because this part of the application was found inadmissible by the Chamber.[144] In subsequent cases, however, the ECtHR has provided more details on requirements which the dedicated mechanisms for review of whole life sentences should meet in order to comply with Article 3 of the ECHR.

The first case to come before the ECtHR after the Grand Chamber's judgment in *Vinter*[145] was the case of *Laszlo Magyar v Hungary*.[146] In the material case the only mechanism through which a prisoner sentenced to life without parole could have been released was presidential clemency. The Second Section of the Court had no hesitation in finding that in Hungary life imprisonment without parole did not meet the requirement of reducibility under Article 3 of the ECHR.[147] The Court's holding was based on the arguments that the clemency law provided no specific guidance on criteria based on which the President makes clemency decisions, and nor was she/he required by that law to provide reasons for her/his decisions.[148]

In principle, the Court did not exclude the possibility that the requirement of reducibility of life imprisonment without parole could be met by a power of pardon. However, in a case such as this the pardon law should have the following essential features. First, it should be sufficiently clear in regard to criteria and conditions that the prisoner should fulfil in order to be considered for release. Second, it should guarantee proper consideration of the changes of circumstance in a particular case and the progress towards rehabilitation made by the prisoner.[149]

In the next case, which was *Harakchiev and Tomilov v Bulgaria*,[150] the ECtHR found that the presidential power of clemency is sufficient to give a whole life prisoner hope of regaining her/his freedom. The Court was satisfied that the Constitutional Court articulated that while executing the power of pardon the president should comply with principles of non-arbitrariness, equity, humanity, compassion, mercy, and take into account the health and family circumstances of a prisoner.[151]

144 *Vinter v United Kingdom* [GC] (n.43) para.132.

145 ibid.

146 *Laszlo Magyar v Hungary* App no 73593/10 (ECtHR, 20 May 2014).

147 ibid para.58.

148 ibid para.57.

149 ibid para.58.

150 *Harakchiev and Tolumov v Bulgaria* ECHR 2014-III 391.

151 ibid para.258.

Furthermore, a pardon commission was set up to considered the applications of prisoners in a transparent manner and according to criteria published in advance. The commission published annual reports in which it provided both statistical data on considered applications and criteria under which these applications were assessed. According to these criteria the commission had regard to all circumstances of the case, including the crime committed, the time already served, the degree to which the aims of punishment had been attained, and the prisoner's prospects of personal development, including the risk of reoffending.[152] The ECtHR regarded such a degree of certainty and transparency as sufficient to satisfy the requirements of Article 3. The Court came to this conclusion in spite of the fact that there was no obligation to provide reasons in every pardon decision. Moreover, the decisions could be reviewed only by the Constitutional Court upon a motion of specifically authorised agents.[153]

In the subsequent cases, the ECtHR reaffirmed that both executive and judicial forms of review of whole life sentences met the requirement of reducibility of sentence in the meaning of Article 3.[154] Moreover, the Court re-stated that while the States Parties enjoy a margin of appreciation in regard to the time of the review, this margin is not unlimited. A whole life imprisonment will be regarded as irreducible within the meaning of Article 3 if a prisoner would be required to serve 40 years before she/he could be eligible to apply for review of her/his life sentence.[155]

The Grand Chamber, in its judgment in the case of *Murray v the Netherlands*,[156] summarised and reaffirmed the requirements relating to the review of whole life sentences articulated by different Chambers of the ECtHR in different cases. According to the judgment, the review mechanism must comply with the following principles. First, the grounds and rules of the review should have a sufficient degree of clarity and certainty. Furthermore, the grounds of review laid down in the domestic legislation must comply with the grounds set out in the ECtHR's case law. This means that the availability of pardon on the ground of ill-health or old age would not meet the requirement of reducibility of life sentences.[157]

Second, the assessment of the necessity of continued imprisonment must be based on objective criteria which were known to the prisoner as she/he served the sentence. These criteria include resocialisation (special prevention), deterrence (general prevention) and retribution.[158]

Third, the review must be accompanied by sufficient procedural guarantees. Such guarantees must at least include an obligation to disclose to a prisoner

152 ibid para.259.

153 ibid para. 258–259.

154 *Trabelsi v Belgium* App. no 140/10 para.115 (ECHR, 4 September 2014); *T.P. and A.T. v Hungary* App nos 37871/14 and 73986/14 , para.38 (ECtHR, 4 October 2016).

155 *T.P. and A.T. v Hungary* (n.153) paras 45–50.

156 *Murray v the Netherlands* [GC] (n.149).

157 *Murray v the Netherlands* [GC] (n.140) para.100; *Vinter v United Kingdom* [GC] (n.43) para.128

158 *Murray v the Netherlands* [GC] (n.140) para.100; *Vinter v United Kingdom* [GC] (n.43) para.119.

the materials on which the decision is made, a requirement to give reasons for refusing an application for early release, and finally, a refusal to order early release should be amenable to judicial review in the courts.[159]

Developments in the US

There have also been some developments in the US in relation to the Constitutional requirement of reducibility of life sentences. However, in contrast to Europe, these developments concerned only the reducibility of life sentences imposed on juveniles. In the case of *Graham v Florida*[160] the Supreme Court held that the Eighth Amendment of the US Constitution prohibits imposition on juvenile offenders of life without parole sentences for non-homicide crimes. Two years later, in the case of *Miller v Alabama*,[161] the Supreme Court found that imposition of mandatory life sentences on juveniles, even for homicide offences, violates the Eighth Amendment.

In contrast to its approach to the Eighth Amendment challenges regarding excessiveness of prison sentences, where the Court adopted case-by-case approach,[162] in cases concerning juvenile life without parole sentences (JLWOP) the Court adopted a categorical approach. This means that not only the sentences in particular cases were found unconstitutional, but also the legislation which authorised such sentences.

The judgments of the Supreme Court outlawing of JLWOP for non-homicide offenders and prohibiting its mandatory application for homicide offenders relied on several factors relating to the type of punishment and the specific category of offender. The Court observed that JLWOP is the second most severe sentence after the death penalty, with which it shares some common characteristics which no other sentence has. Like the death penalty, life without parole is irrevocable in the sense that it takes away the liberty of the offender without giving him/her a chance to regain it.[163] Furthermore, according to the majority opinion, juveniles up to 18 years old are less culpable than adults. They are different from adults in the sense that they 'lack maturity and have underdeveloped sense of responsibility', 'are more vulnerable or susceptible to negative influences and outside pressures, including peer pressure', and their characters are still in the process of formation.[164]

The Court went on to consider the four purposes of punishment, i.e. retribution, deterrence, incapacitation and rehabilitation against JLWOP. It found that because of their immaturity, vulnerability and inherent capacity to change, juveniles convicted for non-homicide offences do not deserve to be deprived

159 *Murray v the Netherlands* [GC] (n.140) para.100; *Kafkaris v Cyprus* [GC] (n.85) para.105; *Laszlo Magyar v Hungary* (n.146) para.57.

160 *Graham v Florida* 130 SCt 2011 2023 (2010).

161 *Miller v Alabama* 132 S Ct 2455 (2012).

162 See e.g. *Solem v Helm* (n.50).

163 *Graham v Florida* (n.160) 2028.

164 ibid 2026.

of liberty for life without a chance to regain their freedom.[165] In relation to deterrence, the Court observed that 'the same characteristics that render juveniles less culpable than adults suggest that juveniles will be less susceptible to deterrence'.[166] Moreover, according to the Court, incapacitation as an aim of punishment cannot justify JLWOP. This statement of the Court is also rooted in the Court's finding of juveniles' inherent capacity for change. Because of this capacity, the high risk of reoffending at the time of sentencing does not allow the Court to conclude that the juvenile offender will be a risk for the rest of her/his life.[167]

Finally, the most critical component of the judgment is recognition of juvenile offenders' constitutional right to rehabilitation. The judgment states that 'states should give defendants like Graham some meaningful opportunity to obtain release based on demonstrated maturity and rehabilitation'.[168] However, it falls short of explaining what the right to rehabilitation entails. Some of the Court's arguments suggest that the prison authorities are obliged to help the prisoner to achieve rehabilitation by providing rehabilitation services and treatment.[169] On the other hand, the Court seems to say that rehabilitation will be achieved as a result of maturing.[170] Ultimately, the Court did not detail what the states should do in order to fulfil their obligation to provide rehabilitation opportunities. Justice Kennedy stated that 'it is for legislatures to determine what rehabilitative techniques are appropriate and effective'.[171]

In a subsequent case, *Miller v Alabama*, the Supreme Court held that the Eighth Amendment prohibits JLWOP sentences not only for non-homicide offenders, but also for homicide offenders, if the imposition of such a sentence is made mandatory by the law.[172] In coming to this conclusion the majority again relied on the same distinctive features relating to the personality of juvenile offenders and the nature of life sentence without possibility of release. In *Graham v Florida* the Court distinguished non-homicide offenders from those who kill, intend to kill or foresee that life will be taken. The Court stated that the former are 'categorically less deserving of the most serious forms of punishment than are murderers'.[173]

By contrast, in *Miller* the emphasis was put on the commonality among all juvenile offenders in terms of their immaturity and vulnerability. According to the Court, because of these features, even for homicide offenders individualised sentencing is required for the 'imposition of the harshest possible penalty for

165 ibid 2027.
166 ibid 2028.
167 ibid 2029.
168 ibid 2030.
169 ibid 2030, 2033.
170 ibid 2029.
171 ibid.
172 *Miller v Alabama* (n.161) 2455.
173 *Graham v Florida* (n.160) 2027.

juveniles' in order take into account the possible role of their immaturity and vulnerability in the commission of the crime.[174]

The decisions of the US Supreme Court discussed above are important developments in advancing the limits of State power to punish. However, these developments have a limited scope. The decisions of the Court exclude individuals who were 18 years old or older at the time of the commission of the crime as well as juveniles whose JLWOP sentences for homicide offences were imposed by a judge on a discretionary basis. The rationale for banning the imposition of JLWOP demonstrates that these limitations cannot hold ground.

In these cases the US Supreme Court attributed inherent capacity to change only to juveniles. The Court relied on peculiarities relating to the personality of juvenile offenders, the role of their immaturity and vulnerability in the commission of a crime. In the relevant judgments the Court recognised that the personality of juveniles is not yet fully developed. This factor gives rise to two independent but interconnected justifications which supported banning JLWOP for the above-mentioned categories of juvenile offender. The first justification is that immaturity and vulnerability to negative influences impact juveniles' decisions to engage in criminal behaviour. The second justification of the ban is that the rehabilitation of juvenile offenders is still possible, because their personality is not yet fully developed.

The Court believed that immaturity and vulnerability are characteristics attributable to all juveniles. It accepted the role of these characteristics in the commission of crimes and therefore it banned sentences which foreclose on the possibility of atonement and rehabilitation of juvenile offenders. It should be noted that giving a chance of atonement and rehabilitation does not mean that all juvenile offenders will achieve this aim and will be released. In contrast to the general nature of the rule in relation to the imposition of the sentence, the release of these offenders will be still based on a discretionary decision which will take into account all relevant circumstances of an individual case. There will be those who will take their chance of rehabilitation and regain their freedom after atoning for their crimes, but there could be many more who will not. In summary, banning the preclusion of rehabilitation of young offenders is based on the rationale that it is better to give the chance of regaining the right to freedom to every young offender irrespective of whether they will rehabilitate themselves, rather than to deny regaining the right to freedom to the few individuals who will do so.

This rationale is not compatible with the idea of excluding juveniles whose JLWOP sentences for homicide offences were imposed by a judge on a discretionary basis. As mentioned, immaturity and vulnerability of juveniles have a two-pronged role in banning JLWOP. First, it is believed that these factors affect decisions to engage in crimes. If this were the only justification for the ban, it could be said that the issue of whether these characteristics, indeed, influenced the commission of crime could be determined to some degree at sentencing. Therefore, excluding juveniles whose JLWOP sentences for homicide offences

174 *Miller v Alabama* (n.161) 2475.

were imposed by a judge after consideration of all relevant circumstances of the case, including the role of immaturity and vulnerability in the commission of the crime, might seem justifiable on the ground of the severity of the crime.

However, this was not the only justification of the prohibition. The Court believed that juveniles cannot be precluded from a possibility of regaining freedom based on rehabilitation, because they have a capacity for personality change and could return to society to leave a crime-free life after rehabilitation. Therefore, precluding some individuals with the same capacity on the basis of the gravity of crime seems unjustifiable. Although the sentence is not mandatory (i.e. is imposed after consideration of all the circumstances of the case, including the role of immaturity and vulnerability in the commission of the crime), on the basis of the gravity of the committed crime no judge or expert witness can ever predict how the juvenile's personality will change in, let us say, 25 years. The gravity of the committed crime is not helpful in this regard. To decide whether or not a person is rehabilitated is in no way an easy decision, but it will be much easier to make retrospectively.

Similarly, excluding adults from the ban on life without parole (LWOP) sentences is also unjustifiable. It cannot be excluded that some adults who committed horrible crimes at the age 18 or over may be able to change and lead a crime free-life after serving 25 or more years. If banning JLWOP has the purpose of not precluding juveniles who will be able to change from regaining the right to liberty, rather than all juveniles, such an opportunity should be not denied to adults.

Furthermore, banning JLWOP on the basis that juveniles have the capability of personality change means that at some point of the sentence a parole board or a similar body shall make a decision on whether or not to release the prisoner based on certain factors, including the result of the rehabilitation process. However, the Court was very short and sometimes inconsistent in articulating how the rehabilitation would be achieved. Moreover, it did not elaborate on the type of procedure and the due process safeguards which would be appropriate for this kind of review. These issues were left entirely to the discretion of the states.

Conclusion

States are authorised to imprison people as a punishment for a crime. This limitation of the right to liberty is explicitly authorised in many international and regional human rights treaties and national Constitutions. The limitation makes no exemption on the basis of old age. However, as discussed in this chapter, human rights put certain limits on the power of States to punish offenders. Despite differences in legal frameworks and different judicial tests used for assessment of similar cases, both the countries which are bound by the ECHR and those across the Atlantic, such as the US and Canada, recognise that deprivation of the right to liberty for a crime should not undermine human dignity.

This requirement entails respecting the principle of proportionality, i.e. the means of achieving the aims of the punishment should not undermine the right to liberty to such a degree as to amount to degradation of human dignity.

Furthermore, the method and manner of administration of sentences should comply with civilised standards, humanity and decency. And finally, respect for human dignity forbids depriving a human being of the hope to atone for her/his crime, to rehabilitate him/herself and regain the right to liberty at some time in the future.

The last limitation, which is generally known as the right to hope, is grounded on the recognition of humans' inherent capacity for personal development and change. This means that even the most serious offenders cannot be assumed to be 'beyond redemption' and locked up until they die. A chance to regain freedom should be given to a human being because hopelessness destroys the human spirit and consequently human dignity. Before various courts and tribunals, the right to hope has been relied upon to argue against the type of life imprisonment which is known in Europe as whole or natural life imprisonment and in the US as life without parole.

In the US the reliance on the right to hope in litigation before the US Supreme Court resulted in recognition that the Eighth Amendment of the US Constitution prohibits imposition of LWOP sentences on juveniles who commit non-homicide offences as well as on those homiciders on whom the imposition of LWOP is mandatory. The decisions of the US Supreme Court are important developments in advancing the limits of State power to punish. However, these developments have a limited scope. The decisions of the Court exclude individuals who are 18 years old or older as well as juveniles whose LWOP sentences for homicide offences were imposed by a judge on a discretionary basis. Moreover, the US Supreme Court left entirely unelaborated the issues of the content of the right, the identity of the decision-maker and procedural safeguards that must accompany the review in order to prevent arbitrariness in the decision.

By contrast, litigation based on the right to hope has resulted in more robust changes in Europe. The developments in the case law of the German Federal Constitutional Court, and more recently in ECtHR jurisprudence, has brought a recognition that the right to hope requires that a possibility of review and a prospect of release should be given to all prisoners. This requirement must be respected even in those cases where imposition of a whole life sentence is already justified on the grounds of punishment and deterrence. This approach recognises that with time the need for retribution and deterrence will not necessarily remain unchanged.

This recognition on the part of the ECtHR imposes a legal obligation on the Contracting States to have in place a review mechanism equipped with adequate procedural guarantees in order to check whether, after the passage of time, the continued imprisonment still serves a legitimate purpose and, if it does not, order the release of the prisoner. Furthermore, States must provide prisoners with the means necessary to enable their rehabilitation.

2 Extending the right of review to elderly and seriously ill prisoners

Abstract

As interpreted by the European Court of Human Rights, Article 3 of the European Convention of Human Rights requires courts to review whole life sentences after prisoners have served a considerable part of the sentence, presumably 25 years. The review has two independent aims. In the first place, the aim of making review available is to offer to whole life prisoners a hope of regaining their freedom. Moreover, it aims to prevent punishing the prisoner disproportionately more severely than is justified by the legitimate aims of punishment. This chapter analyses the applicability of the rationale of the right to review to the situation of prisoners whose mandatory custodial term is longer than their actuarial or clinical life expectancy, and those who are otherwise seriously ill. The analysis demonstrates that a serious illness and the likelihood of dying in prison may impact the severity of the sentence, making continued imprisonment unlawful. Therefore, as in whole life imprisonment cases, when prisoners are likely to die in detention or are otherwise seriously ill the fundamental nature of human dignity requires a review of continued imprisonment in order to prevent punishing the prisoner grossly more severely than is justified by the legitimate aims of punishment.

The Grand Chamber's judgment in the case of *Vinter*[1] is ground-breaking not only because of its findings, but also for the reasoning of the Grand Chamber and its implications for Article 3 of the European Convention on Human Rights (ECHR) in general. The Grand Chamber of the European Court of Human Rights (ECtHR) has recognised that the ECHR does not prohibit the imposition of life sentences on adult offenders, especially for serious crimes such as murder. However, life sentences in Contracting States should be reducible, i.e. should afford a possibility of review and a prospect of release in order to be compatible with Article 3 of the ECHR.[2]

Indeed, the grounds on which the Court found a violation of Article 3 encompass a remarkable mixture of independent but at the same time interrelated

1 *Vinter and others v United Kingdom* [GC] ECHR 2013-III 317.
2 ibid para.106.

factors. The judgment suggests that the review of whole life sentences is required for two interrelated but independent reasons.

The first ground for this requirement is to afford a prisoner the hope of regaining her/his freedom. This is required because depriving a human being, including those who have committed the most serious crimes, of the hope of regaining freedom by rehabilitating her/himself 'would be to deny a fundamental aspect of their humanity and, to do that, would be degrading'.[3] It is prohibited to deprive a human being of the hope of regaining her/his right to freedom because all human beings possess the fundamental capacity for personal development and change, which cannot be excluded even for those who have committed the most serious crimes.

The second ground is to prevent punishing the prisoner grossly more severely than is justified by the aims which necessitated the imposition of the sentence. According to the Grand Chamber, at the imposition stage a life sentence might be justified as punishment/retribution, deterrence, public protection and rehabilitation, which are legitimate penological goals. While many of these aims of punishment will be present when a whole life sentence is imposed, the balance between them 'is not necessarily static and may shift in the course of the sentence'.[4] The balance between the aims of punishment may shift because of that capacity for change which all human beings possess, including the worst criminals. Thus, , even when it is a justified punishment at the time of its imposition, whole life imprisonment 'with the passage of time … becomes a poor guarantee of a just and proportionate punishment'.[5] Therefore, Article 3 of the ECHR imposes a legal obligation on the Contracting States to have in place a review mechanism to check whether, since imposition of a whole life sentence, the progress made by the prisoner towards rehabilitation is so significant that continued imprisonment can no longer be justified by the legitimate aims of punishment.[6]

According to the Grand Chamber, it is 'axiomatic that a prisoner cannot be detained unless there are legitimate penological goals for that detention'.[7] The Grand Chamber did not specify which of the ECHR rights would be violated if a prisoner continued to be detained without legitimate penological goals. However, the lawfulness of the deprivation of the right to liberty of a person convicted for a crime is ensured by Article 5(1)(a).[8]

In order to be lawful, in addition to being imposed after conviction by a competent court, imprisonment should be lawful in a substantive and procedural sense. Lawfulness in this sense has been interpreted by the ECtHR to refer, essentially, to national law requiring national authorities to comply with substantive and procedural requirements of the respective laws. However, lawfulness also

3 ibid per Judge Power-Forde.
4 ibid para.111.
5 ibid para.112.
6 ibid para.119.
7 ibid para.111.
8 European Convention on Human Rights 1950 (ECHR) (Council of Europe).

requires compliance with the purpose of Article 5, which is to protect individuals from arbitrariness.[9] To comply with the purpose of Article 5 a domestic law authorising deprivation of liberty must be sufficiently accessible and precise.[10] Furthermore, apart from formally falling within one of the grounds prescribed under Article 5(1), deprivation of liberty should comply with the purpose of the ground on which it is carried out,[11] be in a good faith[12] and not be disproportionate to its purpose.[13]

Indeed, jurisprudence from different jurisdictions demonstrates that apart from the constitutional prohibition of cruel, unusual, inhuman or degrading punishment in some cases, the prohibition of arbitrariness was considered to be a source of prohibition of grossly disproportionate punishments.[14] However, in the case of *Vinter* both Chambers of the ECtHR found that punishments which are grossly disproportionate to the aims pursued would violate Article 3 of the ECHR.[15] Therefore, it could be concluded that the Court considered that continued imprisonment of a whole life prisoner would be grossly disproportionate in violation of Article 3 if the review revealed that it was no longer justified by the legitimate aims of punishment.

In spite of this conclusion, it is important to highlight that, in terms of human rights, the essence of imprisonment without legitimate goals of punishment is unlawful deprivation of liberty. However, such a situation would reach the threshold of degrading punishment in violation of Article 3 of the ECHR when it was grossly disproportionate, i.e. could not be justified by any of the legitimate goals. As the jurisprudence demonstrates, human dignity could be violated through an aggravated violation of another Convention right.[16]

The above rationale of the right to review under Article 3, which the ECtHR articulated in connection with whole life imprisonment, is also applicable to the case of elderly prisoners whose mandatory custodial terms are longer than their actuarial or clinical life expectancy, and those who are otherwise seriously ill.

9 See e.g. *Amuur v France* ECHR 1996-III 850 para.50.
10 *Gusinskiy v Russia* ECHR 2004-IV 129 para.62.
11 ibid paras 70–78.
12 *Bozano v France* Series A no 111 para.55.
13 See e.g. *Winterwerp v Netherlands* (1979) Series A no 33 para.39; *Guide on Article 5 of the Convention: Right to liberty and security* (2nd edn, Council of Europe/European Court of Human Rights 2014); Jim Murdoch, 'Safeguarding the Liberty of the Person: Recent Strasbourg Jurisprudence' (1993) 42(3) *The International and Comparative Law Quarterly* 494; Stefan Trechsel, 'Right to Liberty and Security of the Person' (1980) 1 *Human Rights Law Journal* 88; David J Harris, Michael O'Boyle and Colin Warbrick, *Law of the European Convention on Human Rights* (2nd edn, Oxford University Press 2009).
14 See e.g. Dirk van Zyl Smit and Andrew Ashworth, 'Disproportionate Sentences as Human Rights Violations' (2004) 67(4) *Modern Law Review* 541, 543.
15 *Vinter v United Kingdom* [GC] (n.1) para.102
16 See e.g. *East African Asians v United Kingdom* App nos 4403/70–4419/70 and 14 others, 62 para.209 (Commission Decision, 14 December 1973); *Abdulaziz, Cabales and Balkandali v UK* App no 9214/80; 9473/81; 9474/81 (ECtHR, 28 May 1985) para.91; *Smith and Grady v United Kingdom* ECHR 1999-VI 45 para.121.

Indeed, both grounds on which review is required, i.e. prohibition of depriving of the hope of release and preventing continued imprisonment which is not justified by the legitimate aims of punishment, are present in the case of prisoners whose mandatory custodial term is more than their remaining actuarial or clinical life expectancy. Although the issue of hope is not relevant to the situation of non-fatally ill prisoners, in their case the requirement of review is based on the ground of preventing continued imprisonment which is not justified by the legitimate aims of punishment. As demonstrated, this is a self-standing ground for review.

Like whole life prisoners, those whose mandatory custodial term is more than their remaining life expectancy should not be deprived of the hope of regaining their freedom. Indeed, at least some, if not the majority, of these prisoners were not even sentenced to life imprisonment. Furthermore, a change of circumstances which may shift the balance between the aims of punishment, is possible both in the case of elderly prisoners whose mandatory custodial terms are longer than their actuarial or clinical life expectancy, and those who are otherwise seriously ill. And finally, in the case of these prisoners the impact of the likelihood of dying in prison and of serious illness may compensate for the minimum time, presumably 25 years, which whole life prisoners are required to serve before the review of their continued imprisonment. Thus, it could be argued that the right to review under Article 3 should also be extended to prisoners whose mandatory custodial terms are longer than their actuarial or clinical life expectancy, and those who are otherwise seriously ill. However, in order to substantiate the above statement a detailed analysis of the issues – the hope of regaining freedom, rehabilitation and the impact of old age and serious illness on the severity of punishment – is required.

Hope of regaining freedom

As demonstrated, the two reasons for the Article 3 requirement of a review of whole life imprisonment are to offer hope of regaining freedom and to ensure that punishment does not become disproportionately more severe during the administration stage. The issue of hope of regaining freedom is also relevant to those prisoners whose mandatory custodial term is more than their remaining actuarial or clinical life expectancy. As with whole life imprisonment, in these cases human dignity prohibits the State 'forcefully to deprive a person of his freedom without at least providing him with the chance to someday regain that freedom'.[17] However, the situation in which the life expectancy of the offender is less than the minimum custodial part of the sentence is slightly different from *de jure* whole life sentence. In the latter case the opportunity for release does not depend on the longevity of the prisoner. In the case of a *de jure* whole life sentence the concept of *de jure* means that even if the prisoner surpasses all expected limits of longevity she/he cannot outlive the prison term. As the Grand Chamber put it, 'the punishment becomes greater with time: the longer the prisoner lives,

17 *Vinter v United Kingdom* [GC] (n.1) para.113.

the longer his sentence'.[18] This factor of certainty that the sentence is for life, i.e. independent of the longevity of the offender, is missing in cases when a mandatory custodial term of either a determinate or an indeterminate prison sentence is more than the remaining actuarial or clinical life expectancy of the offender.

Actuarial life expectancy is not an exact measure, but rather the average number of remaining years of life at a particular age calculated on the basis that age-specific mortality rates remain at their most recently measured levels.[19] However, a more exact measure or great demographic expertise is not necessary to calculate, for instance, that a minimum term of 25 years at the age of 82 amounts to a *de facto* irreducible life sentence.[20] While there will be a few individuals who will live a little longer than expected, from the perspective of justice it seems plausible to take the average point, i.e. life expectancy, as a threshold for the right to review and to deal with nuances of individual cases in the process of the review.

Furthermore, not to provide a chance of regaining freedom within the commonly known average duration of human life, to a prisoner whose actuarial life expectancy is less than the mandatory custodial part of her/his determinate or indeterminate prison term, would be contrary to the principle of legal certainty. Legal certainty is one of the elements of the rule of law which is a constituent part of the common heritage of the Member States of the Council of Europe (CoE).[21] In the case of *Vinter*, the Grand Chamber articulated that it would be contrary to legal certainty to make the prisoner serve an indeterminate number of years before he can raise the question that, in terms of reducibility, the 'legal conditions of his sentence fail to comply with the requirements of Article 3'.[22] Similarly, it would be contrary to the principle of legal certainty to make the prisoner serve the sentence, hoping that she/he will regain or will be given an opportunity to regain his freedom if against all odds she/he lives longer than the vast majority of his counterparts.

Furthermore, the aim of the opportunity to regain freedom is broader than allowing a prisoner to die at home.[23] Therefore, if a *de facto* life prisoner is given the opportunity of review within her/his life expectancy, and after release does not die immediately at the age predicted by actuarial calculations, neither the aims of punishment nor any other principles that govern the punishment of offenders would be diminished.

Similarly to actuarial life expectancy tables, clinical predictions of life expectancy due to fatal illness are not exact.[24] Furthermore, it is difficult to know what

18 ibid para.112.

19 Samuel H Preston, Patrick Heuveline and Michel Guillot, *Demography: Measuring and modeling population processes* (Blackwell 2001) 35–38.

20 See e.g. *R. v Lowe* (2014).

21 See e.g. *Brumarescu v Romania* ECHR 2001-I 155 para.61; European Convention on Human Rights (n.8) preamble.

22 *Vinter v United Kingdom* [GC] (n.1) para.122.

23 ibid para.127.

24 See e.g. Bric A Williams, 'Balancing Punishment and Compassion for Seriously Ill' (2011) 155(2) Ann Intern Med 122, 124.

the future holds in terms of development of new medication and methods of treatment of particular diseases. However, the arguments advanced above in support of the review on the ground of actuarial life expectancy are equally relevant to the review on the ground of fatal illness. These arguments demonstrate that uncertainty over actuarial and clinical life expectancy is not an obstacle to extending the right of review to prisoners whose life expectancy is less than the minimum custodial part of the sentence. The issue of uncertainty can be dealt with during the review itself. It should be noted that the above points are irrelevant to extending the Article 3 right to review of continued imprisonment of prisoners who are seriously but not fatally ill.

Rehabilitation

Although the hope of regaining freedom is an important component of the right to review of whole life imprisonment, it is not the only ground. Prohibition of denying such hope is based on the belief that even those who committed the worst crimes are capable of rehabilitation.[25] The concept of rehabilitation, as it is understood by the Court, should be discussed in more detail in order to see whether it applies to elderly prisoners who serve fixed or indeterminate sentences with longer mandatory custodial terms than their natural life expectancy, and those who are terminally or otherwise seriously ill.

The Grand Chamber's judgment in the case of *Vinter* makes it clear that there is a danger that a whole life sentence which was a proportionate punishment at the time of the imposition may become grossly disproportionate, i.e grossly more severe, because the balance between the aims of punishment is susceptible to change.[26] However, Article 3 would not be violated if the release were denied because the prisoner continued to pose a danger to society.[27] Whereas the prospect of release should not be ruled out because of a person's capacity to change her/his personality, whether or not the whole life prisoner would be released depends on the real change of balance between the need for further punishment, deterrence, public protection and rehabilitation.

It is explicit in the judgment that the capacity for change of personality or for rehabilitation is one of the critical factors in the possible shift of balance between the aims of punishment. Apparently, when talking about rehabilitation as one of the aims of punishment, the Court did not have in mind the concept of rehabilitation in the broad meaning of the term as it is considered in the penological literature.[28] Rather, the Court considered that the aim of rehabilitation would be achieved when the prisoner no longer posed a danger to society, i.e. rehabilita-

25 *Vinter v United Kingdom* [GC] (n.1) para.114.
26 ibid para.111.
27 ibid para.108.
28 See e.g. Antony Duff, *Punishment, communication, and community* (Studies in crime and public policy, Oxford University Press 2001) 5.

tion and public protection were considered as two sides of the same coin.[29] The Court considered that, especially in serious cases which attract life sentences, if this aim could be achieved at all, it would require a long prison term. According to comparative and international law materials reviewed by the Court, such a term could be around 25 years.[30]

A similar change of circumstances is also possible in cases where the mandatory part of a fixed or indeterminate prison term is more than the remaining life expectancy (actuarial or clinical) of the prisoner and when a prisoner is otherwise seriously ill. In these cases the ground for possible change in the balance between the aims of punishment is serious illness or advanced age. It is very likely that such prisoners will cease posing a danger to society. This argument is strongly supported by empirical research. It has been demonstrated that age is the most reliable indicator of low recidivism; the age–crime curve strongly supports the idea that the older prisoners are at release, the less likely it is that they will reoffend.[31] The likelihood of reoffending declines even further with the time served before release; in the category of prisoners over the age of 60 who have served four to 10 years in prison before release, the reoffending rate is 4.8%, in contrast to 36.9% of those aged 18–20.[32]

Furthermore, serious illness is another component which decreases the risk of reoffending. Although this claim apparently has not been empirically verified, common sense suggests that elderly, seriously ill prisoners, by virtue of their reduced capacity, would be even less likely to reoffend than those who are elderly and fit. This common-sense claim is indirectly supported by the fact that respective prison regulations in England require the medical opinion regarding the prisoner's ability to escape to be taken into account in the risk assessment in cases of outside hospital escorts and bedwatch.[33]

Denying hope of regaining freedom, even to people who committed the most egregious crimes, is regarded as degrading. There is a belief that even such persons can rehabilitate themselves and cease posing a danger to society. However, those who were sentenced to a whole life sentence would require a long time in prison in order to achieve this aim.

By contrast, in the case of elderly prisoners whose mandatory part of a fixed or indeterminate prison term is more than their remaining actuarial life expectancy and those who are terminally or otherwise seriously ill, such a long prison term would not be required for ceasing to pose a danger to society. In the case of

29 See e.g. *Vinter v United Kingdom* [GC] (n.1) para.47, 108.

30 ibid para.120.

31 House of Commons Justice Committee, 'Older prisoners: Fifth Report of Session 2013–2014' (Volume I: Report, together with formal minutes, oral and written evidence, London 2013) 40; Michael Gottfredson and Travis Hirschi, 'The True Value of Lambda Would Appear to be Zero: An Essay on Career Criminals, Criminal Careers, Selective Incapacitation, Cohort Studies, and Related Topics' (1986) 24(2) *Criminology* 213.

32 House of Commons Justice Committee (n.31) 40.

33 Prisons and Probation Ombudsman for England and Wales, 'Fatal incidents investigation: restraints' (2013). Learning lessons bulletin 2 2, accessed 9 October 2015.

whole life prisoners, a catalyst for possibly ceasing to pose a danger to society is rehabilitation, while in the case of elderly and seriously ill prisoners it is their age and/or serious illness that makes them less prone to reoffending. However, the term which a whole life prisoner will be required to serve before a review will be conducted is not only to achieve rehabilitation of the prisoner, but also punishment and deterrence.

According to the Court, the aims of punishment and deterrence could justify the imposition of a whole life sentence, but could not rule out the prospect of release. Therefore, after the passage of, presumably, a 25-year period it should again be checked whether the time already served has been sufficient to achieve these aims. The time component which is also required for the purposes of punishment and deterrence is missing in the case of elderly and seriously ill prisoners. While there may be no need to continue their punishment in order to protect the public, the aims of punishment and deterrence may still require that they continue to serve the punishment imposed by the court. However, the aims of punishment and deterrence in the case of above mentioned categories of elderly prisoners might also be achieved earlier than was envisaged by courts at the time of the imposition of the sentences: the impact of old age and illness on the severity of the punishment may make punishment more severe than would otherwise be the case.

Measurement of punishment severity: objectivism, subjectivism and a hybrid approach

The measurement of the severity of punishment is an issue of utmost importance, because to achieve the same aims different types or quantity of punishment would be required, depending on the case at hand. Three broad approaches to the measurement of severity of punishment are objectivism,[34] subjectivism,[35] and a hybrid approach.[36]

34 See e.g. Dan Markel, Chad Flanders and Gray, 'Beyond Experience: Getting Retributive Justice Right' (2011) 99(2) *California Law Review* 605; Dan Markel and Chad Flanders, 'Bentham on Stilts: The Bare Relevance of Subjectivity to Retributive Justice' (2010) 98(3) *California Law Review* 907; David Gray, 'Punishment as suffering' (2010) 63(6) *Vanderbilt Law Review* 1619; Mara F Schiff, 'Gauging the Intensity of Criminal Sanctions: Developing the Criminal Punishment Severity Scale (CPSS)' (1997) 22(2) *Criminal Justice Review* 175; Andrew von Hirsch, *Censure and sanctions* (Oxford monographs on criminal law and justice, Clarendon 1993) 33–35.

35 See e.g. Bronsteen, John, Buccafusco, Christopher and S. Masur, 'Retribution and the Experience of Punishment' (2010) 98(5) *California Law Review* 1463; Bronsteen, John, Buccafusco, Christopher and Masur, Jonathan, 'Happiness and Punishment' (2009) 76(3) *University of Chicago Law Review* 1037; Adam J Kolber, 'The Comparative Nature of Punishment' (2009) 89(5) *Boston University Law Review* 1565; Adam J Kolber, 'The Subjective Experience of Punishment' (2009) 109(1) *Columbia Law Review* 182.

36 See e.g. David J Hayes, 'Penal Impact: Towards a More Intersubjective Measurement of Penal Severity' (2016) 36(4) *Oxford J Legal Studies* 724; David Hayes, 'Proximity, pain, and State punishment' [2017] *Punishment & Society*, published online 27 March 2017; 10.1177/1462474517701303.

Objectivism

Objectivists measure the severity of punishment by relying on standard interests or freedoms that are intended to be affected by imposition of a particular type of punishment. For instance, von Hirsch suggested that the living standard analysis which he articulated in connection with gauging crime severity could also be applied in relation to gauging punishment severity.[37] According to this approach, if a certain interest, which a particular punishment interferes with, is 'an important interest – in the sense of its importance as standardized means to achieving a certain living-standard', deprivation of such interest is severe irrespective of the perception of a particular individual.[38] Von Hirsch proposed scaling punishments in accordance with the importance of interests and the degree to which these interests are intruded upon. The more important the negatively affected interest is, the severer the penalty.[39] Von Hirsch also argued that the measurement of punishment severity should not seek to account for the personal sensitivities of particular individuals.[40]

Similarly, Schiff used a concept of liberty, i.e. freedom of movement and freedom of choice, as common denominator for deprivations which to some degree are caused by any type of punishment. Based on this approach she constructed a quantitative scale of relative severity of punishment.[41]

Despite arguing that the measurement of punishment severity should not depend on how particular individuals experience punishment, von Hirsch and Ashworth endorsed the principle of equal impact of punishments. According to these authors, when certain handicaps of an offender would make punishment significantly more severe, the 'sanction should be adjusted in order to avoid its having undue differential impact on him'.[42] The equal impact principle aims not to make an offender suffer less than the deserved punishment, but to ensure that offenders do not suffer more punishment than deserved by avoiding the differential impact that punishment can have on an offender because of certain handicaps. This principle applies only to unusual cases 'that diverge from the norm significantly, that would speak for attending to those unusual features and, if appropriate, modifying the sentence to ensure there is not an unequal impact'.[43]

As mentioned above, von Hirsch suggested measuring severity of punishments through analysis of living standards, where severity is gauged by reference to the importance of the interests upon which the sentence typically impinges without taking into account individual experiences of offenders.[44] However,

37 von Hirsch (n.34) 34.
38 ibid 35.
39 ibid 34.
40 ibid 35.
41 Schiff (n.34)
42 Andrew von Hirsch and Andrew Ashworth, *Proportionate Sentencing: Exploring the Principles* (Oxford University Press 2005) 172
43 ibid.
44 ibid.

he argued that under living-standard analysis offenders with certain handicaps would suffer a greater setback of their interests if the sanction which was normally imposed in similar cases was applied in their cases. Therefore, in such cases less severe punishment 'under an equal-impact theory would be designed merely to eliminate this increment in severity'.[45] The equal impact principle would apply to offenders with certain handicaps sentenced to penalties with demanding routines, such as imprisonment, that will make normal sentences imposed in like cases unduly onerous for such offenders.[46] It is, however, acknowledged that, as with the assessment of seriousness and severity in normal cases, in unusual cases living-standard analysis could not produce a precise calculation of added interest setback, rather it offers 'an approximate norm in dealing with unusual situations'.[47]

Subjectivism

The objectivists' focus on the formal side of punishment rather than on the content has generated considerable criticism. The critics focused on objectivists' failure to account for substantive rather than formal justice.[48] According to critics, by focusing only on the formal side of punishment objectivists misrepresent the institution of punishment. All major accounts of punishment accept that punishment is a hard treatment or deprivation, i.e. something which, if not harmful, is at least unpleasant.[49] Unpleasantness is inevitably a product of subjective experience. Failure to recognise that the same punishment affects different individuals differently, ultimately results in different substantive outcomes for those offenders whom, in comparison with others, the same punishment affects differently by virtue of their personal situation. This compromises objectivists' own promise of punishing like cases alike.[50]

It is true that choosing to focus on a single formal metric such as liberty makes it possible to create a monolithic scale of deprivations. This makes comparisons of severity simple and straightforward. However, in order to fit in the scale, any deprivation or pain which could not be accommodated by this metric should be discarded. In order to 'safely' discard all pains which do not fit within the single metric of liberty, objectivists tend to give the pain an objective qualification by focusing only on intended pains.[51] This approach, in its turn, raises the question

45 ibid 173.

46 ibid.

47 ibid 172.

48 Jesper Ryberg, *The Ethics of Proportionate Punishment: A Critical Investigation* (Library of Ethics and Applied Philosophy vol.16, Kluwer Academic Publishers 2004) 140.

49 Andrew Ashworth, *Sentencing and criminal justice* (Law in context, 5th edn Cambridge University Press 2010) 95; T McPherson, 'Punishment: Definition and Justification' (1967) 28(1) *Analysis* 21.

50 Jesper Ryberg, 'Punishment and the Measurement of Severity' in Jesper Ryberg and JA Corlett (eds), *Punishment and ethics: New perspectives* (Palgrave Macmillan 2010) 74–82.

51 Hayes (n.36), 735.

of delimitation of intended and unintended pains of punishment. Moreover, by focusing on liberty as a metric for measurement of punishment severity, objectivists presume that liberties are equally important for everybody, disregarding the idea that freedoms could be differently valued by each individual.[52]

Some critics of objectivism argue that measurement of punishment severity cannot ignore its impact on an individual and its desirability. Their approach to measurement identifies unpleasant features of punishment through inquiring into individual experiences of the punished. It attempts to reveal the way punishment affects offenders during and beyond serving the sentence. Studies adopting this approach tend to come up with a catalogue which shows incidents and variation of pains without accounting for the quantity in terms of relative severity compared one to another and in terms of impact on offenders' life. However, these studies were not able to offer a scale of punishment severity which could enable meaningful comparisons.[53] They recognise that experience of pain depends on many different factors, such as offenders' previous experiences, expectations and ability to adapt to different situations. In order to enable meaningful measurement of punishment severity, some authors suggest that the experiences of penal subjects during punishment should be compared to their previous 'baseline conditions'.[54]

The idea that the same punishment affects individuals differently depending on their personal characteristics is not new. Surprisingly, it was Bentham who brought forward this idea and elaborated a list of characteristics which may affect the punishments' severity. According to Bentham:[55]

> It is further to be observed, that owing to the different manners and degrees in which persons under different circumstances are affected by the same exciting cause, punishment which is the same in name will not always either really produce, or even so much as appear to others to produce, in two different persons the same degree of pain:

therefore,

> That the quantity actually inflicted on each individual offender may correspond to the quantity intended for similar offenders in general, the several circumstances influencing sensibility ought always to be taken into account.

52 ibid 736.

53 See e.g. Ioan Durnescu, 'Pains of Probation: Effective Practice and Human Rights' (2010) 55(4) *International Journal of Offender Therapy and Comparative Criminology* 530 ,534–538.

54 See e.g Kolber, 'The Comparative Nature of Punishment' (n.35); Kolber, 'The Subjective Experience of Punishment' (n.35).

55 Jeremy Bentham, *An introduction to the principles of morals and legislation* (Dover philosophical classics, Repubn of Oxford Clarendon 1907, Dover 2007) 182.

He listed the following 32 'circumstances influencing sensibilities':[56]

> 1. Health. 2. Strength. 3. Hardiness. 4. Bodily imperfections. 5. Quantity and quality of knowledge. 6. Strength of intellectual powers. 7. Firmness of mind. 8. Steadiness of mind. 10. Moral sensibility. 11. Moral biases. 12. Religious sensibility. 134. Religious biases. 14. Sympathetic sensibility. 15. Sympathetic biases. 16. Antipathetic sensibility. 17. Antipathetic biases. 18. Insanity. 19. Habitual occupations. 20. Pecuniary circumstances. 21. Connexions in the way of sympathy. 23. Radical frame of body. 24. Radical frame of mind. 25 Sex. 26. Age. 27. Rank. 28. Education. 29. Climate. 30. Lineage. 31. Government. 32. Religious profession.

Bentham suggested that the judge ought to adjust the sentence taking into account the sensibilities of offenders, because according to his theory the punishment ought to be no more or less than is necessary to outweigh the expected profit of the crime.[57]

A hybrid approach

Like penal objectivism, the account of penal subjectivism has a number of gaps that affect this model's potential of producing a comprehensive and practical method of measuring penal severity. Apart from the above shortcomings, the model's ability to generalise and accurately predict future experiences is questionable. Furthermore, it does not try to delimit pains resulting from the penal intervention and those which exist in an offender's life independently of the penal intervention.[58]

Despite all shortcomings, research into the pains of punishment has made undeniable the existence of routine pains that accompany State punishment. These pains can arise both from the State's actions and those of non-State actors. The problem of whether these pains should be considered part of punishment remains a topic of heated debates between objectivists and subjectivists.[59] Against this background a hybrid approach to this issue is suggested by Hayes.[60]

Hayes argued that ignoring the fact that punishment is routinely accompanied by pain equals a refusal to acknowledge the way in which it is currently practised. He defined pains of punishment as 'a personal experience of physical, mental, or emotional suffering by a penal subject arising from their punishment by agents of a criminal justice system'.[61] In order to add an objective element to the concept of pains of punishment and aid its delimitation from other pains that exist in

56 ibid 44–45.
57 ibid 179.
58 Hayes (n.36), 4.
59 See e.g. Markel and Flanders (n.34).
60 Hayes (n.36).
61 ibid 5.

the life of a penal subject during the punishment, Hayes suggested a taxonomy of pains based on how closely they can be attributed to the State. In this model pains of imprisonment are categorised into four groups. The first are ***direct*** pains which are directly intended by the State; this is followed by ***oblique*** pains which, though not directly intended, are foreseeable at the time of the imposition of punishment; these are followed by ***contextual*** pains, which are unintended but have a causal relationship with the penal intervention; and finally, there are ***unrelated*** pains which exist in the life of a penal subject independently of the penal intervention.[62]

According to Hayes it is easy to identify pains that fall into the first and the last category, i.e. directly intended and unrelated. For instance, any type of punishment intends to deprive or at least limit to some extent individual freedoms such as freedom of movement, freedom of choice, etc. In the category of unrelated pain, one can count, for example, personal bereavement which coincidentally exists during the punishment and is not related to it.[63]

In the category of ***oblique*** pains fall pains such as an offender's inability to find a job after serving the punishment, or eviction from social housing as a result of conviction. These harms are not the aim of the State agents, but are 'sufficiently proximate to the state agents' intention to allow us to take them into account when determining penal severity'.[64] Hayes further classified oblique pains into two groups: ***general*** and ***specific***. To the general group belong pains such as diminished employability, which routinely accompanies criminal conviction; research demonstrates that in comparison to non-convicted job seekers, the job search for ex-offenders lasts on average two years longer, although it should not be assumed that this time period will be exactly two years in every case.[65]

By contrast, ***specific oblique*** pains are a virtual certainty in every case in a specific class of cases. For instance, eviction from housing in the case of conviction might be prescribed in the housing arrangement of the convicted person. Although the judge may not wish it, she/he will be certain of this consequence.[66]

As to unrelated pains, they coincidentally exist in the life of a penal subject during the punishment. However, they could be intensified or give rise to other pains, because of the punishment. In order to accommodate these pains Hayes came up with the category of ***contextual*** pains. For instance, personal bereavement of the penal subject because of the death of a terminally ill family member is unrelated to the punishment. However, the pain of loss will intensify when a prisoner cannot spend last hours with a dying family member, because she/he is in prison.[67]

Furthermore, Hayes relates to contextual pains those potential pains which are indirect consequences of punishment, such as pains arising from loss of contact

62 ibid 6.
63 ibid 7.
64 ibid 8.
65 ibid.
66 ibid 9.
67 ibid 10.

with friends and family, absence from key developmental periods of children, etc. Unlike unrelated pains, contextual pains bear indirect connection to the punishment. Hayes's point of distinction of contextual pains from oblique pains is that the latter category is relatively accurately foreseeable as a 'virtual' certainty of the actions of the penal agents, while the former 'is not necessarily foreseen or even foreseeable by the sentencing authorities'.[68] However, the sources of contextual pains are 'still proximate to the State in that pains are caused by penal intervention'.[69] Hayes does not argue that the responsibility for contextual pains could be attributed to the State. Rather, his concern is to demonstrate the proximity of those pains to the penal intervention and their impact on penal severity. Therefore, the definition of causation here is broader than in substantive criminal law.[70]

Hayes accepts that his model does not offer a means for ranking pains of punishment. His taxonomy of pains is not a scale; it does not assume that all penal subjects will necessarily suffer contextual, oblique or unrelated pains or will experience these pains in the same way. Furthermore, contextual or oblique pains may inflict more suffering on a penal subject than direct pains of punishment. Hayes argues that the aim of his model is only to provide a useful heuristic for classifying the pains and enabling the progression of discussion on the issue of which pains of punishment should be taken into account in measuring the punishment severity.[71]

However, he proposes some ways in which these pains could be taken into account in policy and practice. According to Hayes, general *oblique* pains (e.g. ex-offenders' employability) should be taken into account at least to some extent at the policy-making level. He suggest that with reference to social science research the policy-makers can calculate some general reduction of sentences in order to account for general oblique pains which to some extent affect all offenders. As to specific oblique pains, these could be taken into account only at the level of sentencing, because they are less generalisable.

By contrast, caution should be exercised in accounting for contextual pains in the measurement of severity of sentence. Contextual pains are more complex than oblique pains. Social experiences are usually affected by multiple causes and it might be virtually impossible to separate different sources of pains. It might be difficult even for offenders to categorise the sources of their pains, while any attempt to do this arbitrarily is vulnerable to research bias. In summary, contextual pains are inaccessible to sentencing authorities and are insufficiently foreseeable. They cannot be objectivised in the way the oblique pains can. Therefore, they should be either ignored or given some regard on the basis of rough estimates at the cost of legal certainty. According to Hayes, his account of penal severity 'can

68 ibid.
69 ibid.
70 ibid 11.
71 ibid 7.

assist in development of a more socially accurate criminal justice system that is more capable of doing justice in the context'.[72]

Hayes argued that adoption of a proximity-based model would not require any alteration of the role of the judiciary, because subjective circumstances have always been taken into account at sentencing through judicial discretion. However, he stated that personal mitigation, as it exists in England and Wales, could not be a mechanism for implementing a proximity-based model: personal mitigation provides a class of contextual factors leaving a judge with a wide discretion, but little guidance as to how much weight should be given to each factor. In order to become a mechanism for implementation of a proximity-based model, the present system of personal mitigation should be fine-tuned to allow weighting of individual factors.[73]

Furthermore, Hayes argued that the role of personal mitigation is limited in the present sentencing model. This can be taken into account to fine-tune the punishment only after the harm and culpability have already been determined based on factors which focus heavily upon criminal acts rather than a convict's circumstances. According to Hayes, this approach limits the ability of personal mitigation to affect overall penal severity and places more emphasis on policy-makers in guiding judgments at sentencing.[74] He argues that in order to implement a proximity-based model judges need to take a more holistic approach by looking at the offender's conduct in comparison with 'the pains that the sentence is likely to inflict on the specific individual in her unique contexts, insofar as the court is aware of them'.[75] This requires not necessarily new mechanisms, but rather a different approach as to how the existing mechanisms are used in practice.[76]

Impact of old age and/or serious illness on severity of punishment

Regardless of whether or not one agrees with Hayes' model, it is impossible to disagree with the fact that the same punishment may cause suffering of different degrees depending on the personal circumstances of offenders. The question is not whether the pains of punishment should be considered as part of the punishment, but rather how the pains stemming from different personal circumstances should be categorised and how the impact of these circumstances could be neutralised or mitigated. Hayes' idea of categorisation of pains based on the proximity to the State's intention might be a useful first step towards achieving this aim. However, this model seems to have some gaps. The present discussion will focus on gaps which are more relevant for the purpose of this book, leaving aside other issues such as the appropriateness of attempting to neutralise or mitigate all pains of punishment through sentence reduction.

72 ibid 12.
73 ibid 14.
74 ibid.
75 ibid.
76 ibid 15.

The relevant matter of discussion in this book is that the model proposed by Hayes is entirely forward-looking; the categories are built on the bases of generalisability and foreseeability of pains at the time of policy-making or sentencing. By focusing on the proximity of pains to the intention of the State at the time of policy-making or sentencing, this model puts some very acute pains in a category of less relevant pains. This will result in their being given less regard in the measurement of the punishment's severity. Suppose that a prisoner suffering from cancer is driven a long way three times a week to receive life-saving treatment in a civilian hospital. She/he is shackled both in the security van and during the treatment in the hospital. In this case, it could not generally be said that the illness itself arises from or is related to imprisonment. However, the pains of illness are intensified owing to the prisoner's transfers, handcuffing, etc. Even if the information about the offender's illness is available to sentencing authorities, the pains stemming from the impact of an illness on the prisoner's experience or the impact of the imprisonment on the development of the illness are not a virtual certainty at the time of sentencing, i.e. these pains are not sufficiently foreseeable. Therefore, in Hayes' model these pains would be considered as contextual pains.

Similarly, pains of elderly prisoners (whose sentences are longer than their life expectancy) stemming from the prospect of dying in prison would also be classified as contextual pains. In cases where the imposed sentence surpasses the actuarial or clinical life expectancy of the offender (in cases where the information about a terminal illness is available at sentencing), the pains stemming from these sources could be foreseen at the time of sentencing. However, they are not sufficiently foreseeable: a certain individual may surpass expected limits of longevity or in cases of terminal illness may live longer than expected owing to the development of new medication and methods of treatment, or individual trajectories of the development of disease.

Hayes' model suggests that such pains should either be ignored or be given some regard on the basis of rough estimates at the cost of legal certainty.[77] Moreover, such limited regard to the pains related to the illness of the offender could be given only if the information about the illness exists at the time of sentencing. It seems that this model leaves out entirely the situation when a prisoner becomes ill during the punishment. Therefore, it disregards the impact on the measurement of punishment severity of those pains which stem from the illness that was not known to the sentencing authorities.

A better approach, particularly for taking into account the severity of punishment pains arising from the likelihood of dying in prison and the impact of terminal or otherwise serious illness, will be to allow retrospective consideration of the impact of these pains on the severity of the punishment. Indeed, the review of ECtHR case law demonstrates that the Court has recognised the impact of serious medical conditions and the likelihood of dying in prison on the severity of imprisonment. A similar position emerges from the review of English case law. The review demonstrates that attempts are made to remove differences of

77 ibid 12.

impact of a punishment arising from serious medical conditions of a defendant and the likelihood of a defendant's dying in prison owing to either old age or fatal illness. Courts reduced sentences to make allowance for such circumstances if they were informed about them at the time of sentencing. When such circumstances have arisen or intensified during the execution of sentences, attempts have been made to take these pains into account in the severity of punishment retrospectively.

Impact of old age: the approach of the ECtHR

In several cases before the ECtHR the applicants raised the issue of compatibility of continued deprivation of liberty with Article 3 because of the impact of very old age or a serious medical condition on their prison experience.[78] In these cases, applicants based their Article 3 complaints about continued imprisonment on both their advanced age and their state of health, and the incompatibility of these with prison conditions. Therefore, in the case law of the ECtHR, the issue of impact of old age on the severity of punishment and consequently the compatibility of continued imprisonment in view of old age almost always appears in conjunction with the issue of health. A close analysis is required in order to distinguish the position of the ECtHR in relation to the each issue.

Although applications challenging the compatibility of continued detention with Article 3 of the ECHR had been brought by elderly detainees earlier,[79] the first such challenge on the ground of old age appears to have been made in the case of *Priebke v Italy*.[80] The applicant, who was over the age of 85, complained *inter alia* that in view of his extreme old age keeping him in prison was inhuman and degrading and therefore contrary to Article 3 of the ECHR. However, the ECtHR stated that, although incarceration of an 85-year-old might fall within the scope of Article 3, in the particular case the treatment of the applicant did not attain the minimum level of severity to reach the threshold of degrading punishment. This conclusion was based on the fact that the applicant was imprisoned for only a short time and had a satisfactory state of health. Moreover, Italian authorities had taken measures necessary to protect the applicant's well-being.[81]

Similar findings have emerged from other ECtHR decisions. In both *Sawoniuk v United Kingdom* and *Papon v France*, which came after *Priebke*, the ECtHR explicitly stated that the ECHR contains no prohibition against the imprisonment of elderly persons, but also noted that 'under certain circumstances the detention of an elderly person over a lengthy period might raise an issue under Article 3'.[82] Subsequent case law on the subject demonstrates that this approach

78 See e.g. *Priebke v Italy* (dec.) no. 48799/99 (ECtHR, 5 April 2001); *Sawoniuk v United Kingdom* (dec.) no. 63716/00 ECHR 2001-VI 375; *Papon v France (no. 1)* (dec) ECHR 2001-VI 459.

79 *de Varga-Hirsch v France* [1983] 33 DR 158.

80 *Priebke v Italy* (n.78).

81 ibid.

82 *Sawoniuk v United Kingdom* (n.78); *Papon v France (no. 1)* (n.78).

has become one of the general principles by which the ECtHR assesses relevant claims.[83]

It should be highlighted that these cases were declared manifestly ill-founded, and therefore inadmissible for consideration of the merits, because the Court found that the claims were not supported by the facts of the case. Indeed, none of these cases presented a situation in which the custodial term which the prisoners needed to serve before automatic or discretionary release was longer than the prisoner's life expectancy. In the case of *Priebke*, by the time the ECtHR considered the admissibility of the application, the prisoner had been released from prison after being held for no more than three months. Thus, it is not surprising that the ECtHR held:[84]

> In view of the short length of time involved, the applicant's satisfactory state of health and the care taken by the Italian authorities in monitoring the situation, the treatment to which he had been subjected following his conviction had not attained the minimum level of severity required to fall within the scope of Article 3. The application was therefore manifestly ill-founded.

In the case of *Sawoniuk v United Kingdom*, the 80-year-old applicant had been sentenced to mandatory life imprisonment in 1999 for war crimes committed during World War II and had spent more than two years in prison by the time of the application. While declaring the complaints under Articles 3 or 5 in relation to the applicant's sentence and detention manifestly ill-founded, the ECtHR held, *inter alia*, that it could not be said that the applicant's imprisonment was without any prospect of release. It stated that although no tariff had yet been fixed by the Home Secretary, the Lord Chief Justice recommended a tariff of only five years. Furthermore, the ECtHR pointed to the specific mechanisms available to the applicant that could be used to reduce the sentence if the tariff fixed by the Home Secretary were unreasonable.[85]

Finally, Maurice Papon, a 90-year-old man who had been in prison for more than three years serving a sentence of 10 years, complained *inter alia* that any form of imprisonment of a man over the age of 90 constituted in itself and in its essence a breach of Article 3 of the ECHR. Although the possibility of early release was neither directly raised by the applicant nor deliberated by the ECtHR, in its inadmissibility decision the Court pointed out the various ways in which the French authorities could intervene if the applicant's health 'taken together with his extreme old age were to worsen'.[86]

83 *Mouisel v France* ECHR 2002-IX 219 38; *Matencio v France* no 58749/00 76 (ECtHR, 15 January 2004); *Sakkopoulos v Greece* no 61828/00 39 (ECtHR, 15 January 2004); *Farbtuhs v. Latvia* no 4672/02 53 (ECtHR, 2 December 2004).

84 *Priebke v Italy* (n.78).

85 *Sawoniuk v United Kingdom* (n.78).

86 *Papon v France (no. 1)* (n.78).

In these cases it was not directly argued that owing to advanced age or likelihood of dying in prison the sentences impacted the offenders disproportionately more severely turning into *de facto* whole life sentences. However, it is evident that the ECtHR did not regard the sentences at stake as irreducible. It pointed to the various remedies available that could be used to release the applicants before the mandatory custodial part of the sentence was served.[87] Although, in relation to these cases, the ECtHR stated that 'none of the provisions of the Convention expressly prohibits imprisonment beyond a certain age', it did not exclude the possibility that 'under certain circumstances, the detention of an elderly person over a lengthy period might raise an issue under Article 3'. The court pointed out that 'regard is to be had to the particular circumstances of each specific case'.[88]

A more direct indication of the recognition of the impact of old age on the severity of sentence can be found in a recent case of *Khamatokhu and Aksenchik v Russia*.[89] The Grand Chamber of the ECtHR recognised that exempting adults aged 65 and over from life imprisonment was a legitimate justification for differentiated treatment in the context of sentencing policy.[90] Under Russian legislation, life-sentenced prisoners have a prospect of release after serving 25 years.[91] However, the Court articulated that exempting adults aged 65 and over from life sentences was a measure to ensure the compatibility of life imprisonment with the requirement of reducibility under Article 3. The Court stated that providing a maximum age limit for the imposition of life imprisonment is one of several ways of complying with the reducibility requirement of Article 3.[92]

The statement of the Court that exemption of adults aged 65 and over from life sentences is a way of complying with requirement of reducibility under Article 3 is a recognition of the impact of old age on the severity of punishment. This statement demonstrates that the Court is concerned that, in comparison to younger lifers, in the case of adults aged 65 and over the requirement of review after 25 years could not be regarded as providing a real prospect of release, because they are likely to die before the review.

Impact of a serious medical condition: the approach of the ECtHR

The ECtHR has developed detailed rules for the assessment of the impact of a serious medical condition on the severity of punishment, i.e. compatibility of continued imprisonment in cases of fatally or otherwise seriously ill prisoners. As the case law demonstrates, in both categories the ECtHR generally applies the same standard regardless of whether the illness is fatal in the short term or otherwise serious. The starting position of the ECtHR is that Article 3 of the ECHR

87 *Papon v France (no. 1)* (n.78); *Priebke v Italy* (n.78); *Sawoniuk v United Kingdom* (n.78).

88 *Papon v France (no. 1)* (n.78); *Priebke v Italy* (n.78); *Sawoniuk v United Kingdom* (n.78).

89 *Khamtokhu and Aksenchik v Russia* [GC] App no 60367/08 and 961/11 (ECtHR 24 January 2017).

90 ibid para.70.

91 ibid para.17.

92 ibid para.81.

cannot be interpreted as laying down a general obligation to release prisoners on the ground of ill health.[93] However, Article 3 imposes an obligation on the State to protect the health and wellbeing of prisoners by, *inter alia*, providing them with the necessary medical assistance.[94] Furthermore, Article 3 requires the State to ensure that conditions of detention are compatible with human dignity and that 'the manner and method of execution of the measures imposed do not subject him to distress or hardship of an intensity exceeding the unavoidable level of suffering inherent in detention'.[95]

Furthermore, the ECtHR has recognised that the health of the detainee is 'among the factors to be taken into account in determining how a custodial sentence is to be served', in particular in regard to the continued detention of persons who are living with a fatal illness or whose condition is permanently incompatible with prison life.[96] In subsequent cases the ECtHR clearly stated that 'Article 3 may require the release of a detainee only in exceptional cases and under certain conditions, where his or her health is absolutely incompatible with detention'.[97]

As mentioned, Article 3 requires States to provide requisite medical assistance and secure conditions of detention compatible with human dignity. In order to assess the compatibility of health status with the continued detention of the applicant, in addition to this general requirement, the ECtHR has developed an assessment test consisting of three additional factors: (a) the condition of the prisoner, (b) the quality of care delivered, and (c) the advisability of maintaining the detention in view of the applicant's health status. [98] To observe how the ECtHR applies the above standards in particular cases, it is necessary to carry out a detailed analysis of relevant cases.

The requisite medical assistance

The quality of medical assistance provided to prisoners remains the most difficult element to address in assessing whether the prisoner has received the requisite medical assistance provided for in Article 3. The ECtHR stated that it should be comparable to the care provided to the general public, but not to the health

93 See e.g. *Kudla v Poland* [GC] ECHR 2000-XI 197 paras 93–94; *Mouisel v France* (n.83) para.40; *Sakkopoulos v Greece* (n.83) para.38; *Holomiov v. Moldova* App.no. 30649/05 (ECtHR, 7 November 2006) para.112; *Grishin v Russia* App no 30983/02 (ECtHR, 15 November 2007) para.71; *Enea v. Italy* [GC] ECHR 2009-IV 163 para.58; *Chaykovskiy v. Ukraine* App no 2295/06 (ECtHR, 15 October 2009) para.54.

94 See e.g. *Kudla v. Poland* [GC] (n.93) para.92-94; *Kalashnikov v Russia* ECHR 2001-XI 197 para.95

95 See e.g. *Kudla v Poland* [GC] (n.93) para.94; *Mouisel v. France* (n.83) para.40.

96 See e.g. *Mouisel v France* (n.83) paras 43–44; *Matencio v France* (n 83) para.76; *Sakkopoulos v Greece* (n.83) para.38; *Farbtuhs v Latvia* (n.83) para.52; *Gülay Cetin v Turkey* no. 44084/10 para.103 (ECtHR, 5 March 2013).

97 See e.g. *Chaykovskiy v Ukraine* (n.93) para.55; *Grishin v Russia* (n.93) para.71.

98 *Chaykovskiy v Ukraine* (n.93) para.55; *Sakkopoulos v Greece* (n.83) para.39; *Enea v Italy* [GC] (n.93) para.59 *Farbtuhs v Latvia* (n.83) para.53.

treatment available in 'the best civilian clinics'.[99] According to the ECtHR, in order to comply with the requirements of Article 3, the authorities must provide ill prisoners with prompt and accurate diagnosis and care.[100] Furthermore, where the medical condition requires regular and systematic supervision, involving a comprehensive therapeutic plan aimed at ensuring adequate treatment of the illness and preventing further aggravation, should be provided.[101] However, the ECtHR reserves considerable flexibility in assessing the adequacy of prison health care, preferring a case-by-case determination rather than setting general standards.[102]

The care provided to ill prisoners was found to be adequate in all cases where the authorities complied with medical recommendations regarding the treatment required by a prisoner. In the case of *de Varga-Hirsch v France*, the complaint was found to be manifestly ill-founded. Although the health of the applicant was poor and became worse in custody, the national authorities ordered 10 expert opinions regarding the health of the applicant and provided the treatment required.[103] Furthermore, when it was found that the applicant needed treatment which could not be administered in prison, he was transferred to a civilian hospital where he received the necessary treatment. In coming to its decision, the European Commission also took note of the available reports that the applicant had himself contributed to the worsening of his health by refusing to undergo insulin treatment and not properly following the prescribed diabetic diet.[104]

Similar lessons have also emerged from other ECtHR judgments. In *Chartier v Italy* the application was also judged manifestly ill-founded. Although the European Commission recognised the seriousness of the health condition of the applicant, it was satisfied that the authorities provided him with care appropriate to his state of health, constantly monitored the situation and transferred the applicant to civilian hospitals when necessary care was not available in prison.[105]

In the case of *Sakkopoulos v Greece*, the applicant had undergone triple bypass surgery, suffered from heart failure and diabetes requiring a special diet and treatment with daily medication. However, the ECtHR concluded that his nine months of pre-trial detention was not in violation of Article 3 because he was provided with appropriate treatment in a prison hospital and was transferred to a civilian hospital after suffering a heart attack in detention.[106]

99 *Mirilashivili v Russia* (dec.), no. 6293/04 (ECtHR, 10 July 2007).

100 See e.g. *Khatayev v Russia* App no. 56994/09 (ECtHR, 11 October 2011) para.83; *Yevgeniy Alekseyenko v Russia* App no. 41833/04 (ECtHR, 27 January 2011) para.100.

101 See e.g. *Hummatov v Azerbaijan* App nos. 9852/03 and 13413/04 (ECtHR, 29 November 2007) para.109, 114; *Popov v Russia* App no. 26853/04 (ECtHR, 13 July 2006) para.211; *Sarban v Moldova* App.no. 3456/05 (ECtHR, 4 October 2005) para.79.

102 *Aleksanyan v Russia* no. 46468/06 140 (ECtHR, 22 December 2008).

103 *de Varga-Hirsch v France* (n.79) 213–214.

104 ibid 195–200.

105 *Chartier v Italy* (1982) 33 DR 41 49–51.

106 *Sakkopoulos v Greece* (n.83) 36–46.

In *Enea v Italy* the ECtHR found that there was no violation of Article 3. Despite the fact that the applicant suffered from a number of diseases which progressed during imprisonment, the Court was satisfied that the authorities fulfilled their obligations under Article 3 by providing him with medical services appropriate to his state of health and conducting a series of medical checks, tests and specific examinations in the prison hospital over a lengthy period.[107]

In *Grishin v Russia*[108] the claim of violation of Article 3 on the basis that the treatment provided to the applicant in detention was inadequate to his needs was found manifestly ill-founded. The ECtHR stated that while it was prepared to accept that 'in principle the resources of the penitentiary system are limited compared to those of civil clinics', the facts of the particular case did not suggest that the disparity between the treatment available in civil clinics and that provided to the applicant 'was so great as to have adversely affected the applicant's state of health or to have caused him suffering'.[109]

Conditions of detention of seriously ill detainees

The second component assessed by the ECtHR in the category of cases under discussion is the issue of whether the conditions of detention meet the special needs of a seriously ill or disabled prisoner. According to the ECtHR, the positive obligation under Article 3 'to ensure that a person is detained in conditions which are compatible with respect for his human dignity'[110] requires the State authorities to provide conditions meeting the special needs of the prisoner 'if they decide to place and keep a disabled person in detention'.[111]

The court found a violation of Article 3 on this basis in the case of *Price v the United Kingdom*.[112] In this case, a severely disabled person who also suffered from kidney problems was detained for three and a half days, one night of which was spent in a cell in a police station and the rest at the prison health care centre. The night in the police cell she had to spend in her wheelchair, because 'the bed was hard and would have caused pain in her hips' and 'she was unable to use the toilet since it was higher than her wheelchair and therefore inaccessible'.[113] The applicant also complained of being constantly cold, although she was wrapped with blankets by the officer on watch and a visiting doctor.[114] In regard to her three days at the prison health care centre, the applicant submitted that on one occasion she had to remain in a toilet for three hours until 'she agreed to allow

107 *Enea v Italy* [GC] (n.93) 57–67.
108 *Grishin v Russia* (n.93).
109 ibid para.76.
110 *Kudla v Poland* [GC] (n.93) para.94.
111 *Z.H. v Hungary* App no 28973/11 (ECtHR 8 November 2012) para.29; *Farbtuhs v Latvia* (n.83) para.56.
112 *Price v United Kingdom* ECHR 2001-VII 153.
113 ibid para.8.
114 ibid paras 9–10.

a male nursing officer to clean her and help her off the toilet', while on another occasion her bedclothes were removed in the presence of male officers.[115]

In regard to these complains the ECtHR stated:[116]

> [T]o detain a severely disabled person in conditions where she is dangerously cold, risks developing sores because her bed is too hard or unreachable, and is unable to go to the toilet or keep clean without the greatest of difficulty, constitutes degrading treatment contrary to Article 3 of the Convention.

Subsequent case law demonstrates that the threshold for fulfilling the obligation to provide conditions meeting the special needs of seriously ill prisoners is rather high; to fulfil this obligation it is not enough to ensure that the special needs of this category of prisoner are merely met, they should be met in a professional manner and the conditions should be adjusted to a degree to allow the prisoner as much self-reliance as possible.

This approach of the ECtHR can be clearly observed in the case of *Farbtuhs v Latvia*.[117] In this case an 85-year-old man who was suffering from various serious diseases and required assistance for some activities of daily living was kept in prison for about two years. The ECtHR found a violation of Article 3 despite the efforts of Latvian authorities to adjust the conditions of imprisonment to his needs. Indeed, the Latvian authorities took careful measures to assess the health and functionality of the applicant and ensure that the conditions of detention were appropriate; the medical report concluded that the health of the applicant was not incompatible with detention given that he was kept under regular medical supervision and provided with assistance for activities of daily living.[118] Moreover, the authorities not only placed the applicant in the prison infirmary, where he was assisted in activities of daily living by staff and outside working hours by designated volunteer inmates, but he was also regularly allowed to have family members stay with him for 24 hours as an exception to prison rules.[119]

Furthermore, the ECtHR itself emphasised that the applicant made no complaints regarding specific conditions of his detention, such as the state of the premises, lighting, ventilation, heating or daily diet.[120] Moreover, he did not dispute the special conditions and treatment with which he was provided in the prison infirmary.[121] As to the quality of care which he received outside working hours and at weekends, although it was true that during these periods he was assisted by fellow inmates who according to the applicant sometimes 'refused to cooperate', the applicant did not point to any such occasion.[122]

115 ibid para.15.
116 ibid para.30.
117 *Farbtuhs v Latvia* (n.83).
118 ibid 11.
119 ibid 60.
120 ibid 55.
121 ibid 39–44.
122 ibid 46.

In finding a violation of Article 3 the ECtHR stated:[123]

> The Court doubts the appropriateness of such a solution, leaving as it did the bulk of responsibility for a man with such a severe disability in the hands of unqualified prisoners, even if only for a limited period. It is true that the applicant did not report having suffered any incident or particular difficulty as a result of the impugned situation; he merely stated that the prisoners in question sometimes 'refused to cooperate', without mentioning any specific case in which they had refused. However, the anxiety and unease which such a severely disabled person could be expected to feel, knowing that he would receive no professional assistance in the event of an emergency, in themselves raise a serious issue from the standpoint of Article 3 of the Convention.

The ECtHR has maintained this high standard in more recent cases, reaffirming that leaving a seriously ill person who is deprived of his liberty to rely on cellmates for assistance in fulfilling the activities of daily living amounts to degrading treatment in violation of Article 3.[124]

Furthermore, the Court also found a violation of Article 3 in cases where the conditions of detention did not allow a disabled person to be self-reliant as far as possible. In the case of *Cara-Damiani v Italy,* the court explicitly stated that 'the detention of a disabled person in a facility where he cannot move on his own, as in the material case, for such a long period constitutes degrading treatment prohibited by Article 3 of the Convention'.[125] In this case, one of the three independent grounds for finding a violation of Article 3 was the fact that the applicant, a wheelchair user, was held for more than two and half years in an ordinary prison block where, owing to architectural barriers, he was not able to move around on the wheelchair or use facilities such as toilets without assistance.[126] It is worth emphasising that, as in the case of *Farbtuhs,* the applicant did not detail any specific incidents which would have made him feel humiliated. It was not the case that the applicant was unable to use the facilities; he was not able to use the facilities without assistance. This further demonstrates that the above statement of the ECtHR relates to the fact of imprisonment in conditions where the prisoner cannot be self-reliant rather than to any specific incident.

The issue of overall compatibility of medical conditions with deprivation of liberty

As stated earlier, in cases disputing the overall compatibility of continued imprisonment of persons with a serious medical condition with Article 3, the ECtHR

123 ibid para.60.

124 See e.g. *Engel v Hungary* App no. 46857/06 (ECtHR, 20 May 2010) para.27, 30.

125 *Cara-Damiani v Italy* no. 2447/05 72 (ECtHR, 7 February 2012); See also *Vincent v France* App no. 6253/03 (ECtHR, 24 October 2006) para.103.

126 *Cara-Damiani v Italy* (n.125) 71.

also assesses whether, in the view of an applicant's situation, further enforcement of the sentence amounted to violation of Article 3.

The starting position of the ECtHR in such cases is that Article 3 of the ECHR cannot be interpreted as laying down a general obligation to release persons deprived of their liberty on the ground of ill-health.[127] Nonetheless, both the former Commission and the Court acknowledged that, regardless of the availability of necessary medical care, 'detention per se inevitably affected prisoners suffering from serious disorders'.[128] In early cases the ECtHR reiterated the Commission's position in the case of *Chartier v Italy*,[129] namely that the proper administration of criminal justice in particularly serious cases may require remedies in the form of humanitarian measures in order to alleviate the effects of the detention or to terminate it as soon as circumstances require.[130]

However, in the case of *Mouisel v France*,[131] the ECtHR apparently reversed its position that remedies to alleviate the effects of the detention on seriously ill detainees or to terminate it are required exclusively on humanitarian grounds. After taking note of developments in the CoE (3rd General Report of the European Committee for the Prevention of Torture and Inhuman or Degrading Treatment or Punishment (CPT) and the Committee of Ministers' Recommendation No. R(98) 7), France's legislation (referring to the law allowing suspension of the sentence if the prisoner's state of health is not compatible with further enforcement of a sentence) and its own case law the ECtHR stated that:[132]

> health, age and severe physical disability are now among the factors to be taken into account under Article 3 of the Convention in France and the other member States of the Council of Europe in assessing a person's suitability for detention.

Furthermore, the ECtHR stated that the requirement to take into account health, age and severe disability in assessing a person's suitability for detention gives practical expression to its statement articulated in the case of *Selmouni v France*.[133] In this case the Court stated that the 'increasingly high standard being required in the area of the protection of human rights and fundamental liberties correspondingly and inevitably requires greater firmness in assessing breaches of the fundamental values of democratic societies'.[134]

127 See e.g. *Kudla v Poland* [GC] (n.93) paras 93–94; *Mouisel v France* (n.83) para.40; *Sakkopoulos v Greece* (n.83) para.38; *Holomiov v Moldova* (n.93) para.112; *Grishin v. Russia* (n.93) para.71; *Enea v Italy* [GC] (n.93) para.58; *Chaykovskiy v Ukraine* (n 93) para.54.

128 *Mouisel v France* (n.83) para.38 citing *Chartier v Italy* (n.105) para.53.

129 ibid.

130 See e.g. *Papon v France (no. 1)* (n.78).

131 *Mouisel v France* (n.83)

132 ibid para.38.

133 *Selmouni v France* ECHR 1999-V 149 para.101.

134 *Mouisel v France* (n.83) para.43.

In more recent cases, after stating that there is no general obligation under Article 3 to release detainees on health grounds, the ECtHR states that 'Article 3 may require the release of a detainee only in exceptional cases and under certain conditions, where his or her health is absolutely incompatible with detention'.[135] According to the ECtHR, when assessing the overall compatibility of a detainee's health with continued detention, in addition to previously discussed factors (i.e. the adequacy of medical assistance and care provided), two further factors should be considered: the seriousness of the prisoner's medical condition and the advisability of maintaining the detention measure in view of the state of health of the applicant.[136]

The advisability of continuing deprivation of liberty in view of the state of health of the applicant

In order to raise the issue of overall incompatibility of continued detention with Article 3, the medical conditions of a prisoner need to be particularly serious. In *Mouisel* the applicant had been 80% disabled, suffering from chronic lymphocytic leukaemia (a type of blood cancer) which had been aggravated by the stress of being ill and had affected his life expectancy, causing his health to decline notwithstanding with the treatment provided.[137] Similarly, in *Gülay Cetin v Turkey*[138] and *Tekin Yildiz v Turkey*,[139] applicants were suffering respectively from advanced cancer with a short-term fatal diagnosis and from Wernicke-Korsakoff syndrome consisting of loss of certain cerebral functions.[140] In many other cases, however, medical conditions were not short-term fatal but still very serious.[141]

In cases where a prisoner suffers from a serious illness, the provision of necessary care is not enough to satisfy the requirements of Article 3; the overall compatibility of further enforcement of detention also needs to be considered. For instance, in the case of *Mouisel v France*, neither the measures taken by the authorities (such as providing the applicant with numerous examinations, cancer treatment in civilian hospitals, transfer to a prison closer to the civilian hospital and his assignment of an individual cell), nor the fact that the applicant had himself contributed to the deterioration of his health by not consenting to a particular treatment, were considered to be sufficient to comply with the requirements of Article 3.[142] An approach similar to one applied in this case can be observed in

135 *Chaykovskiy v Ukraine* (n.93) para.55; *Grishin v Russia* (n.93) para.71.

136 *Chaykovskiy v Ukraine* (n.93) para.55; *Sakkopoulos v Greece* (n 83) para.39; *Enea v Italy [GC]* (n.93) para.59.

137 *Mouisel v France* (n.83) 17.

138 *Gülay Cetin v Turkey* (n.96).

139 *Tekin Yildiz vTurkey* no.22913/04 (ECtHR 10 November 2005).

140 *Gülay Cetin v Turkey* (n.96); *Tekin Yildiz vTurkey* (n.139).

141 *Farbtuhs v Latvia* (n.83); *Scoppola v Italy* no. 50550/06 (ECtHR, 10 June 2008); *Cara-Damiani v Italy* (n.125); *Contrada v Italy (no.2)* no. 7509/08 (ECtHR, 11 February 2014).

142 *Mouisel v France* (n 83).

other cases, suggesting that in addition to providing ill prisoners with necessary care, the authorities also need to consider whether, in view of his or her state of health, the applicant should continue to be detained.[143]

In cases where the authorities continued to detain a person whose state of health was unequivocally found by medical experts to be incompatible with imprisonment, the ECtHR was more likely to find a violation of Article 3. In *Mouisel v France*, expert medical opinion recorded a deterioration in the health of the applicant and, referring to the difficulties of providing cancer treatment while he was detained in prison, recommended that the applicant be 'looked after in a specialised unit'.[144] While examining the compatibility of the applicant's continued detention with Article 3 of the ECHR, the court observed that it was evident from the medical reports that the applicant's health was continuing to deteriorate and that the prison was not equipped to deal with this. However, the prison authorities did not take any special measures, such as transferring the applicant to a hospital or 'any other institution where he could be monitored and kept under supervision, particularly at night'.[145]

The same reasoning can be observed in the case of *Farbtuhs v Latvia* where expert medical opinion (which was based on examinations conducted after the applicant had already spent more than six months in prison) unequivocally recommended early release from prison.[146] Similarly, in *Contrada v Italy*, the ECtHR found a violation of Article 3, stating that 10 medical certificates which consistently and unambiguously concluded that the applicant's health status was not compatible with the prison regime had been disregarded by domestic authorities.[147]

In *Scoppola v Italy* the ECtHR emphasised that the domestic court recognised that the applicant's further detention in prison was incompatible with his health, changing it to detention at home.[148] However, this decision was not implemented because it appeared that the applicant did not have a suitable home, and therefore the applicant remained in prison where his continued detention, according to the domestic court, constituted inhuman treatment. According to the ECtHR, in this situation, if the applicant could not have been kept under home detention, the authorities should have either transferred him to a suitable prison or hospice or 'defer[red] execution of a sentence that had become tantamount to treatment contrary to Article 3 of the Convention'.[149]

Furthermore, continued detention would be found in violation of Article 3 if an applicant required a specific medical treatment which was not available in prison. Indeed, this was a separate ground for finding a violation of Article 3

143 *Farbtuhs v Latvia* (n.83); *Scoppola v Italy* (n 141); *Cara-Damiani v Italy* (n.125); *Contrada v Italy (no.2)* (n.141).
144 *Mouisel v France* (n.83) 17.
145 ibid 45.
146 *Farbtuhs v Latvia* (n.83) 21.
147 *Contrada v Italy (no.2)* (n.141) 82.
148 *Scoppola v Italy* (n.141) 46–47.
149 ibid 50.

in the case of *Cara-Damiani v Italy*. In this case, the ECtHR emphasised that although in December 2005 the applicant was moved to the prison wing for disabled prisoners, the rehabilitation treatment which he required to avoid further deterioration of his locomotor skills was not available even in this unit.[150]

Despite the availability of several medical reports asserting that the applicant needed rehabilitation treatment which was not available in prison but could be provided in specialised centres, the domestic courts refused an application filed as early as in February 2005 regarding suspension of the applicant's sentence or placement of the applicant under house arrest in a specialised hospital. The ECtHR considered that the 2008 decision of the Bologna court to grant the applicant house arrest in a hospital for six months (subsequently extended to two and a half years) to undergo required rehabilitation treatment in addition to surgery, confirmed that the treatment required by the applicant was not available in prison and could be provided only in a specialised centre.[151] The ECtHR concluded that in circumstances when the care needed by the applicant was not available in prison, his continued detention against the advice of doctors had reached the minimum level of severity to constitute inhuman treatment in violation of Article 3.[152] The ECtHR found that in the view of conclusions reached in the material case, the Italian authorities had violated Article 3 of the ECHR and subjected the applicant to inhuman and degrading treatment.[153]

Similarly, in finding a violation of Article 3 in the case of *Scoppola v Italy*, the ECtHR emphasised that despite the finding of a domestic court that the applicant's continued detention was incompatible with his health because the care he required could not be provided in the prison, the applicant continued to be held in the same conditions for more than a year.[154] The authorities proposed moving him to a prison which had a unit for disabled prisoners, but this did not take place until more than a year after the decision. In these circumstances the ECtHR emphasised that the applicant had not been able to walk since 1987 and was suffering from many other diseases which made his further detention in prison incompatible with his state of health, and that continuing to deprive him of his freedom in prison amounted to inhuman treatment.[155]

In contrast, the ECtHR is less likely to find a violation of Article 3 in cases where either medical reports contain some uncertainty regarding the compatibility of continued imprisonment with the health of a prisoner or where there are contradictory medical opinions regarding this issue. In *de Varga-Hirsch v France*, all the medical experts who examined the applicant noted that, in view of the applicant's advanced age and state of health, his continued detention involved some medical risks. However, the majority of experts stated that the

150 *Cara-Damiani v Italy* (n.125) 71.
151 ibid 74.
152 ibid 77.
153 ibid 78.
154 *Scoppola v Italy* (n.141) 51.
155 ibid 46–47.

treatment required by the applicant's state of health could be provided in prison or in a prison hospital. Only one expert opinion stated that the 'state of health of the applicant was not compatible with imprisonment, because the treatment for diabetes was not available at the prison hospital'.[156] The European Commission acknowledged that the health of the applicant was poor and became worse in detention, but it found that the application was manifestly ill-founded because this situation did not amount to an arguable claim under Article 3.[157] In coming to this decision the European Commission articulated that none of the expert medical opinions stated definitively that applicant's health was incompatible with detention.[158]

Furthermore, in *Chartier v Italy*, in the period between 1976 and 1982 at least six medical opinions from different experts were filed recommending transfer to a specialised clinic because the health of the applicant continued to deteriorate in the prison environment and the treatment needed was unavailable there or was difficult to administer. Only one report in 1982 found that the condition of the applicant had stabilised.[159] Although the European Commission recognised the seriousness of the health situation of the applicant, it was satisfied that the condition of the applicant was described as stable in the last available medical report, and therefore held the application to be manifestly ill-founded.[160]

The implications of the ECtHR's approach

The ECtHR explicitly stated that the Convention contains no prohibition against the imprisonment of elderly persons. However, it also noted that 'under certain circumstances the detention of an elderly person over a lengthy period might raise an issue under Article 3'.[161] In a more recent case the Grand Chamber of the ECtHR stated that providing a maximum age limit for the imposition of life imprisonment is one of several ways to comply with the reducibility requirement of Article 3.[162] This statement is a direct indication of the recognition of the impact of old age or the likelihood of dying in detention on the severity of the punishment. It implies from this statement that, in contrast to younger life prisoners, the review after serving 25 years does not provide adults aged 65 and over with the prospect of release, because for them 25 years would already be an irreducible life sentence. Although the case concerns imposition of the sentence, and thus the issue of the impact of old age on the severity of the sentence was articulated in regard to sentencing, the Court did not rule out retrospective adjustment of the severity of the sentence. It stated that not imposing a life sentence on adults aged 65 and over is only one of the ways of complying with

156 *de Varga-Hirsch v France* (n.79) 195–200.
157 ibid 214.
158 ibid 213–214.
159 *Chartier v Italy* (n.105) 18–35.
160 ibid 49–51.
161 *Sawoniuk v United Kingdom* (n.78); *Papon v France (no. 1)* (n.78).
162 *Khamtokhu and Aksenchik v Russia* [GC] (n.89) para.81.

the reducibility requirement, which means that a review of an already imposed sentence on this category of prisoners after they reach certain age is also an acceptable way of adjusting the impact.

As to the impact of serious illness on the severity of punishment, the analysis demonstrated that in exceptional cases, where the health of a detainee is absolutely incompatible with deprivation of liberty, Article 3 may require their release,[163] i.e. a retrospective adjustment of the severity of the punishment based on the impact of a serious medical condition. The absolute incompatibility threshold depends on three components, the first of which is the seriousness of the medical condition of a detainee. To fall within the scope of the first component of absolute incompatibility the medical condition should be declared either incompatible with further detention or very serious and requiring treatment in a specialised unit.[164]

When the seriousness of the illness is established, the ECtHR further examines measures taken by the authorities on the basis of medical reports. In essence, the ECtHR looks at whether the authorities reviewed the fitness of the detainee to further serve a particular measure. Although the ECtHR primarily assessed whether the measures undertaken by authorities were sufficient to comply with Article 3, rather than the availability of a formal mechanism for release in domestic legislation, the case law of the ECtHR contains many indications that a legal procedure should be available to review retrospectively the continued deprivation of liberty in the view of serious illness.

First, in some cases the ECtHR noted that although at the time of the submission the applicants were not eligible to apply for release on the ground of serious illness, subsequent legislative changes introduced procedures for review which constitute sufficient guarantees to ensure the protection of prisoners' health and wellbeing. Article 3 of the ECHR obliges the States to reconcile the legitimate requirements of custodial sentence with protection of prisoners' health and wellbeing.[165]

Indeed, in the case in *Mouisel v France*, the applicant did not complain about the lack or ineffectiveness of the release mechanism. However, the ECtHR reviewed developments in domestic legislation, noting that recent changes increased the power of judges to grant ordinary parole in cases 'where the prisoner has to undergo treatment'.[166] Furthermore, the new law on the rights of patients allowed prisoners with life-threatening or other serious medical conditions which are incompatible in the long term with their continued detention, to apply to a court for a suspension of the sentence.[167] Based on these developments the ECtHR stated:[168]

163 See e.g. *Chaykovskiy v Ukraine* (n.93) para.55.

164 See e.g. *Mouisel v France* (n.83) para.45; *Farbtuhs v Latvia* (n.83) para.21; *Contrada v Italy (no.2)* (n.141) para.82; *Scoppola v Italy* (n.141) paras 46–47; *Tekin Yildiz v Turkey* (n.139) paras 78–79.

165 *Mouisel v France* (n.83) para.44; *Matencio v France* (n.83) paras 80–81.

166 *Mouisel v France* (n.83) para.43.

167 ibid para.26,43.

168 ibid para.44.

> The Court notes that the procedural arrangements introduced by the laws of 15 June 2000 and 4 March 2002 have provided for new remedies before the judge responsible for the execution of sentences, enabling prisoners whose health has deteriorated significantly to apply to be released at short notice; those remedies are available in addition to the possibility of applying for a pardon on medical grounds, which the French President alone is empowered to grant. It considers that these judicial procedures may provide sufficient guarantees to ensure the protection of prisoners' health and wellbeing, which States must reconcile with the legitimate requirements of a custodial sentence. However, it must be acknowledged that those procedures were not available to the applicant during the period of detention considered by the Court and that the State's only response to his situation was to refuse his applications for a pardon on medical grounds without stating any reasons. As the Government noted, the applicant could not have been released on parole until he satisfied the eligibility requirements – that is to say, not until 2001. Moreover, the possibility of applying to have his sentence suspended did not exist at the time of his detention.

In fact, at the time when the ECtHR considered this case, the applicant had already benefited from early release introduced by the new legislative amendments. The amendments made him eligible for parole on the ground of his illness. Therefore, the question before the Court was to determine whether the continued imprisonment of the applicant in the period from his diagnosis until release from prison attained the minimum level of severity to fall within the scope of Article 3.[169]

The ECtHR reiterated the statements concerning the availability of remedies in the domestic legal order in the case *of Matencio v France*.[170] The reasoning of the ECtHR in these cases demonstrates that the availability of legal mechanisms which enable the review of the necessity of further imprisonment of seriously ill prisoners under domestic legislation is very important for the protection of the rights under Article 3 of the ECHR. However, neither in the case *Mouisel* nor in *Matencio* was the ECtHR confronted with the issue of whether the lack or ineffectiveness of a domestic legal procedure amounted to a violation of Article 3 or any other Articles of the ECHR.

In other cases concerning the compatibility with Article 3 of continued deprivation of liberty of seriously ill persons, procedures for release based on serious illness were available and, indeed, the applicants made good use of them. In *Farbtuhs* the initial application to a court requesting early release on the basis of serious illness and several subsequent appeals were rejected on the ground that the medical conditions of the applicant did not fall within conditions that allow early release on this ground. After almost a year of a litigation, a domestic court ordered the early release of the applicant on the ground of illness, basing the

169 ibid para.45.
170 *Matencio v France* (n.83).

decision on the fact that the health of the applicant had further deteriorated.[171] In *Tekin Yeldiz* a violation of Article 3 was found on the ground that the applicant, whose sentence was suspended because of the incompatibility of continued imprisonment with his health, was recalled to prison even though his health had not improved.[172]

Furthermore, the ECtHR also found a violation of Article 3 in the case of *Scoppola*. Although the applicant was serving a life sentence, the domestic court granted him detention at home for one year on the ground that his state of health required care which could not be provided in prison. According to the domestic court this situation made continued imprisonment tantamount to punishment contrary to Article 3. This decision, however, was set aside because the applicant did not have a home adapted to his needs. According to the ECtHR the domestic court's decision to set aside a decision to change imprisonment to home detention violated the rights of the applicant under Article 3 of the ECHR because it failed to consider any alternative arrangements. Under domestic legislation, for instance, the court was authorised to defer the execution of a sentence that had become tantamount to treatment contrary to Article 3 of the Convention. [173]

Similarly to the case of *Mouisel*, in the case of *Contrada*, by the time of the ECtHR's decision the applicant's request for suspension of imprisonment had already been granted by a domestic court. However, while finding a violation of Article 3, the ECtHR questioned the previous decisions of domestic courts to reject sentence suspension requests on the basis that the applicant's health conditions were not serious, or not impossible or extremely difficult to deal with in prison. According to the ECtHR, such reasoning appears to be questionable, especially given the results of medical examinations to which the applicant was repeatedly subjected.[174]

The case law on the subject contains yet more indications that the ECtHR has recognised the impact of serious illness on the severity of imprisonment and the possibility of retrospective adjustment of the severity of the punishment. Strong support for this argument is provided in the case of *Gülay Cetin v Turkey*.[175] In this case, after spending three years in detention, the applicant was diagnosed with cancer. Although she had been convicted of murder, because of pending appeal processes her prison sentence had become final after she had already spent five years in detention. During pre-trial detention the successive applications to release the applicant on bail on the ground of her medical condition had all been rejected, despite being supported by medical evidence of her deteriorating health. The Court substantiated the rejection of 20 bail applications on the basis of the seriousness of the offence and other general grounds supporting the application

171 *Farbtuhs v Latvia* (n.83) paras 24–27.
172 *Tekin Yildiz vTurkey* (n.139).
173 *Scoppola v Italy* (n.141) paras 12–19, 50.
174 *Contrada v Italy (no.2)* (n.141) para.85.
175 *Gülay Cetin v Turkey* (n.96).

of pre-trial detention.[176] Furthermore, because the sentence had not yet become final, the applicant was ineligible for either a presidential pardon – which can be granted on the basis of old age, incurable disease or disability – or suspension of execution of the sentence.[177]

In finding a violation of Article 14 (prohibition of discrimination) in conjunction with Article 3, the ECtHR stated that the facts of the case fell well within the scope of Article 3 and there was also an unjustified difference in treatment between terminally ill pre-trial detainees and those serving a final sentence with regard to the protection of their dignity: under the applicable legislation, pre-trial detainees were ineligible for the various forms of release on the ground of terminal illness which could benefit only those serving final sentences.[178] Furthermore, the ECtHR stated that those domestic legal mechanisms designated specifically to review the continued deprivation of liberty in view of serious illness are important guarantees of the protection of the health and wellbeing of prisoners and are able to meet the requirements of Article 3 of the ECHR. However, these measures were not applied in the case of the applicant until her sentence had become final, although it appeared that in theory these provisions by analogy apply also to pre-trial detainees.[179] The reasoning of the ECtHR clearly indicates that the Court recognises the impact of a serious illness on the severity of imprisonment and the possibility of retrospective adjustment of the severity of the punishment.

The approach of the English courts

Primary legislation in England and Wales has listed some factors that have an impact on determining the severity of punishment. Under the Criminal Justice Act 2003 the age of an offender is a factor capable of impacting the severity of punishment in murder cases.[180] This has been interpreted by the Lord Chief Justice to relate 'to physical capacity on release or the likelihood of the defendant dying in prison'.[181] In contrast, the physical illness of the offender is not a specifically defined statutory factor in determining the sentence for a particular offender. However, the Court of Appeal delivered two guideline judgments on the issue. The application of the principles articulated by the Court of Appeal in the guideline judgments can be observed in many cases decided by the Court.

Serious medical condition as ground for sentence reduction

In 1997 the Court of Appeal in the case of *Bernard*[182] delivered a guideline judgment on the reduction of sentences on the ground of the ill-health of the

176 ibid para.21.
177 ibid para.28,41.
178 ibid 126–133.
179 ibid paras 131–132.
180 Criminal Justice Act 2003, Sch.21(11)(g).
181 Cited in *R v Sullivan* [2005] 1 Cr App R (S) 67, 325.
182 *R v Bernard (Basil Mortimer)* [1997] 1 Cr App R (S) 135.

offender. It reviewed a number of its past decisions dealing with the same issue. Despite concluding that the decisions were not easily reconcilable, based on these cases the Court of Appeal set out the following principles:[183]

> (i) a medical condition which may at some unidentified future date affect either life expectancy or the prison authorities' ability to treat a prisoner satisfactorily may call into operation the Home Secretary's powers of release by reference to the Royal Prerogative of mercy or otherwise but is not a reason for this Court to interfere with an otherwise appropriate sentence (Archibald Moore);
> (ii) the fact that an offender is HIV positive, or has a reduced life expectancy, is not generally a reason which should affect sentence (Archibald Moore and Richard Moore);
> (iii) a serious medical condition, even when it is difficult to treat in prison, will not automatically entitle an offender to a lesser sentence than would otherwise be appropriate (Wynne);
> (iv) an offender's serious medical condition may enable a court, as an act of mercy in the exceptional circumstances of a particular case, rather than by virtue of any general principle, to impose a lesser sentence than would otherwise be appropriate.

In this guideline judgment, the Court of Appeal is keen to stress that an offender's serious medical condition cannot be seen as a general ground of excuse from or reduction of an otherwise appropriate punishment, even if the condition is difficult to manage in prison. Instead, the Court of Appeal states that a case-by-case approach should be adopted which ties the reduction of sentence due to serious illness to exceptional features of a particular case rather than to illness in general.[184] This demonstrates that reducing a sentence on this ground is left to the discretion of sentencing courts.

The Court of Appeal is also keen to distinguish situations relating to the serious medical condition of the offender, which can be dealt with by a sentencing court or on appeal, from situations which fall within the jurisdiction of the executive. It states that medical conditions which generally limit the life expectancy of the offender, possibly resulting in the death of the offender while still in prison, or for which the Prison Service is unable to provide appropriate treatment, fall under the jurisdiction of the executive.[185]

This judgment does not offer a particular test as how the courts should exercise discretion to decide whether the features of a particular case are exceptional, warranting reduction of a sentence, and, if so, how much reduction is warranted. However, the relevant case law of the Court of Appeal offers insights into this and also sheds light on the issue of the delineation between the jurisdiction

183 ibid 138.
184 *R. v Green (Paul Palmerston)* [1992] 13 Cr App R (S) 613, 615.
185 *R. v Bernard (Basil Mortimer)* (n.182) 138.

of courts and the executive with regard to the serious medical condition of an offender.

It is apparent that in the case law the nature of the illness, the ability of the prison service to satisfactorily accommodate the needs and treatment of ill prisoners, the seriousness of the crime and the risk of reoffending were the factors that tipped the balance against or in favour of reducing or suspending the sentence on the ground of the ill-health of the offender.

In both *Moore (Archibald)*[186] and *Stark*,[187] the Court of Appeal declined to reduce sentences of five and four years' imprisonment respectively, regardless of the fact that Moore was HIV positive with a likelihood of developing AIDS within two years, while Stark had already developed AIDS. In both cases there were uncertainties about the possible life expectancy of the defendants and no reports demonstrating that the management of the defendants in prison was unfeasible. Furthermore, Stark committed further drug offences while on bail, which allowed the Court to conclude that there was a high risk that as far as his physical condition would allow he would again engage in drug trafficking.

In *Moore* there was no medical evidence demonstrating that the defendant had limited life expectancy. In addition, a hospital asserted that the management of the defendant in prison was 'perfectly feasible', although it would be easier if the defendant were in the community.[188] Against this backdrop, the Court held that, even assuming there was medical evidence regarding the life expectancy of the defendant, it was not the function of the Court to alter the otherwise appropriate sentence based on predictions of life expectancy because of the uncertainties which the future held with regard to the development of new medication and the development of the disease in the particular case.[189] However, the Court did not rule out the possibility that at some point further imprisonment of the defendant would be no longer appropriate either for practical reasons or for reasons of humanity because of his physical condition. When such a situation arose, it would be a matter for the Secretary of State to act according to the situation at hand.[190]

In *Stark* there were two medical reports regarding the life expectancy of the defendant, one of which predicted no more than 12 months' life expectancy while the other set the life expectancy in the range of 18 to 24 months.[191] The Court was asked to reduce the sentence to allow the early release of the offender so he could 'die with dignity and not in prison'.[192] The Court refused to reduce the sentence, emphasising that the life expectancy of the defendant remained uncertain and there was no evidence that the management of his health in prison was not feasible. Furthermore, he was arrested for possession with intent to supply class A drugs and bailed, but committed further drug offences while on

186 *R. v Moore (Archibald James)* [1990] 12 Cr App R (S) 384,.
187 *R. v Stark (Gerrard Michael)* [1992] 13 Cr App R (S) 548,.
188 *R. v Moore (Archibald James)* (n.186) 386.
189 ibid.
190 ibid.
191 *R. v Stark (Gerrard Michael)* (n.187) 549.
192 ibid 550.

bail. Therefore, there was a 'very grave risk that, if this appellant were to be at large as long as his physical condition permitted there would be every risk that he would resort again to drug trafficking'.[193]

This approach can also be observed in other cases in the Court of Appeal. The Court does not consider the reduction of an otherwise appropriate sentence to be correct in the following situation: when, regardless of the existence of serious illness, the life expectancy is uncertain; and it is not plain that the illness makes the experience of imprisonment more onerous or would cause health to deteriorate further because of the impact of imprisonment.[194] Furthermore, in some of its decisions, the Court makes it plain that factors such as the seriousness of the offence and the risk of reoffending are relevant factors to be considered in making decisions on whether the reduction is appropriate.[195]

In contrast, in *Green*,[196] *Leatherbarrow*,[197] *Wynne*[198] and *James Moore*[199] sentences of different lengths were reduced by the Court of Appeal sufficiently to allow early release of the defendants. There were medical reports demonstrating that the defendants had serious illnesses which were difficult to treat in prison, putting their health at risk of further deterioration. Furthermore, there was no issue of persistent offending and it was assumed that the defendants did not pose a risk of further offences.

For instance, in *Green*,[200] although the sentencing court had already taken into account the serious illness of the defendant, reducing an otherwise appropriate sentence of five years to 18 months, the Court of Appeal reduced the sentence even further to allow the immediate release of the defendant.[201] In doing this, the Court took into account the very severe nature of the disease which could result in sudden shock-like states leading to death very quickly in the absence of highly qualified medical intervention. The Court had medical evidence both from the prison doctor certifying that the level of intensive treatment required by the defendant could not be provided in prison and from the doctor who treated the defendant in the community stating that the condition of the defendant had become even worse since his imprisonment, which may have been due to the fact that he had not received proper treatment in prison.[202]

Two factors were critical for the Court in coming to its decision: the serious and life-threatening nature of the disease and the further deterioration of the prisoner's health because the condition was difficult to manage in prison.

193 ibid.
194 See e.g. *R. v Veiga (Jose Dionisio)* [2003] EWCA 2420; *Attorney-General's Reference No 07* [2005] EWCA 1056; *Attorney General's Ref (No. 77 of 2006)* [2006] EWCA Crim 2384.
195 *R. v Veiga (Jose Dionisio)* (n.194) 12.
196 *R. v Green (Paul Palmerston)* (n.184).
197 *R. v Leatherbarrow (Thomas)* [1992] 13 Cr App R (S) 632.
198 *R. v Wynne* (1994) unreported (Court of Appeal).
199 *R. v Moore (James)* [1994] unreported.
200 *R. v Green (Paul Palmerston)* (n.184).
201 ibid 615.
202 ibid.

Although the Court emphasised that the serious and life-threatening disease 'is one of the most powerful mitigating factors', it was keen to stress that the course it had taken was due to the very exceptional features of the case and should not be misunderstood as depreciating the seriousness of drug-dealing offences.[203]

In *Cahill*[204] the Court of Appeal suspended the nine-month sentence for supplying class B and C drugs because the offender had AIDS and an oncological condition which required regular monitoring and treatment in the hospital. Although there were no reports from prison regarding the feasibility of accommodating the needs of the offender while in prison, the Court, relying on medical reports, stated that the very serious condition of the offender, which required supervision in hospital, was an exceptional circumstance which merited suspension of the sentence.[205] In this case the Court of Appeal did not explicitly state other factors which played a role in coming to this decision, but apparently the initial sentence of only nine months indicates that the offence ofdrug dealing in which the offender was involved was not of a very serious nature.

Similarly in *Trevor*,[206] the Court of Appeal reduced the sentence to a degree to allow immediate release of the defendant, although the defendant had already received a sufficiently reduced sentence for causing death by dangerous driving. There were reports from the doctor in charge that the complex medical condition of the defendant would create serious management issues in prison, possibly putting him at significant risk of harm or even death. Although a detailed report from the prison stated that the appellant was coping well in prison and provided a detailed arrangements plan for facilitating complex surgery and treatment in an outside hospital, the Court concluded that, regardless of assurances from the prison service, 'the treatment and the difficulties to which it would give rise make a custodial sentence considerably more onerous for the appellant than would otherwise be the case'.[207]

The Court of Appeal elaborated further principles with regard to the role of offenders' medical conditions in the distribution of sentences in *Qazi*.[208] In *Qazi* the medical condition was not only very serious but also had deteriorated during his time in prison. However, he was transferred to a prison closer to the hospital where he was usually treated and the prison put in place a detailed care plan and other arrangements for his care.[209] The medical condition had already been taken into account by the sentencing judge and on this ground the normal sentence for several counts of large-scale fraud had been reduced to five and a half years' imprisonment. However, the Court of Appeal reduced the sentence by a further

203 ibid.

204 *R. v Cahill (Stephen)* [2009] EWCA Crim 420.

205 ibid 13.

206 *R. v Trevor Norman Clarke* [2010] Cr App R (S) 26.

207 ibid 167.

208 *R. v Qazi (Saraj) and Hussain (Majid)* [2011] Cr App R (S) 8.

209 ibid 40.

six months, apparently based on the balance of the gravity of crime and other aims of the punishment.[210]

In this case the Court of Appeal went on to consider the role of Article 3 of the ECHR at sentencing. The Court reviewed the legal basis of the organisation of health care in prisons in England and Wales and the arrangements required for its implementation in the light of the State's legal obligations under European human rights law. On this basis the Court of Appeal concluded that in discharging its obligations under Article 3 of the ECHR at sentencing, courts should adopt the following approach:[211]

> i) The court is entitled to take into account the fact that there are the arrangements that we have outlined ... above to ensure that prisoners with severe medical conditions in public sector prisons are treated in accordance with their Convention rights, and there are the duties of the Secretary of State of the type set out in Spinks[212]... to release the prisoner if that is the only way a breach of art.3 can be remedied.
> ii) On the basis of those arrangements and their continued operation in practice, a sentencing court need not be concerned in the allocation of a prisoner to a specific prison in the discharge of its duties under art.3. Furthermore, provided that the arrangements that we have set out for the provision of health care under the overall responsibility of the Secretaries of State are maintained and work in practice, a sentencing court does not need to enquire into the facilities in prison for the treatment of a medical condition. The court can be satisfied that there is a proper system for allocation to a prison where health care can be provided in accordance with the procedure we have set out, and that a sentence of imprisonment will not create a risk of a breach of art.3.
> iii) It is only in circumstances where the very fact of imprisonment itself might expose the individual to a real risk of an art.3 breach that the court will be called upon to enquire into whether sentencing a person to custody will mean a breach of art.3. That is a quite different circumstance from the kind of enquiry carried out in Hetherington as to whether facilities in a particular prison were adequate. It is an enquiry that can only arise where there is proper medical evidence before a court that any sentence of imprisonment ipso facto would cause a breach of art.3. We are doubtful if circumstances will ever arise in which such a submission could be made, but if they should ever arise, it would be an exceptionally rare event.
> iv) If any such circumstances should ever arise, then the sentencing court

210 ibid 48.

211 ibid 45.

212 In *R. (on the application of Spinks) v Secretary of State for the Home Department* [2005] EWCA Civ 275 the Court held that the Secretary of State would be obliged to release the prisoner if his continued imprisonment amounted to a violation of Article 3 and the only way to remedy that violation was to release the prisoner.

must be provided with detailed medical evidence with an attached statement of truth by a properly qualified medical expert setting out the ground why imprisonment ipso facto will cause a breach of art.3 ; such a statement must be served on the court and on the Crown Prosecution Service well in advance of the hearing so that the Crown Prosecution Service can, in conjunction with the Secretary of State for Justice, make the appropriate enquiries and produce medical evidence to the court.
v) Once a sentence of imprisonment has been imposed, unless it is to be contended on appeal that the judge should not have imposed a sentence of imprisonment because imprisonment anywhere would ipso facto cause a breach of art.3, the relevance of an appellant's medical condition relates solely to the assessment of the overall length of the sentence in accordance with the principles established in Bernard.
vi) Any issues as to breach of the duties of the Secretary of State in relation to medical treatment and conditions in prison are matters for civil remedies and not for this division of the Court of Appeal.

First of all, these principles and their application by the Court of Appeal in the material case and cases following this one reaffirm the earlier principles articulated in the case of *Bernard*. In particular, the Court was keen to stress again that the medical condition of the offender, even if very serious, cannot be seen as a factor as such excusing the offender from punishment or entitling her/him to an automatic reduction of the sentence. However, when a serious medical condition is evident at sentencing, it is a relevant matter to be considered together with all other circumstances which are relevant to the severity of sentence.

Despite the very serious nature of the illness in the case of *Qazi*, the Court of Appeal granted only some reduction of the sentence which did not result in the early release of the applicant. In other cases, however, the Court reduced the sentence to a degree to allow early release of appellants. For instance, in *Hall*,[213] the medical condition of the offender was very serious and had deteriorated following imprisonment, requiring lengthy intensive treatment in a civilian hospital. Although the condition had stabilised and the care of the appellant in prison was organised, the Court of Appeal stated that post-sentence events demonstrated the gravity of the condition and the potential for unexpected deterioration over a short period. This allowed the Court to reduce the sentence to the term already served (18 months), facilitating immediate release of the applicant.[214]

The difference between this case and the case of *Qazi* seems to be the significantly greater impact of the imprisonment on the defendant. However, even if there is such impact, it could not be an excuse from punishment. In this regard, the Court of Appeal first emphasised that this did not mean that those who are gravely ill or severely disabled, or both, cannot be imprisoned if they commit

213 *R. v Hall (Daniel Patrick)* [2013] 2 Cr App R (S) 68.
214 ibid 442.

serious crimes, even if that would result in 'some loss of the quality of care compared with a self-organised home regime'.[215] As the Court put it: 'their condition cannot be a passport to absence of punishment'.[216]

Second, the Court stressed that the reason for reduction of the sentence in this case was the greater impact of imprisonment on this defendant 'by a margin than it would be on an ordinary appellant'.[217] The Court stated:[218]

> One legitimate aim of sentencing is to preserve, to the extent that one can, some parity of punishment between like offenders. This appellant's life out of prison is made just about bearable by intense care in his own surroundings. Even assuming that he can be provided with care in prison, the impact on him of imprisonment is enormously greater than the impact on any able-bodied, or even significantly disabled, man.

The Court then went on to describe the significantly greater impact of imprisonment on the defendant in material terms.[219]

Third, this decision again demonstrates the significance of balancing retributive and utilitarian factors in view of offenders' medical condition. The Court is keen to emphasise that reducing the sentence for a serious crime (importation of 2.8 kg cocaine, a class A drug) to allow release did not mean lack of punishment in this case because the appellant had already served 18 months of his sentence and had suffered considerably.[220] Furthermore, the Court was concerned that there might be a risk of reoffending in this case. However, to reduce the risk of reoffending, it made a serious crime prevention order requiring the appellant to surrender his passports and banning him from acquiring a new one for a period of three years in order to prevent him from engaging in drug trafficking again.[221]

The Court of Appeal's jurisprudence demonstrates that two types of medical condition were regarded as meriting consideration at sentencing. First, when as a result of serious illness the imprisonment is considerably more onerous for the appellant than would otherwise be the case, but the condition is still manageable in prison.[222] Second, when the illness not only makes the experience of imprisonment more onerous, but also, as in *Green*,[223] there is a further deterioration of health as a result of imprisonment which would not have happened were appropriate treatment provided. When one of these grounds is present, the Court

215 ibid.
216 ibid.
217 ibid.
218 ibid 438.
219 ibid 437.
220 ibid 443.
221 ibid 442.
222 See e.g. *R. v Leatherbarrow (Thomas)* (n.197); *R. v Bernard (Basil Mortimer)* (n.182); *R. v Trevor Norman Clarke* (n.206) 26; *R. v Qazi (Saraj) and Hussain (Majid)* (n.208).
223 *R. v Green (Paul Palmerston)* (n.184); *R. v Hall (Daniel Patrick)* (n.213).

balances it against such factors as the gravity of crime, the need for deterrence and the risk of reoffending.

As a ground for a reduction of the sentence, the second is more compelling for the Court than the first; the Court is more inclined to reduce the sentence in such cases. When considering whether to grant a reduction on the first ground, the gravity of the crime and the other factors play a determining role capable of precluding release. Furthermore, when the Court decides to grant reductions in such cases, in general they do not lead to the early release of the offender.

The Court generally does not suspend the sentence altogether in the second category of cases either; rather, it grants only a reduction of sentence. However, usually it reduces the sentence to a degree to allow the immediate early release of the offender. Furthermore, in these cases the Court also takes into account the gravity of the crime, the issues of deterrence and the risk of reoffending. However, the Court is inclined to consider the time already served as meeting the requirement of punishment at least to some degree and is determined to find alternative solutions to prevent reoffending without depriving the offender of her/his liberty.

Old age and infirmity as grounds for sentence reduction

The majority of cases discussed above relate to non-elderly defendants. Only in the case of *Bernard*, which involved a 63-year-old defendant, was the age an issue emphasised by the Court. Although the Court referred to the offender's old age in conjunction with his illness as the ground for the sentence reduction, no explanation was provided as to why old age was a relevant ground for the reduction of the sentence granted in this case.[224] Unfortunately, the relevance of old age was not reflected in the principles articulated in this case.

While elderly defendants had come before the courts for sentencing on rare occasions in the past, as stated earlier, there has been a dramatic increase in the elderly prison population in England and Wales over the past two decades or so.[225] Some of these prisoners were sentenced to imprisonment when they were already elderly, many for the first time in their lives, for offences committed many years, and in some cases decades, earlier.[226] In many of these cases the issue of old age was put forward as a ground for reduction of the sentence.

It is clear from the decisions of the Court of Appeal that it approves old age and related infirmity as grounds for the reduction of sentences.[227] However, unlike in the case of illness, the Court of Appeal has not delivered a guideline judgment elaborating principles regarding the rationale for such reduction, including the

224 *R. v Bernard (Basil Mortimer)* (n.182) 139.

225 House of Commons Justice Committee (n.31) 5.

226 Elaine Crawley, 'Institutional Thoughtlessness in Prisons and Its Impacts on the Day-to-Day Prison Lives of Elderly Men' (2005) 21(4) *Journal of Contemporary Criminal Justice* 350, 353.

227 See e.g. *R. v John Francis C.* [1993] 14 Cr App R (S) 562; *R. v Bernard (Basil Mortimer)* (n.182); *Attorney General's Ref (No. 77 of 2006)* (n.194); *Attorney General's Reference (No.38 of 2013)* [2014] Cr App R (S) 61; *R. v Taylor* [2015] EWCA 1600.

factors against which the reduction should be balanced, how the factors should be weighed one against another and how much reduction should be granted. The position of the Court in relation to these issues can, however, be clarified to a certain extent by analysing relevant judgments of the Court of Appeal.

Although the Court has not been consistent in its justifications as to why old age is relevant to the length of sentence, in some of its judgments it is implicit that the Court is conscious of the length of the determinate sentence in relation to the actuarial life expectancy. In the case of *John Francis C*, the defendant was sentenced for sexual offences, including rape committed against his grandchildren, over a period of 15 years ending 10 years before his trial.[228] At the time of sentencing the offender was 79 years old and suffered from a number of illnesses, including angina, associated with chronic bronchitis. Although there were no suggestions that, because of his age or ill-health, managing this defendant in custody would not be feasible or that the sentence would be more onerous for him than for the most other offenders, the sentencing judge reduced the normal sentence of 12 years' imprisonment to eight years, referring to the old age and ill-health of the offender. However, the defendant appealed the sentence, arguing that his age and ill-health merited more reduction than was granted by the sentencing judge. Although the Court accepted that at the age of 79 the defendant posed no risk of reoffending, it refused to interfere with the sentence arguing that:[229]

> If we were to reduce it [the sentence] by one, two, three or four years, the point could still be made that this appellant at the age of very nearly 80 might well not be able to live any part of his life in the community again. We consider the reduction that the learned judge made here was as great a reduction as these appalling circumstances could permit. Whether this appellant should be released on compassionate grounds because of his age or because of his health must be matters for the Home Secretary.

Although it is obvious that the justification for sentence reduction in the case of an elderly defendant being sentenced to a determinate term is actuarial life expectancy, the Court of Appeal has disapproved a methodology used by the sentencing judge in calculating the length of the sentence in the case of *Harold S*.[230] In sentencing an 82-year-old defendant for sexual offences lasting over a 10-year period against his granddaughter, including four counts of rape, the judge stated that he bore in mind that the sentence 'is a portion of a person's future life'.[231] Afterwards, referring to actuarial tables and average mortality rates without providing more details, the judge arrived at an equivalent sentence of

228 *R. v John Francis C.* (n.227) 562.
229 ibid 564.
230 *R. v Harold S.* [1998] 1 Cr App R (S) 261.
231 ibid 263.

21 months, which he then increased to three years based on some aggravating factors.[232]

The Court of Appeal assumed that the judge had calculated the sentence taking as a basis of equivalency the life expectancy of a man in his mid-30s where 12 years would equal a third of his life expectancy. Assuming that a man of 82 has life expectancy of approximately five years, the judge had calculated that the appropriate sentence was 21 months.[233] The Court of Appeal, however, disapproved of this way of calculating the sentence, stating that the appropriate method is to determine a sentence that is commensurate with the seriousness of the offence and then adjust it appropriately, taking into account relevant aggravating and mitigating circumstances. In the material case, the mitigating circumstances were the age of the offender and his illnesses which, however, did not make his experience of imprisonment more onerous. On the other hand, the lack of remorse was considered to be an aggravating factor, but it was stressed that it was extremely unlikely that he would commit similar offences in the future. Based on these considerations, the Court of Appeal, like the sentencing judge, arrived at the sentence of three years of imprisonment.[234]

Furthermore, the language of the Court of Appeal in the case of *Fontes*, a man aged 75, clearly reaffirms that the justification for the reduction of the otherwise appropriate sentence based on old age is actuarial life expectancy. While reducing an already reduced sentence of seven and a half years of imprisonment to five years for the importation of large quantity of a class A drug, the Court of Appeal stated that the risk of the offender's 'dying in prison is one which must be taken into account by the court'.[235] In this case the offender had suffered from several hernias, varicose vein problems and arthritis. However, it was mainly the age of the offender that would put him at risk of dying in prison while serving a prison sentence: at the time of release the offender would have been well over 80.

The reasoning of the Court of Appeal in these decisions has the following implications. First, it is obvious that in general the Court takes into account the impact of old age and related infirmity as a ground for sentence reduction. As the reasoning of the Court demonstrates, the actuarial life expectancy becomes a justification for reducing the sentence in cases where a determinate sentence appears to surpass the normal actuarial life expectancy of the offender. The Court ties reduction of the sentence to the age at release. Although, alongside age, the Court also mentions the infirmity and health problems of defendants, the issue of adverse impact of imprisonment on the illness of the offender and/or a more onerous experience of the offender due to illness were not discussed. In these cases illnesses were not the decisive issue for reductions.[236]

232 ibid.
233 ibid.
234 ibid 264.
235 *R. v Fontes* [2006] 1 Cr App R (S) 76, 404.
236 See e.g. *R. v John Francis C.* (n.227); *R. v Bernard (Basil Mortimer)* (n.182); *Attorney General's Ref (No. 77 of 2006)* (n 194); *Attorney General's Reference (No.38 of 2013)* (n.227); *R. v Taylor* (n.227).

In all these cases some reduction of sentence was granted on the ground of age. However, it is clear that although it might be necessary to consider the issue of reduction of the sentence on this ground, judges do not have to grant a reduction. Furthermore, there is no obligation to make an effort to reduce the sentence to a degree which will necessarily be less than the life expectancy of the offender. In this regard the Court of Appeal considers the seriousness of the offence and is careful not to depreciate this both in terms of retribution and deterrence, but the risk of future reoffending seems not to worry the Court: it was often stated that at the very advanced ages in the cases discussed the risk of reoffending is not an obstacle to granting a reduction of sentence. The reasoning of the Court of Appeal indicates that age, however advanced, cannot be seen as an excuse from punishment. The Court often highlights that when sentencing a very old offender to a determinate prison term the risk of the offender's dying in prison must be considered by the court.[237] However, in cases where even big reductions could not equal actuarial life expectancy, it prefers to leave the matter to the Secretary of State, who could release the offender on compassionate grounds.[238]

Old age as a statutory ground for sentence reduction for murder

Under the Criminal Justice Act 2003 the age of an offender is a statutory factor mitigating the severity of the sentence in cases when life imprisonment is mandatory, i.e. in murder cases.[239] For the first time, this Act of Parliament set general principles, including aggravating and mitigating factors, for determination of a minimum term in relation to mandatory life sentences.[240] Section 269(5) of the Act requires the court to 'have regard to' the general principles set out in Schedule 21 when setting a minimum term. According to the respective legislative provision, after determining the starting point for the minimum term, among other factors the court must have regard to the age of the offender in order to set the final minimum term. The offender must serve this term in full before becoming eligible for discretionary parole release.[241] As a factor capable of impacting the severity of a penalty, the age of the defendant was interpreted to relate 'to physical capacity on release or the likelihood of the defendant dying in prison'.[242]

The Lord Chief Justice has stated that section 269(5) of the Criminal Justice Act 2003 imposes an obligation to have regard to the principles set out in Schedule 21, including old age. This does not mean, however, that courts should necessarily alter the normally required minimum term based on the principles set out in this schedule. To comply with the obligation it is enough for the judge to consider these principles. If the judge considers these general principles, but

237 *R. v Fontes* (n.235) 404.
238 *R. v John Francis C.* (n.227) 564.
239 Criminal Justice Act (n.180) Sch.21(11)(g).
240 ibid Sch.21.
241 ibid Sch.21, s.269(5).
242 Cited in *R. v Sullivan* (n.181) 325.

chooses not to follow them, she/he should provide reasons for this. The decision not to take into account aggravating or mitigating factors, including old age, is subject to appeal by the offender or on an Attorney General's reference.[243]

In murder cases the Court of Appeal is explicit about the underlying justifications for old age mitigation and its status. In *Walker*,[244] where a 66-year-old defendant shot and killed his wife during an argument, the Court of Appeal, taking into account all aggravating and mitigating factors, reduced the minimum term of 14 years to 12. The Court regarded the age of the applicant as the major mitigating factor in this case, stating that it was 'concerned and troubled' by the fact that under the minimum term of 14 years the applicant would not be considered for parole until he was 80. According to the Court the mitigating factor of old age is relevant if there is a likelihood of the defendant's dying in prison.[245]

The decision of the Court of Appeal in *Archer*[246] is illustrative. In this case a 55-year-old defendant was sentenced to life imprisonment with a minimum term of 30 years for the murder of a 27-year-old prostitute. The sentencing judge considered the age of the defendant when setting the minimum term, but did not make any reduction to reflect age mitigation. Indeed, he explicitly stated:[247]

> bearing in mind your age of 55, I do not know if in fact you ever will be released. If you are not, you cannot complain. Nasra Ismail was half your age. She was 27 when you took away all the rest of her life.</quote

Counsel appealed against the sentence on the ground of old age, arguing that the defendant would be more than 83 years old before he could be considered for parole if the minimum term was upheld, which created a real risk of his dying in custody before being considered for parole.[248] In support of the argument Counsel relied on Court of Appeal decisions in *Sullivan*[249] and *Walker*.[250]

Based on this ground, the Court of Appeal reduced the minimum term from 30 to 25 years to allow consideration for parole at 78, rather than at 83. In allowing the appeal the Court stated: [251]

> When he [the sentencing judge] came on, however, to consider age, it is quite plain from the words which we have recited that he did not give any credit or allowance in that regard at all, for the reasons that he gave. We are clear that the authorities to which we have been referred by the appellant, and indeed a common sense construction of para.11(g), must mean that one

243 ibid 310.
244 *R. v Walker (John Owen)* [2005] Cr App R (S) 55.
245 ibid 332.
246 *R. v Archer* [2007] 71 Cr App R (S) .
247 ibid 458.
248 ibid.
249 *R. v Sullivan* (n.181).
250 *R. v Walker (John Owen)* (n.244).
251 *R. v Archer* (n.246) 459.

> of the factors which will be taken into account in relation to a sentence as long as 30 years or less, in terms of these kind of serious crimes, is the possibility of the light at the end of tunnel; one that is not given to a prisoner for whom a whole life order is made under para.4 of the Schedule. This offender was not given a whole life order. He was given something less than that, but in practice, as he has said and as Miss Gould has represented on his behalf, it may well be that the sentence he has been given, which does not purport to be a whole life order, will amount to one in practice. If he were considered for parole at 83 and a half he may well not immediately be released, and, if released at that age, or indeed even at a lesser age, he will be nothing like the danger to the public which he might otherwise have been, but he may well never reach that position of being considered for parole by reason of his age.

The decision of the Court in *Archer* demonstrates that, although the Statute does not make a reduction in sentence due to old age obligatory in murder cases, the Court of Appeal will not accept every reason to refuse such a reduction. According to the Court, if the minimum term for murder is not whole life, it should be such as to give the possibility of 'light at the end of tunnel', meaning that a minimum term which is given for the reason of punishment and deterrence[252] should provide a possibility of parole review and release at a point which is less than the actuarial life expectancy of the defendant if she/he does not pose a risk of serious harm to the public after serving the minimum term.

This decision of the Court of Appeal demonstrates that when setting a minimum term for a crime of murder which does not deserve whole life imprisonment, the court should determine a minimum term so as to allow a real possibility of review of continued imprisonment after the minimum term is served. However, as the Lord Chief Justice stated, judges are only required to consider rather than follow the general principles, including the impact of old age, when setting the minimum term for murder. Therefore, they are free to consider and refuse to grant a reduction of the sentence based on old age if there are compelling reasons for so doing. The problems with both the Lord Chief Justice's directions and the subsequent judgment on the issue is that neither articulated the reasons based on which reduction of the sentence based on old age can be rejected.

The judgment of the Court of Appeal in the case of *Derek and Barry Eleners* shed some light on this issue. In this case, 65-year-old Derek Elener was sentenced to life imprisonment with minimum term of 25 years for 12 serious robberies of cash in transit over an eight-year period including one involving the murder of a man who had sought to prevent the robbers fleeing the crime scene.[253] When setting the minimum term, the sentencing judge give insignificant discount for age, stating that 'this was a grave offence, committed during the course of the robbery'.[254]

252 Criminal Justice Act (n.180), s.269.
253 *R. v Sullivan* (n.181) 340.
254 ibid 341.

The sentence was appealed by Derek Elener on the ground that the court did not take into account his age while setting the minimum term. The Court of Appeal stated that in such a case the appropriate starting point is 30 years, which was reduced to 25 years because of his age and guilty plea. Although, regardless of the reduction, such a minimum term for the 65-year-old defendant meant that 'he could never leave prison', the Court of Appeal argued that 'for professional crime of this nature, whatever your age, you must still be severely punished'.[255]

This judgment makes clear that the aims of retribution and deterrence are factors which can override statutory mitigation on the ground of old age. The court will refuse to grant significant sentence reductions to give a defendant the possibility of review after serving the minimum term, if in its opinion the reduction depreciates the seriousness of the crime and undermines deterrence. This is so even in cases where the seriousness of the crime does not formally justify whole life imprisonment. This rationale was clearly articulated by the court in the case of *Sampford*:[256]

> ... clearly age is a mitigating factor. It is a statutory mitigating factor, as is apparent from schedule 21 paragraph 11(g) of the Criminal Justice Act 2003. Advanced age will be relevant in a sentencing exercise such as the one facing [the Judge]. The schedule establishes that, as does Troughton and the other cases cited in Troughton. Neither Troughton nor any other case, nor the schedule, suggests that a court has to do what it can to ensure that a defendant does not die in prison. If nothing else, no court would be in a position to conduct the necessary actuarial exercise. Even if it were, it would not override the requirement of the sentencer to reflect the circumstances of the killing in setting the minimum term. If those circumstances require a minimum which may result in the offender dying in prison, then that will be the minimum term.

The same approach was upheld in other cases, more recently in the case of *Lowe*,[257] who at the age of 82 was sentenced to life imprisonment with a minimum term of 25 years for the double murder of his partner and her daughter with a shotgun. It is evident that the minimum term will take this man far beyond the age which a man in his 80s is expected to reach in the UK. [258] The court obviously did not consider that the crime attained the level of gravity to attract a whole life sentence. However, to give this man a hope of release during his lifetime, the judge would need to sentence him to a minimum term of about five years, which, as the judgment demonstrates, is not conceivable for the court

255 ibid 342.

256 *R v Sampford* [2014] EWCA Crim 1560, para.15.

257 *R. v Lowe* (n.20).

258 Office for National Statistics, 'National Life Tables, United Kingdom: 2012–2014' www.ons.gov.uk/peoplepopulationandcommunity/birthsdeathsandmarriages/lifeexpectancies/, accessed 18 November 2017.

because of the seriousness of the crime and the requirement of deterrence. In such cases, these aims easily override the principle of 'light at the end of tunnel' elaborated by the Court of Appeal. Courts have held that if the circumstances of the case require imposing a minimum term which will make the sentence a *de facto* whole life, that should be the minimum term.[259]

The relevance of old age and fatal illness as grounds for retrospective adjustment of sentences at the stage of administration

As the review of the case law has demonstrated, there are three situations when an offender's old age, or more precisely his remaining life expectancy, was claimed to impact the severity of punishment at sentencing. The first is when life imprisonment is prescribed in law and should be mandatorily imposed. This is relevant only to murder cases. For such cases the age of an offender is a statutory mitigating factor[260] and is considered when a whole life tariff is not warranted and an otherwise appropriate minimum term surpasses the actuarial life expectancy of the offender.[261]

The second situation is when the otherwise appropriate determinate sentence appears to be more than the actuarial life expectancy of the offender. In these cases, the age of an offender is not a statutory prescribed ground for sentence reduction, but, in conjunction with infirmity of the offender, is considered relevant by the Court of Appeal.

The third situation relates to fatal illness, rather than old age, which, however, neither makes the experience of imprisonment significantly more onerous nor does it significantly deteriorate as a result of imprisonment.[262] However, as in the first two situations, the rationale for the claim is the same, i.e. the negative ratio between the remaining life expectancy and the length of an otherwise appropriate sentence.

Although all three situations are put forward by claimants at sentencing and are regarded as relevant for this stage of the criminal procedure by the court and even by the legislator, the reasoning of the Court of Appeal demonstrates that these situations do not make the sentence more severe at the time of imposition. Indeed, they concern the future, more severe than otherwise warranted, impact of the punishment on the offender. In other words, they concern a situation where a punishment, which is based on the balance of all the aims, is warranted at sentencing but ultimately will turn out to be more severe than warranted because it is more likely than not that the offender will die before she/he serves the mandatory custodial part of the sentence.

There is a plenty of support for the argument set out above. The Lord Chief Justice, and subsequently the courts, have interpreted age as a statutory mitigation

259 See e.g. *R. v Sampford* (n.256) para.15.
260 Criminal Justice Act (n.180) Sch.21(11)(g).
261 *R. v Archer* (n.246) 459.
262 See e.g. *R. v Moore (Archibald James)* (n.186); *R. v Stark (Gerrard Michael)* (n.187).

for murder cases because of its relevance to the 'likelihood of the defendant dying in prison'.[263] Indeed, this reasoning is evident in many sentence appeals related to murder cases[264] as well as in cases where an otherwise appropriate determinate sentence is longer than the actuarial life expectancy of the offender.[265] Clearly, the same rationale is relevant in cases where the reason for the negative ratio between the remaining life expectancy and the length of an otherwise appropriate sentence is terminal illness, although the Court of Appeal refused to consider this situation as relevant to sentencing.[266]

Indeed, when refusing to consider reduction of the sentence based on reduced life expectancy due to terminal illness the Court of Appeal stated that:[267]

> (i) a medical condition which may at some unidentified future date affect either life expectancy or the prison authorities' ability to treat a prisoner satisfactorily may call into operation the Home Secretary's powers of release by reference to the Royal Prerogative of mercy or otherwise but is not a reason for this Court to interfere with an otherwise appropriate sentence (Archibald Moore);

This reasoning clearly demonstrates that the Court of Appeal regards the issue of an offender's likely death while still serving the mandatory part of the prison sentence an issue which is relevant not at sentencing, but rather at the administration stage of the sentence. This approach is even more evident in another similar case, in which the Court stated: [268]

> Suppose a very long sentence of imprisonment were imposed, and during the course of that sentence the prisoner contracted some disease such as AIDS. If … submissions were correct it would be open for such a prisoner to file a late notice of appeal and ask this Court to review the sentence. One has only to state that proposition to see that it is untenable.

The Court of Appeal articulated this while considering the issue of the negative ratio of the remaining life expectancy and the length of an otherwise appropriate sentence due to terminal illness in a case where a determinate prison term was considered to be appropriate. However, in principle this approach should also be applicable to consideration of the impact of old age both in cases where life term is mandatory and in cases where a fixed-term prison sentence is appropriate: this approach relates to the rationale in general rather than to its application in a specific case.

263 *R. v Sullivan* (n.181) 325.
264 *R. v Walker (John Owen)* (n.244); *R. v Archer* (n.246).
265 *R. v John Francis C.* (n.227); *R. v Harold S.* (n.230); *R. v Fontes* (n.235).
266 *R. v Bernard (Basil Mortimer)* (n.182) 138.
267 ibid.
268 *R. v Stark (Gerrard Michael)* (n.187) 550.

The above argument appears to be correct, but, contrary to this logic, in murder cases and determinate sentence cases where the negative ratio between the prison sentence and remaining life expectancy was due to chronological age rather than to illness, the Court of Appeal considered this ground as relevant at the sentencing stage. However, the Court has not explained the reason for the different treatment of these comparable, similar situations. The difference in approach cannot be explained by the fact that in the first two situations the likelihood of death is more certain at sentencing than it is in the third situation. Although the Court uses uncertainty over a course of terminal illness and related life expectancy[269] as a reason for refusing to consider this ground at sentencing, like life expectancy in cases of terminal illness, normal actuarial life expectancy can vary in an individual case and increase in general at a different pace, as it has for more than a century.[270]

It is perhaps more useful to link the difference in the approach of the Court of Appeal to the types of the sentence discussed in these situations and with the nature of the respective executive mechanism available at the administration stage of the sentences. The situations deal with different types of sentence: mandatory life where circumstances do not attract a whole life tariff, and determinate terms of imprisonment. In fact, while granting a reduction of the minimum term for the first type of sentence, the sentencing court only brings forward the day of parole review to a date earlier than would otherwise have been appropriate – which, however, does not mean that the prisoner will necessarily be released. Although the reason for granting an earlier opportunity for parole review is also based on the presumption of the future impact of old age on the severity of the punishment, the Court considers that, unless a reduction is granted at sentencing, there will be no possibility to reflect on the possible change in the balance.[271] It is noteworthy that in these cases the Court does not refer to the availability of the executive power of compassionate release as a mechanism to reflect on the possible impact of likelihood of death on the severity of punishment at the administration stage of sentences.[272] It may be assumed that the Court considered this power as not effective in the particular situation; according to the published policy of the Secretary of State, only the terminally ill with three months of life expectancy and severely incapacitated prisoners are eligible to be considered for release under the statutory powers of compassionate release.[273]

In contrast to life sentences, reduction of a determinate sentence necessarily

269 *R. v Moore (Archibald James)* (n.186).

270 Jim Oeppen and James W Vaupel, 'Demography. Broken limits to life expectancy' (2002) 296(5570) *Science* (New York, NY) 1029.

271 *R. v Walker (John Owen)* (n.244) 332; *R. v Archer* (n.246) 459.

272 *R. v Sullivan* (n.181) 340; *R v Sampford* (n.256) para.15; *R. v Lowe* (n.20).

273 A detailed assessment of compassionate release power is conducted in Chapter V of this dissertation; Crime (Sentence) Act 1997, s.30; Criminal Justice Act (n.180), s.248; Prison Service Order 6000 31 March 2005, PSO 6000 (Her Majesty's Prison Service) ch.12.4.1; Prison Service Order 4700 Indeterminate Sentence Manual 2006, ch.12. Indeterminate sentence prisoners compassionate release on medical grounds (Her Majesty's Prison Service).

means early release. It can be argued that the Court of Appeal does not consider it appropriate to grant early release due to a possible change of balance between the aims of punishment which might occur in the future. Furthermore, in such cases the Court refers to the availability of the executive power of compassionate release as a mechanism which can remedy the situation that may occur during administration of the sentence. [274]

The above argument may appear convincing, but there are a few points which contravene its logic. First, if the Court considered it appropriate to deal at sentencing with a likelihood of the death of an elderly defendant in the course of a mandatory life sentence, regarding this as an opportunity for review rather than early release, it should have been granted in all such cases. If the reduction of the minimum term is considered as an opportunity for review, the countervailing factors, i.e. the seriousness of the crime and deterrence, should not be able to override the possibility of review. They should come into play during the review, when the issue of a possible shift in the balance between the aims is under consideration, and override the possibility of release if it appears that there has been no or not enough shift between the aims of punishment to allow early release. However, as shown above, in many such cases the Court of Appeal refused to grant such reductions, referring to the seriousness of the crime.[275]

Second, this approach would have been in conflict with the purpose of the minimum term and the subsequent review in life sentences: the minimum term is imposed for the sole purpose of retribution or punishment and the subsequent review has the sole purpose of assessing the level of risk to the individual or the public if the offender is released[276] rather than assessing a change in the balance between all the aims of punishment, including retribution.

Third, if the Court of Appeal treated the likelihood of the death of an elderly defendant in the course of a mandatory life sentence as an opportunity for review rather than early release, considering the compassionate release mechanism inappropriate for this purpose, it should have refused to grant similar reductions in all determinate sentence cases. In contrast, the Court of Appeal granted reductions in some cases of elderly defendants where the appropriate determinate sentence appeared to be more than their actuarial life expectancy.[277] It cannot be assumed, as with life sentence cases, that the Court regarded the compassionate release mechanism as ineffective, because in some such cases the Court actually referred to this mechanism as an appropriate instrument to deal with the situation at the stage of administration of sentences.[278]

It should be conceded that the Court of Appeal judgments on the issue do not offer a plausible explanation as to why the courts dealt at the sentencing stage

274 *R. v Moore (Archibald James)* (n.186) 386.

275 *R. v Sullivan* (n.181) 340; *R v Sampford* (n.256).

276 Crime (Sentence) Act (n.273) s.28.

277 *R. v John Francis C.* (n.227); *Attorney General's Ref (No. 77 of 2006)* (n.194); *Attorney General's Reference (No.38 of 2013)* (n.227); *R. v Taylor* (n.227); *R. v Harold S.* (n.230); *R. v Fontes* (n.235).

278 *R. v John Francis C.* (n.227) 564.

with a situation which might change the balance between the aims of punishment during the administration of sentences. However, whatever the reason for the Court's approach, it does not weaken the argument that the likelihood of an offender's death in prison could change the balance between the purposes of punishment at the stage of administration of sentences, making an otherwise appropriate sentence more severe. This argument is valid irrespective of whether the likelihood of death is due to normal life expectancy or limited life expectancy due to terminal illness.

The relevance of a serious medical condition as a ground for retrospective adjustment of a sentence at the stage of administration

Physical illness of the offender is not a statutory ground for reduction of sentence. However, the Court of Appeal delivered two guideline judgments on the issue.[279] In this regard there are two situations where the Court considered reduction of the sentence warranted: first, when the management of the offender with a medical condition was difficult in prison, making his experience of imprisonment significantly more onerous than it would otherwise have been;[280] and second, when the medical condition has deteriorated further because of imprisonment.[281]

It is clear that the underlying rationale for reducing an otherwise appropriate sentence in such cases is that the impact of the punishment on the offender due to illness is significantly more severe than would otherwise have been the case. The Court of Appeal stated that in such situations, at sentencing or on appeal, courts may, based on the exceptional features of particular cases, impose a lesser sentence than would otherwise be appropriate.[282] The decisions as to whether or not to grant a reduction of the sentence are taken on the balance of retributive and utilitarian aims of punishment, which may also play a role in how much reduction to grant.

As with the offender's age, the role of a serious medical condition as a ground that may change the balance between the retributive and utilitarian aims of punishment was observed at sentencing. It is clear that if this ground can shift the balance between the aims of punishment at sentencing, it may have the same effect if it intensifies or arises during the administration of the sentence. This is also evident from the approach and the language of the Court of Appeal in cases where, despite the presence of a serious medical condition, its adverse effects were not vivid at the time of sentencing. The Court stated that the latter type of case should be dealt with at the stage of administration of the sentence.[283] Despite this, in exceptional cases the Court of Appeal granted an extension of the

279 *R. v Bernard (Basil Mortimer)* (n.182); *R. v Qazi (Saraj) and Hussain (Majid)* (n.208).

280 See e.g. *R. v Hall (Daniel Patrick)* (n.213).

281 See e.g. *R. v Green (Paul Palmerston)* (n.184).

282 *R. v Bernard (Basil Mortimer)* (n.182) 138; *R. v Wynne* (n 198); *R. v Qazi (Saraj) and Hussain (Majid)* (n.208) 45.

283 *R. v Moore (Archibald James)* (n.186) 387.

appeal period after the offender had already been in prison for many years. This was done in order to consider a reduction of the sentence based on a medical condition which did not warrant reduction of the sentence at sentencing, but deteriorated after the offender had spent three years in prison. It is clear that in its decision-making the Court considers whether there has been a shift in the balance between the retributive and utilitarian aims of punishment in view of the medical condition and the time already spent in prison.[284]

That the balance between the purposes of punishment may also change at the stage of administration of sentences due to a serious medical condition is also evident from the approach of the Court to a situation where after imposition of a sentence of imprisonment it is claimed that the sentence in the prison where the applicant was placed violates Article 3 of the ECHR.[285] The Court of Appeal articulated that such claims are not matters belonging to the stage of appeal, but rather to the stage of administration of sentences, because it is the duty of the Secretary of State to ensure that prisoners with serious medical conditions are provided with necessary care, and if release is the only way to comply with Article 3 of ECHR the Secretary of State has powers to that end.[286]

What remains unclear is the difference between the position of the Court of Appeal in regard to the very same situation when the sentence is appealed based on the principles developed in the case of *Bernard*,[287] i.e. when a reduction of a sentence is requested based on the more onerous impact of imprisonment due to a serious medical condition. The Court stated that in contrast to the issue of Article 3, this is a matter of appeal against a sentence. The difference in the approach of the Court is most probably due to the difference in the nature of the evaluation of the two grounds and the possible result. When the overall length of the sentence is appealed under *Bernard* principles, the Court is evaluating whether the balance between the aims of punishment has changed in view of a serious medical condition. Based on this evaluation, the Court is free to reject, grant some reduction or grant a reduction with the aim of allowing immediate release of a prisoner. In contrast, when the claim is made under Article 3 it does not have the same freedom of choice as in the former case: the decision in the claim under Article 3 will be one of rejecting the appeal or release, which could be granted only if it is the only way to avoid violation of Article 3. This is a more complex issue and probably more appropriate for the administration stage of a sentence.

In summary, it is plain that illness is a universal ground that is relevant both to sentencing and the administration of sentences. If it is present at sentencing the court should consider whether it changes the balance between the aims of punishment, warranting a reduction of an otherwise appropriate term of imprisonment or imposition of an alternative. However, the illness which did not warrant

284 *R. v Davenport (Edward)* [2014] EWCA Crim 835, 17.

285 *R. v Qazi (Saraj) and Hussain (Majid)* (n.208) 45.

286 ibid.

287 *R. v Bernard (Basil Mortimer)* (n.182).

reduction at sentencing may intensify in the course of the sentence, or a prisoner who was healthy at sentencing may become seriously ill during the course of the sentence. In these cases, the issue of whether the serious illness of a prisoner shifts the balance among the aims of punishment and warrants release should be considered at the stage of administration of sentences.

Conclusion

As interpreted by the Grand Chamber of the ECtHR, Article 3 of the ECHR requires States Parties to review whole life sentences after prisoners have served a considerable part of the sentence, presumably 25 years. The review is required because even if the aims of punishment and deterrence could justify imposition of whole life imprisonment, alone they could not justify its implementation until the death of the prisoner; human beings possess a capacity for rehabilitation, and therefore to deny a human being hope of regaining her/his freedom through rehabilitation would be degrading.

This interpretation suggests that the review has two interrelated but at the same time independent aims. In the first place the aim of availability of review is to offer a whole life prisoner hope of regaining freedom. However, the review also has the aim of preventing punishing the prisoner disproportionately more severely than is justified by the aims which necessitated the imposition of the sentence. According to the Court, although whole life imprisonment for a serious crime might be justified by the aims of punishment at the imposition stage, the balance between them might shift over time, making the continued imprisonment unlawful. In the case of whole life imprisonment, the catalyst for change in the balance is the human capacity for rehabilitation which is interpreted by the Court as ceasing to pose a danger to society. In a serious case which attracts a whole life sentence the offender must serve at least 25 years before it can be reviewed whether she/he has rehabilitated her/himself and is no longer a danger to society. However, this term is required not only to achieve rehabilitation of the prisoner, but also punishment and deterrence. These aims might hinder the release of the prisoner at review; however, it is implicit in the judgment that at this stage they may not have as much primacy as at the imposition stage.

The situation of elderly and seriously ill prisoners who serve other than whole life sentences is different from that of whole lifers. The situation of hopelessness plays out differently in cases where the mandatory custodial term of a fixed or indeterminate sentence is longer than actuarial or clinical life expectancy. Moreover, it is not applicable to the situation of seriously ill prisoners.

However, there are similarities in these cases which make the underlying rationale of the requirement of review of continued imprisonment also applicable in cases of elderly and seriously ill. As in whole life sentences, in the case of an elderly prisoner who is likely to die in prison or is seriously ill, a possible shift in the balance between the aims of punishment might occur earlier than is presumed by the imposed punishment. The shift in the balance may make the punishment disproportionately more severe than was appropriate in the particular case.

In contrast to whole life sentences, the possible catalyst for change in cases of elderly and seriously ill prisoners is their age and illness. These prisoners may cease to pose a danger to society because of the age and serious illness. Moreover, these prisoners might not have to serve the term required to achieve the aims of punishment and deterrence in their cases. The impact of old age and serious medical conditions on the severity of the prison sentence may compensate for the length of time necessary to achieve the aims of punishment and deterrence. The impact of these characteristics is taken into account by the ECtHR and English courts.

The Grand Chamber of the ECtHR has recognised that old age or the likelihood of dying in prison impact the severity of punishment. It has stated that providing a maximum age limit for the imposition of life imprisonment is one of several ways to comply with the reducibility requirement of Article 3.[288] It implies from this statement that, in contrast to younger life prisoners, the review after serving 25 years does not provide the elderly with the prospect of release, because for them 25 years would already be an irreducible life sentence.

The issue of likelihood of dying in prison when the imposed sentence surpasses actuarial life expectancy is more or less evident at sentencing, although in these cases it concerns a more severe future impact of the sentence on the offender. The same could be said of dying in prison from a terminal illness that is present at the time of sentencing. The recognition by the ECtHR of the impact of old age on the severity of the sentence was in the context of sentencing. However, the Court did not rule out retrospective adjustment of the severity of the sentence. It stated that not imposing a life sentence on adults aged 65 and over is only one of the ways of complying with the reducibility requirement, which means that a review of an already imposed sentence on this category of prisoners after they reach a certain age is also an acceptable way of adjusting the impact. Moreover, in many cases the Court pointed out the specific mechanisms available to applicants that could be used to adjust the severity of the sentence retrospectively.[289]

In regard to the impact of serious medical conditions on the severity of punishment, the approach of the ECtHR suggests that in the first place attempts should be made to neutralise or mitigate the impact of serious medical conditions on the experience of imprisonment through provision of the requisite medical care in prison and adjustment of prison conditions to fit the special needs of ill prisoners. However, apart from the measures mentioned above, the authorities are required to consider the overall compatibility of a particular medical condition with deprivation of liberty.

This approach of the Court relates both to the stage of sentencing and the administration of sentences. The ECtHR has stated explicitly that before committing a seriously ill person to a prison term a court must ensure that the prison where this person will be detained can meet her/his special needs in a way that punishment will not impact her/him more severely than other people. It implies from the ECtHR's approach that if such conditions are not ensured, courts

288 ibid.

289 See e.g. *Sawoniuk v United Kingdom* (n.78); *Papon v France (no. 1)* (n.78).

should not commit such persons to an immediate prison term, if they are not to violate Article 3 of the ECHR.[290]

When the issue of the compatibility of imprisonment with Article 3 of the ECHR because of a serious illness arose during the administration of imprisonment, the ECtHR reviewed several components of the treatment such as the provision of requisite medical care and compatibility of prison conditions with the health conditions of the prisoner. However, apart from looking at the quality of medical care provided to the applicant and the suitability of prison conditions, the ECtHR has emphasised the importance of legal mechanisms to review the lawfulness of continued deprivation of liberty in view of serious illness.[291] It stated that in exceptional cases, when the health condition is absolutely incompatible with detention, Article 3 may require release. [292]

Similarly, the English Court of Appeal recognised the impact of old age and serious illness on the severity of sentence. The Court interpreted the old age of the defendant as a factor capable of impacting the severity of the penalty to relate 'to physical capacity on release or the likelihood of the defendant dying in prison'.[293] From this interpretation it is clear that this factor relates to the future more onerous impact of punishment on the offender. However, in some cases the sentences were reduced at the stage of sentencing on the ground of the negative ratio between the offender's life expectancy and the length of the sentence. In many other cases courts have refused to reduce sentences based on the same factor, arguing that the situation can be dealt with at the administration stage of the sentence when the more severe impact of the punishment on the offender will have become more certain. [294]

In regard to the impact of a serious medical condition of the offender on the severity of the sentence, like the ECtHR, the Court of Appeal articulated that in the first place such impact should be neutralised or mitigated by provision of the requisite medical care and condition of detention adequate to the fitness of the prisoner. The sentencing courts should consider offsetting the more onerous impact of punishment at sentencing, by not committing a defendant to prison, only when there is sufficient evidence to demonstrate that it is not possible to meet the needs of the prisoner in any of prison facilities.[295] In cases when at the time of the sentencing it was not clear whether, owing to illness, the punishment would impact a prisoner more severely, or whether it would be possible to offset this impact through other arrangements, the courts preferred to leave the issue of dealing with impact of punishment to the Secretary of State.

In summary, it can be stated that the analysis in this chapter supports the extension of the right to review under Article 3 to prisoners whose mandatory

290 *Price v United Kingdom* (n.112) 168–170.
291 See e.g. *Gülay Cetin v Turkey* (n.96) paras 131–132.
292 See e.g. *Chaykovskiy v Ukraine* (n.93) para.55.
293 Cited in *R. v Sullivan* (n.181) 325.
294 See e.g. *R. v John Francis C.* (n.227) 564.
295 *R. v Qazi (Saraj) and Hussain (Majid)* (n.208) 45.

custodial term is longer than their actuarial or clinical life expectancy, and those who are otherwise seriously ill. When imprisonment is for the rest of a person's life, Article 3 requires a review of continued imprisonment to check whether there has been a shift in the balance between the purposes of punishment.[296] It is clear that the aim of the right to review of continued deprivation of liberty in these cases is to give hope of release and also to prevent punishing the prisoner more severely than is justified by the aims of punishment.

There is a similar lack of hope in cases where there is a likelihood of a prisoner's dying in prison owing to fatal illness or advanced age, albeit it is not as certain as in the case of whole life imprisonment. However, unlike in *de jure* whole life cases, the catalyst for a shift in the balance between the aims of punishment in these cases are old age or terminal illness. The issue of hope is not relevant to the situation of non-fatally ill prisoners. Furthermore, the ECtHR has already articulated that in exceptional cases, when continued detention is absolutely incompatible with the state of health of the prisoner, Article 3 may require release. However, as demonstrated, in cases of continued imprisonment of seriously ill prisoners there is a risk that because of the impact of the serious illness on the severity of punishment, the sentence which was lawful at the time of imposition may become unlawful during implementation. This is a self-standing ground of review under Article 3. It has a broader scope than the exceptional requirement of release covering the process of review and has a preventative function.[297] Both in whole life imprisonment and when prisoners are likely to die in detention or are otherwise seriously ill, it is due to the fundamental nature of human dignity that the mere lack of procedure to check whether or not it is protected will constitute a violation of Article 3.

296 *Vinter v United Kingdom* [GC] (n.1) para.119.
297 ibid, per Judge Mahoney.

3 Substantive and procedural elements of review of continued imprisonment of elderly and seriously ill prisoners

Abstract

The extension of the right to review under Article 3 of the European Convention of Human Rights to the continued imprisonment of prisoners whose sentences are longer than their actuarial life expectancy and those who are terminally or otherwise seriously ill raises important substantive and procedural issues. This chapter will demonstrate that in cases of prisoners whose sentences are longer than their actuarial life expectancy the appropriate time for review should be determined with a view to allowing a possibility of regaining freedom rather than dying at home. Whereas, in the cases of terminally or otherwise seriously ill prisoners, the review should be carried as soon as serious illness is diagnosed. Moreover, such review should be accompanied by procedural safeguards prescribed under Article 5(4), because this Article prescribes guarantees against arbitrary deprivation of the right to liberty. It is applicable where the link between the sentencing decision and the continued deprivation of liberty might be broken because of a shift in the balance between the aims that justified detention in the first place. The fundamental interests at stake during the review of continued imprisonment of such prisoners, as well as the principle of the rule of law, require that such review meets the requirements of Article 5(4).

The appropriate time for review of sentences on grounds of old age and serious illness

The likelihood of the death of an offender due to the negative ratio between the length of an otherwise appropriate sentence and the actuarial life expectancy of the offender at sentencing was considered as a ground for reduction of the sentence by courts in England. As the review of the case law demonstrates, the issue has been dealt with in an inconsistent way. It appears that the main reason for refusing to grant a reduction on this ground, even in cases where reductions would have not resulted in early release but merely in early parole review, is the seriousness of the crime.

Furthermore, in some cases the imposition of a sentence of particular severity might be said to have only symbolic meaning when it is clear that the offender's remaining life expectancy would not be enough to serve the mandatory minimum term.[1] Evidently, regardless of the practical effect, the courts were concerned that imposing a significantly lesser term of imprisonment than required by the gravity of the crime would depreciate the function of disapprobation that punishment seeks to express as well as its deterrent effect.

The inconsistent approach of the courts makes it implausible to suggest that the courts considered at sentencing the likelihood of death due to old age during the course of the sentence, because there was no age-based review mechanism at the administration stage of sentences. However, it would be plausible to argue that the issue of the likelihood of dying in the course of the sentence due to a negative ratio between the remaining actuarial life expectancy and the length of the sentence belongs to the administration stage of sentences: this issue concerns the future more severe impact of the sentence on the offender. Therefore, it should be dealt with by a dedicated mechanism allowing a review based on the ground of old age.

Such a mechanism would allow the courts to impose an appropriate sentence necessary to fulfil all relevant aims of punishment, including communication of disapprobation, without worrying about a distant likelihood of a grossly disproportionate impact on the offender. Such a suggestion brings to the fore issues of the age threshold for the review and a minimum term which should be served before the review. In this regard, any suggested threshold would be relative, with some degree of arbitrariness. However, the thresholds can be taken as reference points while the issue of uncertainty can be addressed through a more nuanced decision-making process at the review.

The age threshold for the review should be selected with the view of allowing a possibility of regaining freedom rather than dying at home. Therefore, the threshold should be less than the life expectancy at older ages. For instance, the recent research demonstrates that in England 65-year-old men and women can expect to live an additional 18 to 20 years.[2] Thus, the age of 80 could be regarded as a threshold that would allow review at an age below life expectancy at older ages, providing an opportunity to have some life outside prison if released at this age.

Furthermore, because such a review has the purpose of protecting human dignity, there should be no eligibility exclusions based on the seriousness of the crime committed. However, as sentencing practice demonstrates, in recent years many offenders come before courts for sentencing at even older ages than the selected age threshold for review. If a court sentences a very old offender to a prison term, it would be reasonable to exclude the possibility of immediate or very short-term eligibility to review of the sentence on the ground of old age. In this regard it seems justified to establish a three-year minimum term which needs to be served before a prisoner will become eligible for review of the sentence on

1 *R. v Lowe* (2014).

2 Office for National Statistics, 'National Life Tables, United Kingdom: 2012–2014' http://www.ons.gov.uk/peoplepopulationandcommunity/birthsdeathsandmarriages/lifeexpectancies/, accessed 21 November 2017.

the ground of old age. A three-year minimum term is justified on the basis of life expectancy at older ages,[3] the need for at least some time before the shift in the balance between the goals of punishment could be reviewed, and the requirement to provide an opportunity of regaining freedom.

As to the cases of prisoners whose sentence is potentially for the whole of life because of terminal illness, and the cases of otherwise seriously ill prisoners, the appropriate point of review could be considered to be the presence of a serious illness which may make punishment significantly more severe than appropriate. As mentioned in Chapter 2, a serious medical condition is a ground that is relevant both at the sentencing stage and the administration of the sentence. If it is present at sentencing, the court should consider whether it changes the balance between the aims of punishment, warranting a reduction of an otherwise appropriate term of prison or imposition of an alternative. However, the illness which did not warrant reduction at sentencing may intensify in the course of the sentence, or a prisoner who was healthy at sentencing may become seriously ill during the course of the sentence. In these cases, the issue of whether the serious illness of a prisoner shifts the balance between the aims of punishment and warrants release should be considered at the administration stage of the sentence. In these cases, as well as in the cases of potential whole lifers owing to actuarial life expectancy, the availability of the opportunity for review of continued imprisonment should be clear for the offender at sentencing.

The substance of review of continued deprivation of liberty of elderly and seriously ill prisoners

Another important issue in the context of the right to review of continued imprisonment of elderly and seriously ill prisoners is the substance of the review. It should be highlighted that the existence of the right to review is independent of the right to release; the review does not automatically imply release. However, for the scope of the right to review of the continued deprivation of liberty based on the above mentioned grounds it is important to articulate also the content of the review which is inevitably connected to the rationale of the review. As articulated above, the review is necessitated by the fact that the aims of the punishment which justified it at the imposition of the sentence will not necessarily remain static; the balance between the aims of punishment may shift as the prisoner serves her/his sentence. This shift can be properly evaluated only by reviewing 'the justification for continued detention at an appropriate point in the sentence'.[4]

Following the English Court of Appeal and the Chamber of the ECtHR, the Grand Chamber recognised that the legitimate penological goals are punishment/retribution, deterrence, public protection and rehabilitation. Many of

3 In England men can now expect to live for a further 19 years at age 65, 12 years at 75, six years at 85 and three years at 95. See Public Health England, 'Recent Trends in Life Expectancy at Older Ages: Update to 2014' (2016).

4 *Vinter and others v United Kingdom* [GC] ECHR 2013-III 317 para.111.

these purposes are present at the time of sentencing.[5] It follows that the reviewing body should re-evaluate these goals in view of the prisoner's likelihood of dying owing to actuarial or clinical life expectancy or in view of a serious illness. On the basis of this review the reviewing body should decide whether, in the light of these circumstances and the time already served, the aims of punishment still justify deprivation of liberty in a particular case. If the reviewing body finds that any of the purposes which justified the punishment at imposition justify continued deprivation of liberty, irrespective of likelihood of dying in detention due to old age or fatal illness or the fact that the prisoner suffers from a serious illness, it shall refuse release. However, at the review, the primacy of the aims should be evaluated differently than at the imposition of the sentence. As in *Vinter*, at the stage of review the aims of punishment and deterrence should be considered less primary than they were at sentencing.[6] By contrast, the age/likelihood of dying or serious illness which makes punishment considerably more onerous than is inherent in judicial punishment and the possibility of regaining freedom should be weighty factors in the review.

Procedural safeguards that apply to the review of continued deprivation of liberty of elderly and seriously ill prisoners

As demonstrated, the obligation of review of whole life sentences imposed by Article 3 of the European Convention on Human Rights (ECHR) can and should be extended to prisoners whose sentences are longer than their life expectancy (actuarial or clinical) and those who are seriously ill. The obligation of review raises the issue of procedural safeguards which should accompany the review of whole life sentences and consequently the review of continued imprisonment of prisoners whose sentences are longer than their life expectancy (actuarial or clinical) and those who are seriously ill.

The review mechanism required by Article 3 of the ECHR has two aims: to offer a hope of regaining freedom and to check whether the aims of punishment which justified it at the imposition continue to justify the further implementation of the sentence. The European Court of Human Rights (ECtHR) came to the conclusion that punishments that are grossly disproportionate in relation to the legitimate penological goals would violate Article 3 of the ECHR. However, the review of whether continued imprisonment is justified by legitimate penological goals is in essence a review of the lawfulness of continued deprivation of liberty under Article 5(1)(a). It seems that the ECtHR considered that grossly disproportionate punishment would be an aggravated violation of the right to liberty amounting to degrading punishment within the meaning of Article 3 of the ECHR. Indeed, the jurisprudence of the former Commission and the ECtHR demonstrates that human dignity could be violated through an

5 ibid.
6 ibid.

aggravated violation of another Convention right.[7] For instance, in the case of the East African Asians the Commission found that the UK Government's refusal to allow applicants who were UK citizens of Asian origin to enter and/or remain permanently in the UK constituted a violation of Article 3.[8] According to the Commission:[9]

> the legislation applied in the present case discriminated against the applicants on the grounds of their colour or race. ... discrimination based on race could, in certain circumstances, of itself amount to degrading treatment within the meaning of Article 3 of the Convention ... . [D]ifferential treatment on the basis of race might therefore be capable of constituting degrading treatment when differential treatment on some other ground would raise no such question.

It logically follows that the review which aims to check the lawfulness of continued deprivation of liberty must be equipped with procedural guarantees required by Article 5(4) of the ECHR. This Article, indeed, prescribes a detailed set of safeguards which are applicable to reviews of lawfulness of deprivation of liberty on all grounds prescribed by Article 5(1) of the ECHR including the lawful detention of a person after conviction by a competent court.[10]

The issue of applicability of Article 5(4) to the review of whole life sentences was raised before the Grand Chamber in the cases of *Kafkaris(1)11* and *Vinter*.[12] However, in both cases the Grand Chamber declared the complaints under this Article inadmissible. In the former case, it was not raised in the original submission and therefore fell outside of the scope of the Grand Chamber's jurisdiction,[13]

7 *East African Asians v United Kingdom* App nos 4403/70–4419/70 and 14 others 62, para.209 (Commission Decision, 14 December 1973); *Abdulaziz, Cabales and Balkandali v UK* App no 9214/80; 9473/81; 9474/81 (ECtHR, 28 May 1985) para.91; *Smith and Grady v United Kingdom* ECHR 1999-VI 45 para.121.

8 *East African Asians v United Kingdom* (n.7) 62, para.209.

9 ibid 62, para.297.

10 European Convention on Human Rights 1950, ECHR (Council of Europe) Art.5(4); David J Harris, Michael O'Boyle and Colin Warbrick, *Law of the European Convention on Human Rights* (2nd edn, Oxford University Press 2009) 183; *van Droogenbroeck v Belgium* (1982) Series A no 50 para.54; *Weeks v The United Kingdom* Series A no 114 para.61; *Waite v the United Kingdom* App no 54236/99 (ECtHR, 10 December 2002) para.59; *Hussain v United Kingdom* App no 21928/93 (ECtHR, 21 February 1996) para.60; *Winterwerp v Netherlands* (1979) Series A no 33; *Nikolova v Bulgaria* ECHR 1999-II 203 para.63; *Sanchez-Reisse v Switzerland* A no 107 para.51; *Guide on Article 5 of the Convention: Right to liberty and security* (2nd edn, Council of Europe/ European Court of Human Rights 2014); Jim Murdoch, 'Safeguarding the Liberty of the Person: Recent Strasbourg Jurisprudence' (1993) 42(3) *International and Comparative Law Quarterly* 494; Stefan Trechsel, 'Right to Liberty and Security of the Person' (1980) 1 *Human Rights Law Journal* 88.

11 *Kafkaris v Cyprus* [GC] ECHR 2008-I 223.

12 *Vinter v United Kingdom* [GC] (n.4).

13 *Kafkaris v Cyprus* [GC] (n.11) para.124.

while in the latter case the Grand Chamber's jurisdiction was restricted by the declaration of inadmissibility of this part of the application by the Chamber.[14]

The declaration of inadmissibility of Article 5(4) by the Chamber in the case of *Vinter* is based on the ECtHR's longstanding position that in fixed-term prison sentences and in life sentences which are imposed purely for the purpose of retribution, the requirement of review of lawfulness of the sentence is incorporated in the original sentencing decision of the court.[15] Therefore, an Article 5(4) review does not apply to such sentences, even if domestic laws allow early release in such cases.[16]

In declaring the part of the application regarding Article 5(4) inadmissible in *Vinter*, the Chamber relied on the ECtHR's earlier inadmissibility decision in the case of *Kafkaris v Cyprus (2)*.[17] In this case the applicant complained, *inter alia*, that the mandatory nature of his life sentence and the lack of a mechanism to challenge the lawfulness of his continued detention was a violation of Article 5(4).[18] According to the applicant, the president's power to grant a pardon which was recognised as meeting the requirement of Article 3 in terms of *de facto* and *de jure* reducibility of life sentence[19] did not satisfy the requirements of Article 5(4).[20]

In *Kafkaris (2)*, the First Chamber, in line with the ECtHR's longstanding position, distinguished life sentences imposed purely for the purpose of punishment from those composed of two distinct periods: a minimum term imposed for a punitive purpose and indeterminate detention based on the dangerousness of the prisoner. According to the Court, in the latter case the detention after the punitive term is based on factors such as dangerousness or risk of reoffending, which are subject to change. Therefore, the lawfulness of detention sanctioned by the original sentencing decision is valid only for the punitive period. In order to ensure that the continued detention after the expiration of the punitive period is justified, there should be a procedure compliant with Article 5(4) to review the lawfulness of continued detention and order the release of the prisoner if further detention is not justified.[21]

By contrast, in the cases where the whole life imprisonment is imposed purely for the purpose of punishment, the original sentencing decision incorporates an Article 5(4) review ensuring the lawfulness of the whole life sentence. According to the Chamber, the purpose of retribution, on which the whole life sentence

14 *Vinter v United Kingdom* [GC] (n.4) para.132.

15 *De Wilde, Ooms and Versyp v Belgium* App nos 2832/66; 2835/66; 2899/66 (ECtHR, 18 June 1971) para.83; *V. v United Kingdom* [GC] ECHR 1999-IX 111 para.119; *Stafford v United Kingdom* [2002] 35 EHRR 32 para.87; *Kafkaris v Cyprus (dec.)* App no 9644/09 (ECtHR, 21 June 2011) para.58.

16 *Brown v UK (dec.)* App no 968/04 (ECtHR, 26 October 2004).

17 *Kafkaris v Cyprus (dec.)* (n.15).

18 ibid para.50.

19 *Kafkaris v Cyprus* [GC] (n.11).

20 *Kafkaris v Cyprus (dec.)* (n.15) para.57; *Kafkaris v Cyprus* [GC] (n.11) para.103.

21 *Kafkaris v Cyprus (dec.)* (n.15) para.58.

is based, will remain unchanged during the prisoner's life, ensuring a sufficient link between the original sentencing decision and the continued deprivation of liberty for the whole period imposed by the sentencing court. In such a case, the lawfulness of the original sentencing decision does not depend on the offender's rehabilitation, dangerousness or his risk of reoffending.[22]

The Chamber in *Kafkaris (2)* confirmed the Court's longstanding position in relation to the applicability of Article 5(4) to sentences imposed exclusively for punitive purposes. However, it did not try to explain how this position fits with the reducibility requirement of Article 3 which the Grand Chamber articulated in *Kafkaris(1)*. It is clear that, after the Grand Chamber's judgment in *Vinter*, the reasons given by the Chamber in *Kafkaris (2)* as to the inapplicability of Article 5(4) with regard to life sentences imposed solely for the purpose of punishment have become untenable; the basis of the First Chamber's rejection of the applicability of Article 5(4) to reviews of life sentences imposed for the sole purpose of retribution was based on the argument that the aim of retribution is static and will not change through the whole sentence. Therefore, no issue of lawfulness will arise during the execution of the sentence. Furthermore, it stated that the issues of dangerousness and risk of reoffending are irrelevant for the continued lawfulness of whole life sentences.[23]

By contrast, the finding of the Grand Chamber in the case of *Vinter* that Article 3 requires reducibility of whole life sentences is based on the idea of the dynamic nature of all purposes of punishment, including retribution. According to the Grand Chamber the balance between punishment, deterrence, public protection and rehabilitation, which justified imposition of a life sentence, 'is not necessarily static and may shift in the course of the sentence'. The aims which were primary for the imposition of the sentence may not remain so after a lengthy time into the serving of the sentence. Whether or not the balance between the aims has changed can be determined only by carrying out a review of continued imprisonment.[24]

Furthermore, in the case of *Kafkaris (2)* the First Chamber stated that rehabilitation of the offender and consequently her/his dangerousness and the risk of reoffending are not relevant for the continued lawfulness of a life sentence imposed exclusively for punitive purposes. Therefore, Article 5(4) does not require review of continued imprisonment in such cases.[25] However, this approach clearly contradicts the reasoning of the Grand Chamber, which made the right to rehabilitation one of the main grounds for holding irreducible life sentences to be in violation of Article 3.[26] According to the Grand Chamber, human dignity requires that every offender, irrespective of the nature of her/his crime, be given an opportunity to 'atone for his offence' and one day regain his

22 ibid para.59.
23 ibid.
24 *Vinter v United Kingdom* [GC] (n.4) para.111.
25 *Kafkaris v Cyprus (dec.)* (n.15) para.59.
26 *Vinter v United Kingdom* [GC] (n.4) paras 112–119.

freedom.[27] Irrespective of the primary purpose of imposition of a life sentence, the offender should be given an opportunity of rehabilitation. Based on this and on other purposes which justified the imposition of a life sentence, a review conducted at some point during the sentence will decide whether the offender should continue to be detained or could safely be released.[28]

Despite the reasoning of Grand Chamber in the case of *Vinter*, which clearly demonstrates that Article 5(4) should be applicable to the review of lawfulness of whole life imprisonment, the Third Section of the ECtHR in the very next case on the same matter again declared the complaint under Article 5(4) inadmissible based on the same justifications.[29] Therefore, in other cases on the same subject applicants did not raise the issue of applicability of Article 5(4). Instead, the Court articulated some procedural safeguards which should apply during the review of lawfulness of whole life imprisonment. It attributed these safeguards to Article 3 itself.[30] This approach weakens the protection of the right to liberty and consequently the protection of human dignity, because the procedural safeguards articulated by the Court in relation to whole life cases are weaker than those which are applicable under Article 5(4).

The procedural guarantees that apply to the review of whole life imprisonment are summarised by the Grand Chamber in the case of *Murray v the Netherlands*.[31] According to the Court, the review must be accompanied by an obligation to disclose to a prisoner the materials on which the decision is made, a requirement to give reasons for refusing an application for early release and, finally, a refusal to order early release should be amenable to judicial review in the courts.[32] The Court articulated that in principle both executive and judicial forms of review of whole life sentences could meet the requirement of reducibility of the sentence within the meaning of Article 3.[33] However, if the review is carried out by the executive, the decision to refuse release should be amenable to judicial review.

By contrast, Article 5(4) is more demanding. In addition to the above specified safeguards, it requires that the review be conducted by a court-like body. Although this does not necessarily mean a court of law of a classic nature, it should at least be independent from an executive and the parties of the case.[34] Furthermore, in cases where detention depends on an assessment of detainees' character, mental state and general dangerousness, Article 5(4) requires 'an oral hearing in the context of an adversarial procedure involving legal representation

27 ibid para.112.

28 ibid paras 111–119.

29 *Murray v the Netherlands* App no 47940/99 paras 82–86 (ECtHR, 10 December 2013).

30 See e.g. *Laszlo Magyar v Hungary* App no 73593/10 paras 57–58 (ECtHR, 20 May 2014).

31 *Murray v the Netherlands* [GC] App no 10511/10 (ECtHR, 26 April 2016).

32 *Murray v the Netherlands* [GC] (n.31) para.100; *Kafkaris v Cyprus* [GC] (n.11) para.105; *Laszlo Magyar v Hungary* (n.30) para.57.

33 *Trabelsi v Belgium* App no 140/10 para.115 (ECHR, 4 September 2014); *T.P. and A.T. v Hungary* App nos 37871/14 and 73986/14, para.38 (ECtHR, 4 October 2016).

34 *Weeks v United Kingdom* (n.10) para.61.

and the possibility of calling and questioning witnesses'.[35] The remedy should also provide possibilities for periodic reviews at reasonable intervals.[36] More importantly, the requirements of Article 5(4) could not be met through more than one separate remedy.[37] This means that, if the initial review does not meet the requirements of Article 5(4), the violation of this Article will be found even if the deficiencies of the initial review would have been possible to correct through judicial review of the initial decision.

As the analysis showed after the Grand Chamber's judgment in *Vinter*, the reasons justifying non-applicability of Article 5(4) cannot hold ground. However, in order to more convincingly demonstrate that Article 5(4) is applicable to the review in the above situations, it is necessary to understand and rebut the possible reasons for the attributing procedural guarantees that should accompany the review of whole life imprisonment to Article 3 itself.

Why did the ECtHR attribute procedural requirements to Article 3 itself?

It seems that the roots of attributing to Article 3 the procedural guarantees of the review of whole life imprisonment and ignoring Article 5(4) can be traced to the issue of whether the lack of review in whole life imprisonment is a violation of a substantive or a procedural right. The judgments of the ECtHR in whole life imprisonment cases indicate that the Court treated the lack of review as a procedural violation.

The dissenting minority of judges in the Chamber's judgment in the case of *Vinter38 argued that the absence of a review mechanism that 'would remove the hopelessness inherent in a sentence of life imprisonment' constituted a procedural infringement of Article 3. The Grand Chamber in essence followed the view of the minority, although it did not explicitly state that the lack of review mechanism constituted a procedural violation of Article 3.39*

Furthermore, despite finding that the existing domestic law does not provide an effective remedy before a national authority, the Grand Chamber considered the lack of remedy not under Article 13, which prescribes the right to an effective remedy, but rather under Article 3.[40] Indeed, the ECtHR employed the same approach in cases claiming violation of procedural aspects of Article 3 on the basis of lack of effective investigation into allegations of ill-treatment.[41] This approach

35 *Waite v United Kingdom* (n.10) para.59; *Hussain v United Kingdom* (n.10) para.60.

36 *Winterwerp v Netherlands* (n.10).

37 *Singh v United Kingdom* App no 23389/94 (ECtHR, 21 February 1996) para.69; *Hussain v United Kingdom* (n.10) para.61; *Benjamin and Wilson v United Kingdom* App no 28212/95 (ECtHR, 26 September 2002).

38 *Vinter v United Kingdom* (2012) App no. 66069/09 and 130/10 and 3896/10 (ECtHR, 17 January 2012).

39 *Vinter v United Kingdom* [GC] (n.4).

40 ibid para.130.

41 Harris, O'Boyle and Warbrick (n.10) 573; *Bekos and Koutropoulos v Greece* ECHR 2005-XIII 1; *Corsacov v Moldova* App no 18944/02 (ECtHR 4 April 2016).

is, *inter alia*, explained by the fact that procedural limbs of substantive articles are considered as *lex specialis* in relation to Article 13, imposing stricter due process safeguards. Therefore, the latter, as a rule, is not considered when the former is involved.[42] It seems that the Grand Chamber took the same approach in *Vinter*, considering that the specific nature of the review of continued imprisonment required a more nuanced mechanism than the general right to effective remedy under Article 13. Indeed, this point is supported by the ECtHR's approach in *Kafkaris (2)*.[43] In this decision, the Court stated that the complaint under Article 13 as to the lack of effective national remedy in relation to review of life imprisonment 'is in substance the same as the one made under Article 3 and therefore raises no separate issue'.[44]

Perhaps adding a procedural limb to Article 3 was justified in cases where applicants were not only subjected to treatment prohibited in Article 3 by State agents but were also denied an effective investigation into the matter.[45] The Grand Chamber explained that adopting this approach was due to the fact that the Court was not able to come to a conclusion on whether or not the injuries of applicants were caused by government agents, because authorities failed effectively to investigate the complaints at the relevant time.[46] In this regard, the general right to effective remedy under Article 13 was deemed to be insufficient, because it did not offer strict enough due process safeguards necessary for the effective protection of the right under Article 3.[47]

By contrast, the above described circumstances are not present in cases where the lack of review of continued imprisonment constitutes a violation of Article 3. In these cases it is not possible to imagine a situation where the Court is unable to come to a conclusion on whether or not a violation of Article 3 occurred owing to lack of information substantiating either conclusion. Therefore, for effective protection of the right under Article 3 there is no need to rely on the procedural limb of this Article. In cases where the issue at stake is the availability of review of continued imprisonment, all facts are vivid, making it possible for the Court to come to a conclusion on the issue of whether a mechanism of review is available and whether it offers sufficient procedural safeguards for the protection of the right in question.

Furthermore, although the Court did not attempt to distinguish between substantive and procedural rights involved in these cases, such a distinction is possible and necessary. It should be recalled that the ECtHR found that life

42 Harris, O'Boyle and Warbrick (n.10) 570; *Bekos and Koutropoulos v Greece* (n.41); *Corsacov v Moldova* (n.41).

43 *Kafkaris v Cyprus (dec.)* (n.15).

44 ibid paras 64–65.

45 See e.g. *Assenov and Others v Bulgaria* ECHR 1998-VIII; *Dikme v Turkey* ECHR 2000-VIII 223; *Satik v Turkey* App no. 31866/96 (ECtHR, 10 October 2000); *Bekos and Koutropoulos v Greece* (n.41); *Corsacov v Moldova* (n.41).

46 See e.g. *Ilhan v Turkey* [GC] ECHR 2000-VII 267 paras 87–92; *Labita v Italy [GC]* ECHR 2000-IV 99 paras 131–136

47 Harris, O'Boyle and Warbrick (n.10) 570; *Labita v Italy* [GC] (n.46) para.131.

imprisonment which is *de jure* and *de facto* irreducible violates Article 3 at the time of its imposition.[48] The sentence will be deemed to be irreducible when the domestic law does not provide for the possibility of review of whether or not, on the balance of the aims which justified the imposition of the sentence, the continued imprisonment is still justified.[49] On its face, the lack of possibility of review is a classic example of a procedural violation. However, the analysis conducted by the Grand Chamber in the case of *Vinter*[50] demonstrates a clearly distinguishable substantive component.

The ECtHR found that a sentence of imprisonment which is grossly disproportionate to the aims of the punishment, which include punishment, deterrence, protection of the public and rehabilitation, would violate Article 3 of the Convention.[51] However, even the imposition of whole life imprisonment on an adult offender, especially for a serious crime such as murder, would not be deemed grossly disproportionate within the meaning of Article 3 if the offender would have both the possibility of review of the sentence and a prospect of release.[52] The Grand Chamber specified a number of reasons why there must be both a prospect of release and a possibility of review of a whole life sentence to make it compatible with Article 3.

First, the prisoner cannot be detained unless the aims of punishment are present. Although many of the aims will be present at the time of the imposition of the sentence, the balance between these aims is not necessarily static and may change in the course of the life sentence.[53] Furthermore, the sentence of imprisonment that offers no prospect of release and possibility of review deprives the offender of a possibility to atone for her/his offence: irrespective of any exceptional progress towards rehabilitation, the punishment remains fixed and unreviewable, offering the offender no hope of ever regaining her/his freedom. Depriving a person of hope of release destroys her/his human dignity.[54] Therefore, the Court found that irrespective of the seriousness of the crime all prisoners should be 'offered the possibility of rehabilitation and a prospect of release if that rehabilitation is achieved'.[55]

This reasoning demonstrates that the Article 3 requirement of review has a clearly distinguishable substantive and procedural components. The substantive component is a violation of human dignity which is a result of deprivation of the right to liberty without being given a hope of regaining it by rehabilitation. By stating that, irrespective of the seriousness of a crime, no human being can be deprived of the hope of ever regaining her/his freedom, the Court recognised the indispensable value of human beings and their capacity for personal development

48 *Vinter v United Kingdom* [GC] (n.4) paras 121–122.
49 ibid paras 111–112, 119.
50 ibid.
51 ibid para.102.
52 ibid paras 106,110.
53 ibid para.111.
54 ibid paras 112–113.
55 ibid para.114.

and change. Because every human being possesses a capacity for change, even the worst criminal should not be deprived of the hope of release. Secondly, she/he should be given the possibility of rehabilitation, and finally, after a passage of time, it should be checked whether continued imprisonment is still justified on the balance of the aims which justified its imposition. In this situation hope of release is organically connected to a procedure of review. In order to preserve the hope it should be clear to the offender at sentencing that there is a possibility of review and a prospect of release, i.e. the prisoner should see a 'light at the end of the tunnel'. In summary, the availability of review is required so as not to deprive the offender of hope, but the review itself is required to check whether the continued deprivation of liberty remains justified.

In this regard, in order not to violate the substantive right, i.e. not to deprive a human being of the hope of regaining her/his right to liberty, the grounds and rules of the review prescribed in national legislation must have a sufficient degree of clarity and certainty and must comply with the grounds set out in the ECtHR case law.[56] A violation of the substantive right would be present when the national law does not provide for a review which meets the above requirements. However, when these requirements are met, but the review mechanism does not provide sufficient procedural safeguards, it cannot be said that the offender was deprived of hope. Rather, in this case there is a problem with the effectiveness of the existing remedy.[57] As mentioned, the right to effective remedy before a national authority is prescribed under Article 13. However, because the review aims to check the lawfulness of continued deprivation of liberty, Article 5(4) of the ECHR comes into consideration rather than Article 13; Article 5(4), which is a *lex specialis* in relation to Article 13, specifically prescribes the right to review of the lawfulness of deprivation of liberty.[58]

In addition to the above arguments, the development of the case law in the Member States of the Council of Europe, and specifically in the UK, offers further evidence demonstrating that Article 5(4) shall apply to any type of early release from prison when the liberty interest of an individual is at stake. This includes the review of continued deprivation of liberty required by Article 3.

Applicability of Article 5(4 ECHR to revocation of licence of early released determinate prisoners

It is the longstanding position of the ECtHR that Article 5(4) review does not apply in fixed-term prison sentences even if national law establishes a right to be released early in such cases.[59] The ECtHR has confirmed this position by declaring manifestly ill-founded, and therefore inadmissible, an application submitted

56 See e.g. *Murray v the Netherlands* [GC] (n.31) paras 99–100.

57 See also *Kafkaris v Cyprus* [GC] (n.11) Concurring opinion of Judge Bratza.

58 Harris, O'Boyle and Warbrick (n.10) 570; *Bekos and Koutropoulos v Greece* (n.41); *Corsacov v Moldova* (n.41).

59 *Brown v UK (dec.)* (n.16).

by *Brown*.[60] This application concerned a fixed-term prisoner who was released early on licence and was subsequently recalled to prison following a technical breach of a licence condition.[61] The applicant complained *inter alia* that the decision to recall him to prison without a 'court-like review' of the lawfulness of his continued detention violated Article 5(4) of the ECHR because his recall was not for punitive but for preventative reasons.[62] The applicant further argued that his situation was comparable to that of indeterminate prisoners who are released on licence following a positive recommendation by a Parole Board after serving the punitive term of their sentence. According to the applicant, like these prisoners he was 'lawfully at large', and therefore the lawfulness of his continued detention should be reviewed in line with Article 5(4) if he was recalled to prison.[63]

The ECtHR, however, rejected the applicant's arguments, stating that there is a crucial distinction between the situation of determinate and indeterminate prisoners released on licence. For a determinate prisoner, the lawfulness of detention in Convention terms does not depend on the risk of reoffending, and the fact that he was released before he had fully served his sentence did not change the situation. Therefore, the lawfulness of his recall to prison and continued detention is also ensured by the original sentencing decision and does not require a review in terms of Article 5(4) of the ECHR.[64] In coming to its decision, the Fourth Chamber of the ECtHR referred to the judgments of the Court of Appeal of England on the same matter in the cases of *R.(West) v the Parole Board*[65] and R.(Smith) v the Parole Board as relevant domestic law.[66] In these cases the Court of Appeal rejected the claims of applicants that Article 5(4) applies to the recall of determinate prisoners.[67]

Although the ECtHR rejected the claim that Article 5(4) guarantees apply to the review of continued detention of determinate prisoners, this position no longer holds, at least in the case of the recall of determinate prisoners released on licence: the Court of Appeal decisions on which the ECtHR based its judgment have been reversed by the House of Lords.[68] In the conjoined appeals before the House of Lords, applicants West and Smith argued that Article 5(4) should apply to the procedure of recall of determinate prisoners released on licence, giving a right to oral hearing for the determination of the question whether or not the licence should be revoked, resulting in the return of the prisoner to prison. Before the House of Lords, the respondent Parole Board accepted that in resolving challenges of determinate prisoners against their release it has a public

60 ibid.
61 ibid.
62 ibid.
63 ibid.
64 ibid.
65 *R (West) v Parole Board* [2003] 70 Prison LR.
66 *R (Smith) v Parole Board* [2003] EWCA 1269.
67 *Brown v UK (dec.)* (n.16).
68 *R (Smith and West) v Parole Board* [2005] 1 WLR 350.

duty to act in a procedurally fair manner which will require an oral hearing when there is a dispute about the facts relevant to the determination of the challenge. However the Parole Board strongly resisted that Article 5(4) of the ECHR applies to such reviews or that an oral hearing is required by common law or by the ECHR.[69]

The House of Lords has unanimously rejected the respondent's submissions. In the opinion of Lord Bingham, with which the rest of the House agreed, the recall of determinate prisoners should be governed by the common law requirement of procedural fairness and Article 5(4) of the ECtHR which overlap in this context.[70] Lord Bingham stated in his conclusion that the content of the common law requirement of fairness depends on the interests at stake. In the recall of determinate prisoners the interests at stake are on the one hand the safety of the public and on the other the freedom of the prisoner, albeit 'conditional and to that extent precarious, freedom'.[71] He stated that the freedom in this case is similar to that enjoyed by indeterminate prisoners released on licence. Lord Bingham specified that determinate prisoners who have reached the point in their sentences when they can be released automatically 'have a statutory right to be free: a conditional right, but nonetheless a right, breach of which gives an enforceable right to redress'.[72]

With regard to the ECHR, Lord Bingham stated that it is plain that the initial sentencing decision in the case of determinate sentences satisfies the requirement of lawfulness for the whole sentence; nevertheless, the recall decision must comply with the requirements of Article 5(4).[73] The licence revocation decision should be made by an independent court-like body which can review the lawfulness of recall and order release if the recall is not lawful. Furthermore, as Lord Bingham put it:[74]

> the judicial review of the lawfulness of detention must be wide enough to bear on those conditions which, under the Convention, are essential for the lawful detention of a person in the situation of the particular detainee ... That means, for present purposes, that the Parole Board should be empowered (a) to examine whether circumstances have arisen sufficient in law to justify further detention of a determinate sentence prisoner released on licence and, if so, (b) to decide whether the protection of the public calls for the further detention of the individual detainee. The Parole Board is empowered to discharge those functions. Its review will in my opinion satisfy the requirements of article 5(4) provided it is conducted in a manner that meets the requirement of procedural fairness already discussed.

69 ibid 353.
70 ibid 365.
71 ibid 360.
72 ibid.
73 ibid 362.
74 ibid 363.

Although these requirements could not be interpreted to mean granting an oral hearing in all cases where a prisoner contests the recall, the oral hearings cannot be limited to cases where it is assumed that it may affect the outcome of the decision. According to Lord Bingham:[75]

> Even if important facts are not in dispute, they may be open to explanation or mitigation, or may lose some of their significance in the light of other new facts. While the board's task certainly is to assess risk, it may well be greatly assisted in discharging it (one way or the other) by exposure to the prisoner or the questioning of those who have dealt with him. It may often be very difficult to address effective representations without knowing the points which are troubling the decision-maker. The prisoner should have the benefit of a procedure which fairly reflects, on the facts of his particular case, the importance of what is at stake for him, as for society.

In the same case Lord Slynn went further, stating that he was persuaded by the counsel of the applicants that the determinate sentences where prisoners have a right to be released early consist of two parts. An early released determinate prisoner has only a conditional right to his freedom under licence ('more circumscribed in law and more precarious than the freedom enjoyed by the ordinary citizen'). However, the recall and the revocation of her/his licence is not empowered by the initial sentence of the trial judge, but is a new decision on deprivation of liberty. Therefore, the prisoner in such cases is 'entitled to take proceedings by which the lawfulness to that detention can be decided speedily by a court under article 5(4)'.[76]

Although the *West* judgment relates only to recall of determinate prisoners, the arguments relied upon by their Lordships are similarly applicable to all release decisions. Indeed, a trend can be observed in England towards extending the applicability of Article 5(4) to all release decisions.

Applicability of Article 5(4) to the early release of determinate prisoners

The Court of Appeal of England has extended the applicability of Article 5(4) to the conditional early release of determinate prisoners.[77] The most relevant decision in this group of cases is the decision of the Court of Appeal in the case of *Johnson*.[78] Johnson was a determinate prisoner who was eligible for release by the Parole Board after serving half of the sentence. However, the Secretary of State failed to supply the necessary documents to the Parole Board in a timely manner, as a result of which the Parole Board held a hearing and released the

75 ibid 362.

76 ibid 367.

77 *R (Johnson) v Secretary of State for the Home Department* [2007] 1 WLR 1990; *R (O'Connell) v Parole Board* [2007] 2591 EWHC (Admin).

78 *R (Johnson) v Secretary of State for the Home Department* (n.77).

prisoner some eight and a half months after he had become eligible for review of his continued imprisonment.[79]

In this case the prisoner argued that the delay of his parole hearing violated his rights under Article 5(4) of the ECHR, which required determination of the lawfulness of his detention speedily by a court and his release if the detention was not lawful. Relying on judicial decisions in cases of indeterminate prisoners, the applicant argued that, like the tariff part of indeterminate sentences, the part of the determinate sentence during which the prisoner is not eligible for parole is for the purpose of punishment. After this point, the Parole Board shall 'speedily' decide whether continued imprisonment is necessary for the protection of public. Although continued imprisonment after the prisoner becomes eligible for parole is still justified by the original sentence, Article 5 (4) applies to this latter part requiring speedy review of the lawfulness of continued detention.[80]

This argument is also supported by the legislative criteria which the Secretary of State is required to have regard to when giving directions to the Parole Board and the directions issued by the Secretary of State. According to the s.32 (6) of the Criminal Justice Act 1991, the criteria which 'the Secretary of State must have particular regard to are the need to protect the public from serious harm from offenders; and the desirability of preventing commission by them of further offences and of securing their rehabilitation'.[81] In addition, the directions given by the Secretary of State required the Parole Board, while making decisions on early release, to 'consider primarily the risk to the public of further offences being committed at the time when the prisoner would otherwise be in prison and whether any such risk is acceptable'.[82]

The Secretary of State, in line with the general position of the ECtHR and the decision of House of Lords in *Giles*,[83] argued that there is a fundamental difference between determinate and indeterminate sentences in terms of applicability of Article 5(4). In the former, the review of lawfulness of the whole sentence is incorporated in the original sentencing decision.[84]

However, the Court of Appeal distinguished the decision of the House of Lords in *Giles*,[85] pointing out that the prisoner in that case argued that he should have been considered for parole not at the halfway point of his sentence, but earlier: although for a determinate number of years, his sentence was longer than commensurate with the seriousness of his offence because the sentencing judge considered him dangerous.[86] Furthermore, the Court noted that in this case no issue related to the delay from the statutorily prescribed point of parole review

79 ibid 1993.

80 ibid 1994–1996.

81 Criminal Justice Act 1991.

82 *R (Johnson) v Secretary of State for the Home Department* (n.77) 1994.

83 *R (Giles) v Parole Board* [2004] 1 AC 1.

84 *R (Johnson) v Secretary of State for the Home Department* (n.77) 1996–1997.

85 *R (Giles) v Parole Board* (n.83).

86 *R (Johnson) v Secretary of State for the Home Department* (n.77) 1997.

was put before the House of Lords.[87] Deriving support from House of Lords' decisions in *West*,[88] and partially in *Clift*,[89] the Court of Appeal held that:

> So far as delay in an application coming before the Parole Board is concerned, or so far as there being delays from which it follows that different prisoners with determinate sentences are having their hearings before the Parole Board dealt with at different periods of time after their eligibility date, that same arbitrariness is present in the determinate sentence prisoner context. It is that arbitrariness which, in Convention terms, would, in my view, render the sentence unlawful, and falls within the ambit of article 5(4).

The above developments demonstrate that there is a clear tendency to extend the reach of the common law requirement of fairness and, indeed, Article 5(4) to all decisions where the freedom of an individual is at stake. However, the House of Lords reversed the Court of Appeal's judgment on the same matter in the case of *Black*,[90] putting this development on hold.

The issue before the court in this case was the compatibility of the s.35(1) of the Criminal Justice Act 1991 with Article 5(4) of the ECHR. At the time, unlike in the cases of indeterminate prisoners and determinate prisoners serving less than 15 years, s.35(1) preserved the power of the Secretary of State to refuse to follow the recommendation of the Parole Board to release on licence determinate prisoners serving 15 years or more, after such prisoners have served half of the sentence.[91] On the surface, the disputed issue in this case relates solely to the identity of the decision-maker. However, this issue and the issue of applicability of Article 5(4) of the ECHR in this context are dependent on whether the original aim of a determinate sentence is sufficient to justify the lawfulness of the whole sentence in cases when there is an applicable early release scheme.

In the case of *Black*,[92] the majority of the Lords agreed with the opinion of Lord Brown that, although with regard to a small fraction of prisoners preserving the power of the Secretary of State not to release a determinate prisoner following a positive recommendation of the Parole Board may be an anomaly, it is not incompatible with Article 5(4) of the ECHR. This conclusion of Lord Brown is based on his belief that for determinate sentences the original sentencing decision incorporates review of the lawfulness of deprivation of liberty for the whole term of imprisonment imposed by the court at the sentencing stage. Therefore Article 5(4) is in principle not applicable, irrespective of the fact that domestic law provides for the possibility of early release at some point before the whole sentence imposed by the sentencing court has been served.[93]

87 ibid 1998.
88 *R (Smith and West) v Parole Board* (n.68).
89 *R (Clift) v Secretary of State for the Home Department* [2007] 1 AC 484.
90 *R (Black) v Secretary of State for Justice* [2009] 2 WLR 282.
91 ibid 284.
92 ibid.
93 ibid.

In coming to this conclusion Lord Brown particularly relied on the case law of the ECtHR.[94] Furthermore, he relied on several dicta from the House of Lords' decisions on similar but not identical issues, such as passages from Lord Bingham's speech in *West*,[95] where he emphasises the essentially punitive purpose of determinate sentences, and in *Clift*,[96] where again Lord Bingham stressed that:

> a prisoner sentenced to a determinate term of years cannot seek to be released at any earlier time than that for which domestic law provides. During the currency of a lawful sentence, article 5(4) has no part to play.[97]

According to Lord Brown, holding Article 5(4) applicable to the stage of determinate sentences when a prisoner becomes eligible for early release in line with domestic law widens 'the reach of article 5(4) beyond its proper limits, certainly beyond its hitherto recognised scope'.[98] Furthermore, he argued that the fact that the UK has chosen to establish a mechanism of early release from a determinate sentence, specifying the precise point when such prisoners become eligible for release and giving directions to the Parole Board as to how to carry out this task, does not demonstrate that such review is for determination of the lawfulness of the continued imprisonment in line with Article 5(4). There would have been no violation of this Article and the ECHR as a whole even if the State had chosen to 'leave the entire question of release, whether absolutely or on licence, and whether throughout the sentence or only after a given period solely to the executive'.[99]

A distinction has to be made between early release from a determinate prison term and tariff-fixing and determining the length of post-tariff imprisonment in indeterminate sentences. The former is a component of the administrative implementation of sentences, engaging no different issues which can make continued detention unlawful, while during the latter review new issues (such as dangerousness) arise which could potentially affect the lawfulness of continued detention, thereby engaging Article 5(4). Finally, Lord Brown stated that even if he were prepared to accept that, notwithstanding its current position, in the light of new developments in domestic law the ECtHR might be prepared 'to extend the reach of article 5(4) to encompass also determinate sentence prisoners once they become eligible for parole' he would not do that ahead of the ECtHR.[100]

Although the opinion of Lord Brown is supported by the majority of the Lords and is the legitimate interpretation of the law at present, the dissenting opinion of Lord Phillips presents powerful arguments against it. This raises the possibility that the opinion of the majority was simply based on the belief that extending

94 ibid 305–307.
95 *R (Smith and West) v Parole Board* (n.68).
96 *R (Clift) v Secretary of State for the Home Department* (n.89).
97 *R (Black) v Secretary of State for Justice* (n.90) 310–311.
98 ibid 312.
99 ibid.
100 ibid 313.

the reach of Article 5(4) to the phase of determinate sentences when prisoners become eligible for parole should be left to the ECtHR itself.

In his dissenting opinion Lord Phillips referred to the gradual extension of Article 5(4), first to discretionary life sentences, then to mandatory detention of young persons convicted of murder, and subsequently to adults convicted of murder. These developments, according to Lord Phillips, demonstrate that it was not easy for the ECtHR 'to identify the true nature of the English sentencing regime that covers mandatory life sentences'.[101] Although Lord Phillips admitted that the ECtHR had not yet extended the reasoning of its judgments in life sentences to determinate sentences, 'it requires no great leap of reasoning to adopt the same approach' to the part of determinate sentences during which a prisoner is eligible to be released on licence.[102]

As an indication that the ECtHR is gradually moving in this direction, Lord Phillips pointed to some passages from relevant cases. In these cases the ECtHR, while holding applications inadmissible, put forward reasoning which demonstrates that the court could extend the reach of Article 5(4) to the part of determinate sentences during which prisoners are eligible for release. One such case is the ECtHR's decision in *Brown*,[103] where the ECtHR observed that the recall of a determinate prisoner released on licence must be 'in accordance with law'.[104] This recognition makes it 'hard to see why the court did not accept that article 5(4) applied to that issue'.[105] Lord Phillips also argued that the cases where the ECtHR discussed the issue of applicability of Article 5(4) to determinate sentences did not directly engage the issue of the possibility of early release on licence from a determinate sentence under the English sentencing regime.[106]

As further support for the argument that Article 5(4) is relevant to the part of a determinate sentence during which a prisoner is eligible for release on licence, Lord Phillips relied on particular aspects of the English sentencing regime. He stated:[107]

> It has long been part of the English sentencing regime that when a judge sentences a defendant to a determinate sentence of imprisonment there neither is nor is intended to be any expectation on the part of the sentencing judge or the prisoner that the prisoner will serve in prison the whole of the sentence imposed. It is part of our penal policy that, in normal circumstances, prisoners should be released on licence before they have served the full term of their sentences. This implication of our sentencing regime is something that the judge is required to explain when he imposes a sentence of imprisonment. Furthermore, when a judge imposes a determinate sentence he does

101 ibid 287.
102 ibid.
103 *Brown v UK (dec.)* (n.16).
104 ibid.
105 *R (Black) v Secretary of State for Justice* (n.90) 290.
106 ibid.
107 ibid.

> not do so on the basis that the seriousness of the offences requires that the prisoner should be detained for the full period of the sentence. Rather he has regard to the penal effect of the sentence as a whole, having regard to the fact that part of it is likely to be served under release on licence.

Finally, Lord Phillips also relied on the passages from House of Lords' decisions on similar issues where the reasoning of some of the Lords appears to support his line of argument; namely a passage from Lord Bingham's speech in *Giles*,[108] where Lord Bingham articulated that in the case of the applicant who was serving a longer than commensurate sentence, Article 5(4) does not apply because the decision to release the prisoner early does not depend on the executive. According to Lord Phillips, it appears that by saying that 'the sentence left nothing to the executive, since the Parole Board, whose duty is to consider release at the halfway stage of the sentence, is accepted to be a judicial body', Lord Bingham 'considered that the parole decision at the half way stage was one that was required to satisfy article 5(4)'.[109]

Furthermore, he quoted a passage from the speech of Lord Hope in the same decision where he stated that the basic rule set by the ECtHR regarding the non-applicability of Article 5(4) in cases of determinate sentences has been departed from in particular cases. These were those cases where the decision as to the length of the sentence was passed from the judiciary to the executive and there was a danger that, with the passage of time, the factors which informed the original sentence would change. According to Lord Phillips, this observation is perfectly applicable to *Black* where the decision regarding parole is controlled by the executive and 'depends essentially on whether the prisoner still poses a danger'.[110]

The next decision on which Lord Phillips relies to support his dissenting opinion with regard to the applicability of Article 5(4) to the early release of determinate prisoners is the House of Lords' judgment in *West*.[111] He refers to the passages from Lord Bingham's speech where the latter summarised principles upon which the sentencing, licensing and recall regimes are based. These principles demonstrate that early release provisions have the practical effect of relieving prison overcrowding. However, its penal justification is supervised reintegration from custody to freedom when, depending on the compliance of the prisoner with the imposed conditions, the question may arise whether to leave the prisoner on licence or to return her/him to prison.[112]

Furthermore, Lord Phillips relied on the opinion of Lord Slynn in the same case, where Lord Slynn articulated that where a domestic law provides a right to early release from determinate sentences, such sentences should be regarded as consisting of two parts: a custodial part and the licence part. In such cases the

108 *R (Giles) v Parole Board* (n.83).
109 *R (Black) v Secretary of State for Justice* (n.90) 293.
110 ibid.
111 *R (Smith and West) v Parole Board* (n.68).
112 *R (Black) v Secretary of State for Justice* (n.90) 294.

revocation of the licence and return of the individual to prison is a new decision of deprivation of liberty which is not covered by the sentencing decision of the trial judge and should be subject to procedures compliant with Article 5(4).[113]

According to Lord Phillips, theses passages are equally relevant to the role of Parole Boards when considering initial release of determinate prisoners. They demonstrate that even for a determinate sentence, where the domestic sentencing regime establishes the possibility of early release the decision to release on parole is informed by factors such as risk of reoffending and successful reintegration into society. These factors are susceptible to change, which means that even for such sentences the aim of retribution does not justify the whole length of the sentence imposed by the sentencing court.[114]

Finally, to support his dissenting opinion Lord Phillips relies on passages from the decision of House of Lords in *Clift*,[115] where the release of the applicant on parole was subject to the same legislative provision as in the case under consideration. However, in *Clift* the prisoner did not directly argue that the respective provision in domestic law is in conflict with Article 5(4) of the ECHR. Rather, it was argued that preserving the power of the Secretary of State to refuse the release of a prisoner following a positive recommendation from the Parole Board only with regard to determinate prisoners sentenced to 15 years or more is treatment contrary to Article 14 of the ECHR. This claim was rejected because the House of Lords found that the status of the prisoner sentenced to a term of 15 or more years was not a characteristic protected under Article 14. However, it was recognised that Article 5(4) applies to parole release decisions, being capable of bringing Article 14 into play.[116]

According to Lord Phillips, the passages from the speech of Lord Bingham in *Clift* support his view in relation to applicability of Article 5. Lord Bingham stated:[117]

> ... I would agree that the sentences passed on the respective appellants satisfied article 5(1)(a) and provided lawful authority for the detention of the appellants until such time as, under domestic law, their detention became unlawful. Giles [2004] 1 AC 1 established that a prisoner sentenced to a determinate term of years cannot seek to be released at any earlier time than that for which domestic law provides. During the currency of a lawful sentence, article 5(4) has no part to play. But the Secretary of State's argument founders, in my opinion, on a failure to recognise both the importance, in our system, of the statutory rules providing for early release and the close relationship between those rules and the core value which article 5 exists to protect.

113 ibid 295.

114 ibid 294–295.

115 *R (Clift) v Secretary of State for the Home Department* (n.89).

116 *R (Black) v Secretary of State for Justice* (n.90) 295.

117 *R (Clift) v Secretary of State for the Home Department* (n.89) 16–18.

> The Convention does not require member states to establish a scheme for early release of those sentenced to imprisonment. Prisoners may, consistently with the Convention, be required to serve every day of the sentence passed by the judge, or be detained until a predetermined period or proportion of the sentence has been served, if that is what domestic law provides. But this is not what the law of England and Wales provided, in respect of long-term determinate prisoners, at the times relevant to these appeals. That law provided for a time at which (subject to additional days of custody imposed for disciplinary breaches) a prisoner must, as a matter of right, be released, and an earlier time at which he might be released if it was judged safe to release him but at which he need not be released if it was not so judged.
>
> A number of grounds (economy and the need to relieve overcrowding in prisons) have doubtless been relied on when introducing pre-release schemes from determinate sentences such as those under consideration here. But one such consideration is recognition that neither the public interest nor the interest of the offender is well served by continuing to detain a prisoner until the end of his publicly pronounced sentence; that in some cases those interests will be best served by releasing the prisoner at the earlier, discretionary, stage; and that in those cases prisoners should regain their freedom (even if subject to restrictions) because there is judged to be no continuing interest in depriving them of it. I accordingly find that the right to seek early release, where domestic law provides for such a right, is clearly within the ambit of article 5 ...

Based on the above discussed materials, Lord Phillips concluded that, in England and Wales in the case of determinate prisoners who are entitled to release at mid-sentence point, Article 5(1) no longer justifies continued imprisonment and prisoners can challenge the lawfulness of continued imprisonment in line with Article 5(4). As to the case of determinate prisoners whose release is subject to the Parole Board's discretion, they are entitled to release provided they satisfy the criteria for release specified in law. Therefore 'article 5(4) entitles them to judicial determination of that question and timely consideration by the Parole Board will satisfy the requirements of Article 5(4)'.[118]

The dissenting opinion of Lord Phillips was a continuation of the approach of the Court of Appeal discussed above.[119] The fact that, contrary to the decision of the ECtHR, the House of Lords in the case of *Smith and West*[120] recognised that Article 5(4) is applicable to recalled determinate prisoners is very supportive of Lord Phillips's observations. As mentioned, Lord Phillips expressed the opinion that the ECtHR might have difficulties in identifying 'the true nature

118 *R (Black) v Secretary of State for Justice* (n.90) 296.

119 *R (Johnson) v Secretary of State for the Home Department* (n.77); *R (O'Connell) v Parole Board* (n.77).

120 *R (Smith and West) v Parole Board* (n.68).

of the English sentencing regime'.[121] Moreover, 'no great leap of reasoning' was required to extend the approach of ECtHR in relation to life sentences to the part of determinate sentences during which a prisoner is eligible to be released on licence.[122]

Although the House of Lords' decision in *Smith and West*[123] relates to determinate prisoners who were recalled to prison for violation of licence conditions after being released on licence, both the decision of the Court of Appeal in the case of Johnson[124] and the dissenting opinion of Lord Phillips in the case of Black[125] build a very convincing analogy between the initial decision to release on parole a determinate prisoner and determinate prisoners who were recalled to prison. Indeed, the arguments put forward by Lord Phillips in his dissenting opinion persuasively rebut the grounds relied upon by the majority of the House of Lords in arguing that Article 5(4) does not apply to early release decisions in the case of determinate prisoners. The majority also indicated that they might have been prepared to accept the arguments of Lord Phillips, but did not wish to extend the reach of Article 5(4) in domestic law ahead of the ECtHR.[126]

Furthermore, the same rationale can be observed in a more recent case decided by the UK Supreme Court.[127] The Supreme Court strongly reaffirmed that the common law requirement of fairness will in most cases require an oral hearing. Moreover, in the context of recall of early released determinate prisoners and the discretionary release of indeterminate prisoners, this requirement overlaps with Article 5(4) of the ECHR.[128] According to the Court, the applicability of the fairness requirement and consequently Article 5(4) does not depend on the likelihood of achieving a different decision from the one made without following these requirements. Apart from the outcome of the procedure, there are other reasons that necessitate following the requirements of fairness. The first reason is the sense of justice. According to the Court, respect for human dignity requires:[129]

> a procedure which pays due respect to persons whose rights are significantly affected by decisions taken in the exercise of administrative or judicial functions. Respect entails that such persons ought to be able to participate in the procedure by which the decision is made, provided they have something to say which is relevant to the decision to be taken.

The second reason is the rule of law which requires those charged with making decisions in relation to matters of fundamental importance to the individual con-

121 *R (Black) v Secretary of State for Justice* (n.90) 287.
122 ibid.
123 *R (Smith and West) v Parole Board* (n.68).
124 *R (Johnson) v Secretary of State for the Home Department* (n.77).
125 *R (Black) v Secretary of State for Justice* (n.90).
126 ibid 313.
127 *Osborn v Parole Board* [2014] AC 1115.
128 ibid 1132.
129 ibid 1150.

cerned and to society to employ a fair decision-making process, including listening to those individuals 'who have something relevant to say'.[130] Such procedure promotes 'congruence between the actions of decision-makers and the law which should govern their actions'.[131] Finally, the Supreme Court held that the cost of the procedure cannot override the requirement of fairness, because even from the prudential perspective 'procedures which involve an immediate cost but contribute to better decision-making are in reality less costly than they may appear'.[132]

Indeed, the rationale for arguing that Article 5(4) is applicable to life sentences imposed exclusively for punitive purposes, the early release and the recall of determinate prisoners can similarly be extended to the review of continued imprisonment of prisoners whose sentences are longer than their actuarial life expectancy and those who are terminally or otherwise seriously ill.

Conclusion

The main ground of argument in favour of extending the right to review to the three categories of prisoners, i.e. prisoners who are likely to die in custody because of their age, those who are likely to die because of fatal illness and those who suffer from a non-terminal serious illnesses, is the common aim of the review in all three situations. In all three situations the review aims to prevent punishing the offender disproportionately more severely than is justified by the aims of punishment. However, the sources, i.e. old age and illness that may affect the severity of punishment, play out slightly differently in each situation. Therefore, the review should be set in such a way as to fit these differences.

The differences relate to the timing of the review as well as the substantive issues in the light of which the aims of punishment should be re-evaluated. In this regard the review of continued imprisonment of elderly and seriously ill is also different from the review of whole life imprisonment. However, in terms of the identity of the decision-maker and procedural guarantees applicable to the review mechanism there should be no differences. As demonstrated, Article 5(4) guarantees should equally apply to the review of the lawfulness of continued imprisonment of whole lifers, elderly and seriously ill prisoners. The ECtHR has refused to recognise this and has articulated some procedural requirements which it attributed to Article 3 itself. However, this approach weakens the protection of the right to liberty and consequently human dignity. Moreover, the arguments which are advanced to support this approach could not hold the ground.

It is implicit in the decisions of the ECtHR that the refusal to apply Article 5(4) to the review of whole life imprisonment originates from the treatment of the Article 3 requirement of review as a purely procedural violation. However, there is a clearly distinguishable substantive component to the requirement of review. Indeed, it is explicit that the review aims to prevent excessive deprivation

130 ibid.
131 ibid.
132 ibid 1151.

of liberty. When there is no procedure to review a whole life sentence, a human being is deprived of the hope of ever regaining her/his freedom, which is *per se* degrading. However, when such a procedure is in place, but does not afford sufficient guarantees to enable the prisoner to effectively challenge the lawfulness of her/his continued deprivation of liberty, the issue at stake is the effectiveness of the available remedy which is guaranteed by Article 13. In such a situation Article 5(4) should apply, because it specifically prescribes guarantees for challenging the lawfulness of the deprivation of the right to liberty and is a *lex specialis* to a more general right to effective remedy prescribed under Article 13.[133]

Furthermore, the ECtHR refused to apply Article 5(4) to the review of whole life imprisonment, arguing that in the case of a whole life sentence the lawfulness of the deprivation of liberty for the whole duration of the sentence is incorporated into the original sentencing decision, because the sentence is imposed for the purpose of punishment, which is a static aim. However, this claim is in conflict with the Court's own rationale of recognising that Article 3 requires review of whole life sentences.[134] Similarly, as was demonstrated in case of elderly prisoners who are likely to die in custody before serving the mandatory custodial part of their sentence and those who are seriously ill, the balance between the purposes of punishment may shift earlier than was intended at the imposition of the sentence.

The applicability of Article 5(4) to the review of whole life sentences, as well as the review on the ground of old age and serious illness, is also supported by development of the law in this area in the UK, one of the Member States of the Council of Europe. The highest courts in this jurisdiction argued that the fundamental interests which are at stake when the lawfulness of continued detention is reviewed and the principle of the rule of law require such review to meet the common law fairness requirement which in this context overlaps with the requirements of Article 5(4).[135]

Article 3 of the ECHR requires the release of a prisoner based on the ground of likelihood of death in custody due to actuarial or clinical life expectancy if the purposes that justified the sentence at the imposition do not justify continued imprisonment in the light of the likelihood of death. A review based on the likelihood of death is required because continued imprisonment may no longer be justified by the purposes of punishment, i.e. not be in the public interest and, indeed, may become an affront to the prisoner's rights. This indicates that the link between the original sentencing decision and the continued deprivation of liberty in the light of the impact of the sentence on the individual may be broken.

Furthermore, there are fundamental interests at stake in such a review: human dignity, which may be violated through grossly disproportionate deprivation of liberty, and the interests of justice, including public safety. Respect for human

133 Harris, O'Boyle and Warbrick (n.10) 570; *Bekos and Koutropoulos v Greece* (n.41); *Corsacov v Moldova* (n.41).

134 *Vinter v United Kingdom* [GC] (n 4) paras 110–115.

135 *Osborn v Parole Board* (n.127).

dignity and the rule of law requires procedures compatible with Article 5(4) of the ECHR to determine whether the purposes of punishment that justified imposition of a particular sentence on the prisoner justify her/his continued detention in the light of the likelihood of the prisoner's death in custody.

Similarly, the review of the continued deprivation of liberty in cases of seriously ill detainees is necessitated by concern for the protection of the physical and/or psychological wellbeing of detainees. The wellbeing of such detainees may be compromised beyond what is justified by the practical demands of the penal system and the nature of judicial punishment because of the impact of an otherwise appropriate punishment on the detainee due to her/his illness. The interest at stake in this case is also the detainee's human dignity on the one hand and the interests of justice such as retribution, deterrence, incapacitation and/or rehabilitation on the other. Thus, the review of continued deprivation of liberty seeks to find the solution which will reconcile the protection of the health and wellbeing of prisoners with the legitimate requirements of detention. In this case, Article 3 will require the release of the detainee, if it is the only way of protecting human dignity. If the deprivation of liberty continues regardless of the fact that in a particular situation release is the only way to comply with Article 3 of the ECHR, such detention will amount to degrading or inhuman punishment/treatment.

It is clear that serious illness constitutes a significant change in the situation of the prisoner and the purposes which justified imposition of a particular custodial term might not justify its continuation. As in the situations discussed above, the fundamental nature of the interest at stake, i.e. human dignity and respect for the rule of law, will require procedures compatible with Article 5(4) of the ECHR to determine whether release from custody is the only way to reconcile the protection of the health and wellbeing of prisoners with the legitimate requirements of detention.

4 Compliance with substantive and procedural requirements of right to review under Article 3 ECHR: the case of the elderly and seriously ill

Abstract

The right to review will be protected under the law if procedures meeting the requirements of the review are available in the domestic laws of Contracting Parties of the European Convention of Human Rights. This chapter discusses the development of the law of the European Convention of Human Rights relating to compliance of domestic laws with the requirement of review under Article 3. It conducts a detailed analysis of the English compassionate release law which was recognised as a procedure meeting the mentioned requirement of Article 3. Analysis demonstrates that loose executive powers such as this are not capable of meeting the requirements of the right to review of continued imprisonment either in whole life cases or on grounds of old age and serious illness. When the power to decide over the liberty of an individual is vested in the executive which at the same time is responsible for administration of the punishment, the fundamental principle of separation of powers which provides a necessary guarantee against abuse of powers is violated. This deficiency cannot be remedied even by the most rigorous judicial review, because the requirements of Article 5(4) cannot be met through aggregate remedies.

Compatibility of executive powers with requirement of review under Article 3

In *Kafkaris v Cyprus (1)* the Grand Chamber of the European Court of Human Rights (ECtHR) found that life imprisonment of the applicant was not in violation of Article 3 of the European Convention on Human Rights (ECHR) because the presidential power of pardon offered a possibility of release.[1] The Court agreed that the prospect of release for prisoners serving life sentences was limited, because the only possibility for adjustment of life sentences was the presidential power of pardon. Moreover, this power gave unfettered discretion to the President: there were no published criteria or procedures governing the exercise of pardon, no obligation to give reasons for refusing applications, and no possibility to challenge refusal in the courts. Despite these shortcomings of the power

1 *Kafkaris v Cyprus* [GC] ECHR 2008-I 223 paras 103–108.

of pardon, the Court did not find that the applicant had no possibility of release. According to the Court it was clear that life sentences in Cyprus were both *de jure* and *de facto* reducible. There was a legal procedure for review of life sentences. Moreover, the fact that in the past life prisoners were pardoned by the President demonstrated that this power ensured the *de facto* reducibility of life sentences.[2]

Five dissenting judges disagreed with the finding of the Grand Chamber that there was no violation of Article 3 in this case. According to dissenters it was true that the mere limited opportunity of release could not be said to deprive a life prisoner of a prospect of release. However, in order to meet the requirement of reducibility under Article 3 life sentence must also be *de facto* reducible which implies a 'genuine possibility of release'. In the opinion of the dissenting judges the lack of safeguards against arbitrariness prevented the power of pardon from providing a genuine possibility of release. Moreover, various instruments of the Council of Europe (CoE) and other international law sources expressed clear support for the introduction of a parole mechanism with adequate procedural safeguards for the adjustment of long-term and life sentences.[3]

In contrast to the dissenting judges, Judge Bratza took a different approach in his concurring opinion. He agreed with the majority that in the particular case there was no violation of Article 3, because it could not be said that the applicant was deprived of a hope of release; both law and practice give life sentence prisoners the hope of one day regaining their freedom. According to Judge Bratza, the fact that the available mechanism of release did not contain the necessary safeguards against arbitrariness has no significance for the hope of release within the meaning of Article 3. Rather, this situation raises the issue of violation of Article 5(4) of the ECHR.

To support his position Judge Bratza drew an analogy with the ECtHR's judgments in cases of life sentences with minimum terms where the minimum term represents the punishment element of the life sentence. In such cases the Court found that the sentencing decision of the court ensured the lawfulness of deprivation of liberty only for the tariff period, because after the expiry of the tariff the continued imprisonment depends on elements of dangerousness and risk, which are factors prone to change with the passage of time. Therefore, after the expiry of the tariff (minimum term) new issues of the lawfulness of continued imprisonment arise which require review by a body satisfying the requirements of Article 5(4). Judge Bratza accepted that this finding related to life sentences where a tariff was set for the purpose of punishment and deterrence, after which the prisoner can be detained for as long as she/he poses a danger to society. However, he argued that having in place any type of conditional release for whole life prisoners means that the State implicitly accepts that the factors which justified imposition of the sentence are prone to change with the passing of time. Therefore, in the case of such prisoners a conditional release must depend on:[4]

2 ibid para.103.

3 ibid, per Tulkens, Cabral Barreto, Fura-Sandström, Spielmann and Jebens.

4 ibid, per Bratza.

> an assessment of whether the term of imprisonment already served satisfies the necessary element of punishment for the particular offence and, if so, whether the life prisoner poses a continuing danger to society.

Judge Bratza did not elaborate whether in the case of *Kafkaris* the lack of adequate safeguards amounted to a violation of Article 5(4): the Grand Chamber itself refused to consider this issue on the ground that the complaint under this Article was raised after the admissibility decision of the Court. Therefore, the Court found that this complaint was outside of the scope of the case under consideration.[5]

The issue of compatibility of executive powers with the requirement in Article 3 of review and a prospect of release was further debated by the ECtHR in cases coming before the Court after *Kafkaris*. In the case of *Vinter v United Kingdom* the Chamber of the Court expressed doubts whether the Secretary of State's power of compassionate release met the *de facto* reducibility requirement for whole life sentences. However, the Chamber did not find a violation of Article 3, because in its opinion it could not be said that in the case of any of the applicants the continued imprisonment could no longer be justified on any legitimate penological grounds.[6]

By contrast, in the same case the Grand Chamber found that the Secretary of State's statutory power of compassionate release did not meet Article 3 right to review of continued imprisonment of whole life prisoners. The Court did not accept the arguments of the Government that if it could be demonstrated that none of the aims of punishment justifies the continued imprisonment in a *de jure* whole life case, compassionate release exercised in compliance with the ECHR and amenable to judicial review would meet Article 3 review requirements.[7]

The reason for finding that the power of compassionate release in the case of whole life prisoners would not meet the Article 3 requirement for review was the lack of clarity in the domestic law as to applicability of this power to *de jure* whole life prisoners. In the case of *Bibber*,[8] the English Court of Appeal found that this provision could be interpreted in the light of the Human Rights Act 1998 (HRA 1998) to meet the Article 3 requirement to offer a release avenue to whole life prisoners whose continued imprisonment is no longer justified by the aims of punishment. However, the written policy of the Secretary of State was not altered following this judgment.[9] The current policy as set out in the relevant Prison Service Orders (PSOs) allows compassionate release of terminally ill, bedridden or similarly incapacitated prisoners only if they can meet an additional list of very restrictive criteria.[10]

5 ibid para.124.

6 *Vinter and others v the United Kingdom* (2012) App no. 66069/09 and 130/10 and 3896/10 (ECtHR, 17 January 2012) para.95.

7 *Vinter v United Kingdom* [GC] ECHR 2013-III 317 para.130.

8 *R v Bieber* [2009] 1 WLR 223 (Court of Appeal).

9 *Vinter v United Kingdom* [GC] (n.7) para.126.

10 ibid paras 127–128.

Furthermore, Prison Service Instruction (PSI) 4700[11] does not reflect the possibility of being interpreted in the light of the HRA 1998 as also applying to whole life prisoners who would like to seek release on the basis that their continued imprisonment is no longer justified. Therefore, it is not clear whether, in considering an application for compassionate release from a whole life prisoner who does not meet the criteria of the current restrictive policy, the Secretary of State would review the application in line with his published policy or as interpreted by the Court of Appeal in the case of *Bieber*. The Grand Chamber stated that the refusal to release such a prisoner would be open to judicial review:[12]

> … and it could well be that, in the course of such proceedings, the legal position would come to be clarified, for example by the withdrawal and replacement of the Prison Service Order by the Secretary of State or its quashing by the courts. However, such possibilities are not sufficient to remedy the lack of clarity that exists at present as to the state of the applicable domestic law governing possible exceptional release of whole life prisoners.

The Grand Chamber found a violation of Article 3 in the particular case. However, it acknowledged that the compassionate release provision would have met the Article 3 requirement of review in the case of whole life prisoners if the relevant PSI reflected the state of English law in regard to the possibility of release of whole lifers as it was interpreted by the Court of Appeal in *Bieber*.[13]

In his concurring opinion in the Grand Chamber's judgment in the case of *Vinter*, Judge Mahoney highlighted that the Grand Chamber's reason for finding that the power of compassionate release did not meet the reducibility requirement of Article 3 of the ECHR was a lack of clarity in the respective domestic law. He argued that there was no indication in the respective policy document that compassionate release could be interpreted in the light of HRA 1998 as requiring reducibility of the sentence within the meaning of Article 3. He accepted that 'as a matter of English law' the policy document would be overridden by the Secretary of State's obligation to comply with the ECHR. However, the failure to reflect this possibility in the policy document in force would give those affected only a partial picture of the grounds on which the Secretary of State's exceptional power of release could be exercised.[14]

Furthermore, Judge Mahoney suggested that in order to comply with the judgment the respondent government could simply amend the text of the respective PSI. No violation of Article 3 will be found if the text of the PSI is transparent in regard to the possibility of release of whole life prisoners in cases when

11 Prison Service Order 4700 Indeterminate Sentence Manual 2006, Chapter 12. Indeterminate sentence prisoners compassionate release on medical grounds (Her Majesty's Prison Service).

12 ibid para.129.

13 ibid para.125.

14 ibid, per Mahoney.

their continued imprisonment ceases to be justified by the legitimate aims of punishment. However, another option for complying with the judgment is to put in place a dedicated mechanism 'providing for a review of life sentences after a set period, usually after twenty-five years' imprisonment, with further periodic reviews thereafter'.[15]

The developments in the case law regarding reducibility of whole life sentences demonstrate that in order to comply with its obligations under the ECHR the UK Government did not have to take either of the options suggested by Judge Mahoney. On the contrary, the specially constituted panel of the Court of Appeal in the case of *R v McLoughlin*[16] disagreed with the finding of the Grand Chamber, that whole life sentences in England and Wales are irreducible and violate Article 3 of the ECHR.[17] According to the Court of Appeal, the Grand Chamber erred in concluding that the domestic law of England was not sufficiently clear in regard to the prospect of reducibility of whole life orders. The fact that after the Court of Appeal decision in *Bieber*[18] the policy of compassionate release set out in the respective PSI was not revised has no legal consequence. The Court of Appeal concluded that the domestic law is sufficiently clear, requiring the Secretary of State to disregard the policy document and to exercise his power of compassionate release 'in a manner compatible with principles of domestic administrative law and with Article 3'.[19]

The Court of Appeal went further to restate the passages from the case of *Bieber*[20] clarifying the duty of the Secretary of State in regard to the interpretation of the compassionate release law in such a way as to offer a prospect of release to whole life prisoners.[21] According to the Court, if a prisoner demonstrates that, since imposition of her/his whole life sentence, exceptional circumstances justify her/his release on compassionate grounds, the Secretary of State must consider whether such exceptional circumstances indeed justify this.

Moreover, the Secretary of State cannot exercise his discretion by refusing to consider any exceptional circumstance other than those mentioned in the respective policy document. The Secretary of State was bound to read the term 'compassionate release' in a manner compatible with Article 3 and must reason her/his decisions with the references to the circumstances of individual cases. Such decisions of the Secretary of State are subject to judicial review. The Court of Appeal accepted that 'circumstances can and do change in exceptional cases'.[22] However, it refused to specify the exceptional circumstances which would render a whole life sentence no longer justified, because it is difficult to do this in

15 ibid, per Mahoney.
16 *AG Reference (No 69 of 2013) (Ian McLoughlin)* [2014] EWCA Crim 188.
17 *Vinter v United Kingdom* [GC] (n.7).
18 *R v Bieber* (n.8).
19 ibid para.29.
20 ibid.
21 *AG Reference (No 69 of 2013) (Ian McLoughlin)* (n.16) paras 31–34.
22 ibid para.36.

advance, 'given that the heinous nature of the original crime justly required punishment by imprisonment'.[23]

The decision of the specially constituted panel of the Court of Appeal did not in fact provide any new information on the state of English law which was not available to the Grand Chamber at the time of its decision in the case of *Vinter*.[24] It is true that the Grand Chamber stated that despite the decision of the Court of Appeal in *Bieber*[25] the restrictive policy of compassionate release remains in force.[26] Therefore, it was not clear whether, in considering an application for release by a whole life prisoner, the Secretary of State would follow his/her restrictive policy or the decision of the Court of Appeal in *Bieber*.[27] However, other passages clearly demonstrate that the Grand Chamber was perfectly aware that as a matter of English law the Secretary of State would be obliged to apply his power of compassionate release in line with ECHR law interpreting this provision in a manner similar to the Court of Appeal in *Bieber*.[28]

Furthermore, the ECtHR was aware that, if the Secretary of State refused to act in this way, she/he would be obliged to give reasons for her/his decision which would be amenable to judicial review during which the restrictive policy could be quashed or withdrawn by the Secretary of State.[29] When the Grand Chamber stated that English law was not sufficiently clear regarding reducibility of whole life sentences, the Court did not mean that it was not clear for the Court itself. Rather, it meant that the law was not sufficiently transparent for the affected prisoners and prison authorities because the nuances of English law were not reflected in the policy document addressed to them.[30]

Despite the fact that the *McLoughlin* judgment did not change the state of English law that existed before Grand Chamber's decision in *Vinter*, in the subsequent case both the Fourth Chamber and the Grand Chamber of the ECtHR accepted that English law in regard to reducibility of whole life sentences had been clarified. They found that, in the light of the decision in *McLoughlin*, the compassionate release provision could be accepted as offering a prospect of release to whole life prisoners and was compatible with Article 3.[31] Moreover, the Grand Chamber found that English compassionate release law also met procedural guarantees applicable to the review of whole life sentences which were articulated by the ECtHR in the cases that came before the Court after the *Vinter* judgment.[32]

23 ibid.
24 *Vinter v United Kingdom* [GC] (n.7).
25 *R v Bieber* (n.8).
26 *Vinter v United Kingdom* [GC] (n.7) para.126.
27 ibid para.129.
28 ibid para.125.
29 ibid para.129.
30 ibid para.128.
31 *Hutchinson v United Kingdom* App no 57592/08 (ECtHR, 3 February 2015); *Hutchinson v United Kingdom* [GC] App no 57592/08 (ECtHR, 17 January 2017).
32 *Hutchinson v United Kingdom* [GC] (n.31) para.38–69.

It should be highlighted that the finding in the case of *Vinter*, that the power of compassionate release does not meet the requirement of review under Article 3, was based on the fact that the relevant policy document restricted the possibility of compassionate release only to terminally ill, bedridden or similarly incapacitated prisoners.[33] This appears to suggest that, at least in the case of seriously ill prisoners, the power of compassionate release might meet the Article 3 requirement for review: similar grounds are included in the relevant PSOs as grounds based on which a prisoner may be released.[34] The Grant Chamber explicitly acknowledged that the compassionate release provision would have met the Article 3 requirement of review in the case of whole life prisoners if the relevant PSO reflected the state of English law in regard to the possibility of release of whole lifers as interpreted by the Court of Appeal in *Bieber*.[35]

This acknowledgment by the Grand Chamber is based solely on the reasoning of the Court of Appeal on the possibility of interpreting the power of compassionate release in line with Article 3 of the ECHR. The Grand Chamber itself did not assess the power of compassionate release together with its legal corollaries in light of the Article 3 right to review of the continued imprisonment of whole lifers. However, even if this position of the Grand Chamber is accepted as granted, it can be attributed only to the possibility of compliance of compassionate release with substantive requirements of the right to review under Article 3. As the preceding chapters have demonstrated, the procedural guarantees of Article 5(4) are applicable to the Article 3 right to review. Therefore, it is necessary to conduct a detailed analysis of the power of compassionate release and its legal corollaries in order to assess whether this power meets the substantive and procedural requirements of Article 3 review on the grounds of old age and serious illness.

Compassionate release: law, policy and practice

Parliament has established the power of compassionate release applicable to determinate and indeterminate prisoners, including all types of lifers, in different statutes. The provision relating to determinate prisoners, to whom the Criminal Justice Act 1991 applies, is prescribed under s.36 of this statute. This provision applies to both short-term and long-term prisoners sentenced under this Act. Although this provision has been partially repealed and replaced by s.248 of the Criminal Justice Act 2003,[36] it continues to apply to prisoners who were sentenced under the terms of the Criminal Justice Act 1991.[37] According to this law:[38]

33 *Vinter v United Kingdom* [GC] (n.7) paras 127–128.

34 Prison Service Order 4700 Indeterminate Sentence Manual 2006, Chapter 12. Indeterminate sentence prisoners compassionate release on medical grounds (Her Majesty's Prison Service); Prison Service Order 6000 31 March 2005, PSO 6000 (Her Majesty's Prison Service).

35 *Vinter v United Kingdom* [GC] (n.7) para.125.

36 Criminal Justice Act 2003.

37 Criminal Justice Act 1991, see explanatory notes to s.36.

38 ibid, s.36.

> (1) The Secretary of State may at any time release a short-term or long-term prisoner on licence if he is satisfied that exceptional circumstances exist which justify the prisoner's release on compassionate grounds.
> (2) Before releasing a long-term prisoner under subsection (1) above, the Secretary of State must consult the Board, unless the circumstances are such as to render such consultation impracticable.

The difference between the cited law and s.248 of the Criminal Justice Act 2003 is that the latter does not make any distinction between short-term and long-term prisoners in relation to compassionate release. Furthermore, it does not oblige the Secretary of State to consult the Parole Board before releasing a prisoner to whom this provision applies.[39]

The power of compassionate release in relation to those who were sentenced to an indeterminate prison term, including all types of life sentences, is prescribed in the Crime (Sentences) Act 1997.[40] This power is identical to that related to long-term determinate prisoners falling under the jurisdiction of the Criminal Justice Act 1991. It means that in contrast to short-term prisoners subject to the Criminal Justice Act 1991 and prisoners subject to the Criminal Justice Act 2003, the Secretary of State is required to consult the Parole Board before releasing an indeterminate prisoner unless it is impracticable.[41]

The policy of compassionate release: substantive and procedural criteria

The Secretary of State's policy of compassionate release related to determinate and indeterminate prisoners can be found respectively in the Prison Service Order (PSO) 6000[42] and PSI 4700.[43] PSOs and PSIs do not have the status of statutory instruments in the English legal order, but are non-statutory directives which are declarations of the Secretary of State's policy in the respective area.[44]

According to PSO 6000, any determinate prisoner who meets eligibility criteria and has not yet reached her/his release date, be it automatic or conditional, may apply for early release on compassionate grounds irrespective of the length of sentence remaining. In the case of prisoners who have reached their parole eligibility date, compassionate circumstances are considered as part of the general parole process and can be a ground for expediting the process.[45]

According to chapter 12 of PSO 6000, the medical condition or tragic family circumstances of the prisoner are the only possible grounds for compassionate

39 Criminal Justice Act 2003, s.248.
40 Crime (Sentences) Act 1997, s.30.
41 ibid.
42 Prison Service Order 6000 (n.34) 12.
43 Prison Service Order 4700 Indeterminate Sentence Manual (n.34).
44 Stephen Livingstone, Tim Owen and Alison MacDonald, *Prison law* (4th edn, Oxford University Press 2008) 25.
45 Prison Service Order 6000 (n.34) 12.

release. The PSO specifies three types of medical condition which render a prisoner eligible to be considered for compassionate release.

The first is terminal illness where death is likely to occur soon. Although no imperative life expectancy period is specified, the PSO recommends three months as an appropriate period.[46] The second group of medical conditions meriting consideration of compassionate release are those by which a prisoner is bedridden or severely incapacitated, such as being confined to a wheelchair, paralysed or having suffered severe strokes. Apparently the third ground under this heading relates to medical conditions in which 'further imprisonment would endanger the prisoner's life or reduce his or her life expectancy'.[47]

The PSO excludes those prisoners whose medical conditions are self-inflicted, such as those resulting from hunger strikes. Furthermore, if the criteria set out above are not met, the resource and cost implications of maintaining staff on bedwatch duties at an outside hospital/hospice are not grounds to justify release on compassionate grounds.[48]

Furthermore, the PSO 6000 prescribes other mandatory factors which need to be fulfilled in order to qualify an otherwise eligible prisoner to be considered for compassionate release. These factors are:[49]

> (i) The risk of reoffending is past; and
> (ii) There are adequate arrangements for the prisoner's care and treatment outside prison; and
> (iii) Early release will bring some significant benefit to the prisoner or his/her family.

Apart from satisfying these preconditions cumulatively, the applicant should normally claim compassionate release on the basis of facts of which the sentencing or appeal court was not aware.[50] The PSO also specifies some other factors which need to be considered during decision-making, but apparently does not make the decision entirely dependent on those factors. These factors are:[51]

- Whether temporary release under the Prison Rules could significantly reduce the prisoner's and/or family's suffering;
- The length of the sentence still outstanding; the effect on the overall sentence passed by the court if early release is granted; and any remarks which the trial judge made on sentencing which may have a bearing on the question of release;
- The wishes of the prisoner and his/her family and the level of benefit

46 ibid 12.
47 ibid 12.
48 ibid 12.
49 ibid 12.
50 ibid 12.
51 ibid 12.

which would derive to the prisoner and/or the family from permanent release;
- In medical cases, the diagnosis and prognosis; in particular whether there is a specific estimate of life expectancy; and the degree of incapacitation.

The policy on compassionate release for indeterminate prisoners is almost identical to that for determinate prisoners. There are only a handful of relevant differences between the two. First, the PSI 4700 allows only two medical grounds for compassionate release of indeterminate prisoners. These grounds are terminal illness (with three months' life expectancy) and being bedridden or similarly incapacitated, such as being confined to a wheelchair, paralysed or having suffered severe strokes.[52] However, in contrast to determinate prisoners, for indeterminate prisoners medical conditions where 'further imprisonment would endanger the prisoner's life or reduce his or her life expectancy' do not constitute an independent ground for compassionate release.[53] Rather, it is a factor which needs to be satisfied in addition to these grounds. This means that terminally ill prisoners with three months of life expectancy or those who are bedridden or similarly incapacitated need to demonstrate that further imprisonment would endanger their life or reduce their life expectancy.[54] Therefore, it could be stated that the release criteria for indeterminate prisoners are stricter than for determinate prisoners.

A further difference between the compassionate release policy with regard to determinate and indeterminate prisoners relates to the risk of reoffending in eligible prisoners. In this regard, the policy relating to determinate prisoners states that the risk of reoffending should be past. Furthermore, PSO 6000 outlines that one of fundamental principles underlying compassionate release is that it will not put the safety of the public at risk.[55] These are vague definitions which would allow the Secretary of State to reject compassionate release of determinate prisoners if there is even a marginal risk of reoffending of any kind.

The PSI 4700 is more precise in describing the level and the nature of the risk, but it sets a similarly stringent threshold. According to this regulation an indeterminate prisoner who meets the other criteria (discussed above) can qualify for compassionate release if the risk of reoffending (particularly crimes of a sexual or violent nature) is minimal.[56] Although the regulation specifies the nature of the risk in this case, the language of this provision demonstrates that in fact a more than minimal risk of any type of reoffending could preclude releasing an otherwise eligible prisoner on compassionate grounds.

Furthermore, policy documents relating to both determinate and indeterminate prisoners require medical practitioners, in addition to diagnosing the nature

52 Prison Service Order 4700 Indeterminate Sentence Manual (n.34) 12.
53 ibid.
54 ibid.
55 Prison Service Order 6000 (n.34) 12.
56 Prison Service Order 4700 Indeterminate Sentence Manual (n.34) 12.

of the illness and assessing the life expectancy of the prisoner, to evaluate whether the health condition renders the prisoner incapable of committing further crimes, particularly of a sexual or violent nature.[57] Although the policy documents do not exclude those whose health conditions are not such as to render them incapable of re-offending, this requirement demonstrates that compassionate release can be rejected on this ground.

The procedure of compassionate release

The Criminal Justice Acts give few details regarding the early compassionate release procedure. According to the respective regulations, applications cannot be made directly to the Secretary of State: all applications need to be made to prison governors. If a governor supports the application, she/he submits it to the Early Release and Recall Section in the case of determinate prisoners and to the Public Protection Casework Section at the National Offender Management Service (NOMS) in the case of indeterminate prisoners.[58]

PSO 6000 explicitly states that although only the Secretary of State can make a decision releasing a prisoner on compassionate grounds, senior officers in the Early Release and Recall Section have a delegated authority to reject applications.[59] In cases of indeterminate prisoners there is no direct indication of delegated authority to reject applications. However, the wording of the regulation makes it clear that the decisions are made by the Public Protection and Casework Section following consultations with Ministers.[60]

The law does not place any limitations on the number of applications that can be brought by the same applicant nor establish any time period which needs to elapse between applications.[61] Moreover, it states that if an application is successful, the prisoner will be released on licence, making possible the recall of the prisoner if /shehe breaks the conditions of the licence. However, recall is not possible if the health of the prisoner improves or she/he makes an unexpected recovery.[62]

It has been demonstrated that the level of risk of reoffending is one of the essential factors affecting decisions on compassionate release. According to PSO 6000 a determinate prisoner (who meets other eligibility criteria for compassionate release) can be released on compassionate grounds if her/his release will not put the safety of the public at risk.[63] PSI 4700 also makes the compassionate release of an otherwise eligible indeterminate prisoner dependent on the existence of only a minimal risk of reoffending, particularly in relation to crimes of a

57 Prison Service Order 6000 (n.34) App.B.

58 Prison Service Order 6000 (n.34) para.12.5.1; Prison Service Order 4700 Indeterminate Sentence Manual (n.34) para.12.3.1.

59 Prison Service Order 6000 (n.34) para.12.8.1.

60 Prison Service Order 4700 Indeterminate Sentence Manual (n.34) para.12.3.1.

61 ibid para.12.5, 12.8.

62 ibid para.12.13.

63 Prison Service Order 6000 (n.34) para.12.3.1.

sexual or violent nature.[64] Section 248 of the Criminal Justice Act 2003 removed the requirement to consult the Parole Board before releasing long-term and short-term determinate prisoners.[65] However, this requirement is preserved in the case of indeterminate prisoners[66] and those subject to the jurisdiction of the Criminal Justice Act 1991, unless circumstances render such consultations impractical.[67] The respective laws are silent on the particular role of the Parole Board in compassionate release. However, it would be reasonable to assume that the statutory requirement of consultation relates to the risk of further reoffending by a prisoner who is otherwise eligible for compassionate release. It should be noted that the language of the law makes consultation with the Parole Board mandatory unless the circumstances render such consultation impractical. Such circumstances could possibly relate, for example, to the short life expectancy of a prisoner.

It is clear that Parliament reserved the issue of risk assessment in compassionate release cases for the Parole Board. The power of release is vested exclusively in the Secretary of State, who is free to follow or disregard the recommendations of the Parole Board. However, the role of the Parole Board is very important in providing an independent assessment of the risk of reoffending. Despite this legislative requirement, the respective PSO/PSI assigns to prison staff the responsibility for assessing the risk of reoffending in their recommendations to the Secretary of State.[68] Obviously the risk of reoffending is a factor of utmost importance in compassionate release: in spite of the fact that published policy does not make release solely dependent on the issue of risk, without fulfilling this criterion release on compassionate grounds of an otherwise eligible prisoner would not be possible.[69] Therefore, the clear intent of the compassionate release law, together with published policy, is that if a prisoner meets other compassionate release criteria the Secretary of State shall consult the Parole Board before making a decision on release, unless the circumstances render such consultation impracticable.

Interestingly, the Court of Appeal arrived at a different interpretation of this situation. According to the Court's interpretation of this provision, the Secretary of State shall consult the Parole Board when she/he decides that she/he wishes to release a prisoner, before actually putting the decision into operation in order to allow the Parole Board to act as a check on the Secretary of State.[70] According to the Court's interpretation, the opinion of the Parole Board does not have an effect on 'forming' the view of the Secretary of State; if the opinion of the Parole Board

64 Prison Service Order 4700 Indeterminate Sentence Manual (n.34) para.12.2.1.

65 Criminal Justice Act (n.36) s.248.

66 Crime (Sentence) Act (n.40) s.30.

67 Criminal Justice Act (n.37) s.36.

68 Prison Service Order 6000 (n.34) ch.12, p.12; Prison Service Order 4700 Indeterminate Sentence Manual (n 34) ch.12, pp 9–10.

69 Prison Service Order 6000 (n.34) para.12.3.1; Prison Service Order 4700 Indeterminate Sentence Manual (n.34) para.12.2.1.

70 *R.(Spinks) v Secretary of State for the Home Department* [2005] EWCA Civ 275 (Court of Appeal) para.28.

were intended to have an effect on the view of the Secretary of State regarding release, the law would require the Secretary of State to consult the Parole Board before forming a view on compassionate release. Therefore, according to the Court, there is no domestic rule that obliges the Secretary of State to consult the Parole Board, if he/she decides that no exceptional circumstances exist.[71]

The practice of compassionate release

It is not surprising that under this highly discretionary power the number of prisoners released on the above mentioned grounds is 'negligible'.[72] In the period 2004–2013 only 92 prisoners, both determinate and indeterminate, were released on compassionate grounds.[73] Unfortunately, it is neither possible to find out how many prisoners formally met the eligibility criteria for compassionate release, nor how many compassionate release applications were rejected: such data are not collected by the Ministry of Justice.[74]

Although it is not possible to obtain information regarding the number of terminally ill and bedridden or similarly incapacitated prisoners, the number of those who die annually from natural causes (which includes deaths due to either a terminal diagnosis or multiple chronic conditions and old age) stands in stark contrast to the number of prisoners released on compassionate grounds. In the period 2004–2013 only 92 prisoners both determinate and indeterminate were released on compassionate grounds.[75] In the same period 1,208 prisoners died in prison from natural causes.[76] Furthermore, according to information provided to the House of Commons Justice Committee, it is very likely that there were no cases in which a bedridden or similarly incapacitated prisoner was released on compassionate grounds, despite the fact that these prisoners are also eligible for compassionate release.[77] It is clear that the Secretary of State used the power of compassionate release very restrictively, even in respect of those who formally fulfilled the very narrow eligibility criteria.

In 2013 the Minister for Prisons and Probation, while giving evidence to the House of Commons Justice Committee, stated that the reasons behind the infrequent use of the power of compassionate release are public opinion, considerations of victims' interests, the impossibility of precisely determining remaining life expectancy, and the wish of some prisoners to die in prison.[78] The Minister

71 ibid.

72 House of Commons Justice Committee, 'Older prisoners: Fifth Report of Session 2013–2014' (Volume I: Report, together with formal minutes, oral and written evidence, London 2013) 11.

73 Ministry of Justice to Aleksandr Khechumyan (10 October 2014).

74 ibid.

75 ibid.

76 Ministry of Justice, 'Deaths in Prison Custody: England and Wales' (update by December 2014, London 2015). Safety in Custody 1.

77 House of Commons Justice Committee (n.72) 11.

78 House of Commons Justice Committee, 'Older Prisoners: Fifth Report of Session 2013–2014' (Volume II Additional written evidence, London 2013). Justice Committee Reports 32–33.

conceded that he faced difficult decisions regarding the compassionate release of terminally ill prisoners because he needed to meet public expectations of compassion in allowing terminally ill prisoners to go home effectively to die, while at the same time needing to be careful not to release somebody too early.[79]

As the respective laws demonstrate, Parliament entrusted the Secretary of State with broad discretionary powers with regard to the compassionate release of determinate and indeterminate prisoners. Based on this mandate, the Secretary of State sets the policy on how she/he will exercise the power entrusted to her/him by Parliament. Although the statutes give the Secretary of State unlimited discretion in this regard, she/he is bound by her/his published policy, otherwise the decision can be overturned on judicial review.[80] It is possible to observe the approach adopted by the Secretary of State on compassionate release in practice by looking at judicial reviews of the Secretary of State's decisions to refuse compassionate release.

It should be noted that there are not many judicial reviews of the Secretary of State's decisions to refuse compassionate release on the ground of illness. A comprehensive search through legal databases such as Westlaw UK, BAILII and LexisNexis have produced only six relevant decisions, four of which are from the High Court and two from the Court of Appeal.[81] These decisions demonstrate clearly how the very restrictive policy of compassionate release works in practice. Apart from one case where no evidence was presented that the heart condition of the applicant was terminal,[82] in all cases applications were based on the terminal condition of the applicant. Although the policy of the Secretary of State in such cases does not make life expectancy a required criterion, it does recommend three months as appropriate to qualify for compassionate release. However, the decisions demonstrate that in some cases medical professionals are unable to make life expectancy predictions, although the condition is described as terminal,[83] while in others they are able to give only imprecise estimates such as 'months rather than years',[84] or give an estimated median range of life expectancy.[85] Needless to say, in cases of terminal illness where estimated life expectancy was projected to

79 ibid.

80 William Wade and Christopher F Forsyth, *Administrative law* (8th edn, Oxford University Press 2000) 22; *Associated Provincial Picture Houses Ltd v Wednesbury Corporation* [1948] 1 KB 223 (Court of Appeal) 228.

81 *R. v Secretary of State for the Home Department Ex p. Bannori-Shah* [1999] Prison LR 74 (The High Court of Justice); *R. v Secretary of State for the Home Department Ex p. Bannori-Shah* [1999] Prison LR 76 (Court of Appeal (Civil Division)); *R. v Secretary of State for the Home Department Ex p. S (Terence)* [2000] Prison LR 107 (High Court of Justice); *R. (on the application of Spinks) v Secretary of State for the Home Department* [2004] EWHC (Admin) 2916 (Admin) (High Court of Justice); *R. (Spinks) v Secretary of State for the Home Department* (n.70); *Queen (on the application of A.S) v Secretary of State for Justice* [2009] EWHC (Admin) 1315 (High Court of Justice).

82 *R. v Secretary of State for the Home Department Ex p. Bannori-Shah* (n.81).

83 *R. v Secretary of State for the Home Department Ex p. S (Terence)* (n.81) 14–18.

84 *The Queen (on the application of A.S) v Secretary of State for Justice* (n.81) 17.

85 ibid 28.

be more than three months, the prisoner was considered not to meet the required eligibility criteria.[86]

Including a precise life expectancy requirement as a criterion for compassionate release has been criticised as one of the flaws of the compassionate release laws in general. The relevant literature suggests it is difficult to determine life expectancy for a number of diseases, which creates tensions between actual disease trajectories and the requirements of compassionate release. As a result of overreliance on life expectancy, compassionate release is often requested too late and an eligible prisoner dies before a decision is made. Furthermore, the requirement of a predictable, time-limiting life expectancy prognosis excludes patients with some severe, but not end-stage, diseases, some of whom may live for months or years incapable of posing harm.[87]

The other critical factor in the decision-making of the Secretary of State is the risk of reoffending. Again, as the written policy demonstrates, this is formulated in very broad terms, which allows the Secretary of State to reject the application, relying on this ground because in relation at least to indeterminate prisoners who have not yet served the custodial part of their sentence it cannot be said with any certainty that the risk of reoffending is past. Furthermore, as the judicial review cases indicate, to satisfy the Secretary of State's criteria in relation to the risk of reoffending, the medical reports should demonstrate that a prisoner is so disabled by illness as to be not physically able to reoffend.[88]

As with the requirement to predict life expectancy, the requirement to assess whether a prisoner is physically capable of reoffending has been criticised by medical professionals. Predictions of reoffending, if not based on the psychiatric history of the offender, are a matter of criminology rather than medicine; requiring physicians or other medical professionals to predict whether an offender would be physically capable of reoffending puts on these professionals an obligation which is beyond their professional capabilities. Furthermore, for some illnesses physical decline is very difficult to predict: it may often decline sharply shortly before death.[89] Therefore, including such a requirement as a criterion for eligibility for compassionate release puts in doubt whether the policy could be put into practice with any degree of efficacy.

It should be noted that in addition to the medical condition of the prisoner and the risk of reoffending, the Secretary of State can base her/his rejection on several other factors. These are the length of the sentence still outstanding, the effect on the overall sentence passed by the court if early release is granted and any remarks made by the trial judge at sentencing which may have a bearing on the question of release.[90] However, the medical and risk requirements are so

86 *R. (on the application of Spinks) v Secretary of State for the Home Department* (n.81) 22.

87 Bric A Williams, 'Balancing Punishment and Compassion for Seriously Ill' (2011) 155(2) Ann Intern Med 122, 124.

88 *R.(Spinks) v Secretary of State for the Home Department* (n.70) 25; *Queen (on the application of A.S) v Secretary of State for Justice* (n.81) 34.

89 Williams (n.87), 124.

90 Prison Service Order 6000 (n.34) 12.

strict and vague that in none of the cases did the Secretary of State have to rely on other factors to reject an application for compassionate release. It is clear that with such broad and vague criteria it is not difficult to find a reason for rejecting compassionate release even in cases where prisoners satisfy the medical requirements specified in the policy.

As has been demonstrated, the Secretary of State's compassionate release policy and practice are very restrictive. However, in the light of the obligations imposed on the Secretary of State by the HRA 1998, the Grand Chamber of the ECtHR in the case of *Hutchinson* accepted that the power of compassionate release met the requirement of review of continued imprisonment in whole life cases.[91] In order to see whether the course envisaged by the Grand Chamber is, indeed, practical and effective, it is necessary to look at the scope of the obligation to interpret legislation under the HRA 1998 and the judicial review of administrative decisions in English law.

The obligation to interpret the legislation in line with ECHR rights

The HRA 1998 has incorporated the ECHR into the English law, making most of the rights and fundamental freedoms enshrined in the ECHR, subject to any designated derogations or reservations, legally enforceable in English courts.[92] It also requires that courts interpret the Convention rights in line with judgments, decisions, declarations or advisory opinions of the ECtHR, opinions and decisions of the former European Commission of Human Rights and decisions of the Committee of Ministers of the Council of Europe regarding execution of final judgments of the ECtHR.[93]

Moreover, the HRA 1998 requires that 'as far as it is possible to do so, primary and subordinate legislation must be read and given effect in a way which is compatible with the Convention rights'.[94] According to the intention of the Government at the time, this provision authorises courts to disregard established case law whenever it does not take into account Convention rights and establish new precedents in line with the incorporated Convention rights.[95] However, in cases where it is not possible to read and give effect to primary and subordinate legislation in a way compatible with the Convention, the HRA 1998 cannot override such legislation: it is not given a superordinate status which would have allowed overriding provisions of primary legislation in the case of incompatibility with Convention rights. It also cannot affect any incompatible subordinate legislation if the incompatibility arises because of the need to follow the primary

91 *Hutchinson v United Kingdom* [GC] (n.31).
92 Human Rights Act 1998, s.1.
93 ibid, s.2.
94 ibid, s.3.
95 The UK Government, 'White paper on human rights: Rights Brought Home: The Human Rights Bill' (London 1997) 3.

legislation.[96] Giving superordinate status to the HRA was considered to be in conflict with UK constitutional arrangements.[97]

Despite the lack of power to invalidate primary and in some cases secondary legislation, under the HRA 1998 judges of the designated courts have the power to make a 'declaration of incompatibility' if they find that a provision of primary, or in the relevant case of subordinate, legislation is incompatible with a Convention right. However, this declaration neither affects the validity, continuing operation or enforcement of the provision in question nor is it binding on the parties of the particular case.[98] Despite this limitation, the promoters of the Bill envisaged that 'a declaration of incompatibility' by an appropriate court 'will almost certainly prompt the Government and Parliament to change the law'.[99]

Furthermore, s.6 of the HRA 1998 requires public authorities to act in line with a Convention right unless the authority is required to act otherwise by a provision of primary legislation or of secondary legislation which cannot be read or given effect in line with the Convention owing to the requirement of primary legislation. According to this section public authorities are 'a court or tribunal, and any person certain of whose functions are functions of a public nature'.[100]

The HRA 1998 sets out a general obligation to interpret and enforce, as far as possible, primary and secondary legislation – whenever adopted – in a Convention-compatible way.[101] This has vested in public authorities an unprecedented power of interpretation. Unfortunately, s.3(1) of the HRA does not clarify the meaning of the term 'as far as it is possible to do'. For instance, it is unclear whether the Convention shall be called upon only to resolve ambiguity in the legislation or also to interpret the legislation in line with the Convention even if there is no ambiguity. Therefore, the issue of the limit of possibility to interpret primary legislation in line with the Convention is highly disputed.

It was argued that the limit of possibility to interpret legislation in line with the Convention depends on two presumptions that were already in use before the adoption of the HRA.[102] The first is the presumption that Convention rights were to be relied upon for the interpretation of ambiguity in a domestic statute.[103] The second is the presumption that legislation is compatible with common law fundamental rights, which means that general words shall be read in line with those rights, unless it is not possible to do so, because the respective

96 Human Rights Act (n.92), s.3
97 The UK Government (n.95) 2.
98 Human Rights Act (n.92) 4.
99 The UK Government (n.95) 2.
100 Human Rights Act (n.92).
101 ibid, s. 3.
102 See e.g. G Marshal, 'The Lynchpin of Parliamentary Intention: Lost, Stolen or Strained' [2003] *Public Law* 236, 245–246; Richard Ekins, 'A Critique of Radical Approaches to Rights-consistent Statutory Interpretation' [2003] EHRLR 641, 641–642; TRS Allan, 'Legislative Supremacy and Legislative Intention: Interpretation, Meaning and Authority' (2004) 63 *Cambridge Law Journal* 685, 704–707.
103 *R v Secretary of State for the Home Department, ex p. Brind* [1991] AC 696, 747–748.

legislation limits the fundamental rights in question expressly or by necessary implication.[104]

The common law rights presumption is considered to be the stronger of the two presumptions, because it has been in place since the beginning of the interpretative enquiry and operates independently of findings of ambiguity in statutes.[105] Therefore, it is suggested that s.3 of the HRA was adopted with the same presumption as the common law rights presumption, but extended to all rights protected under HRA 1998.[106]

Case law development since the adoption of the HRA 1998 demonstrates that the position of the courts regarding the interpretation of domestic legislation under s.3 of the HRA 1998 has, indeed, fluctuated. In two early cases the House of Lords apparently applied 'the common law rights presumption' in interpreting legislative provisions under s.3 of the HRA. In these cases their Lordships mentioned that s.3 required them to interpret differently otherwise unambiguous statutory provisions.[107] However, they went further to explain that the power of interpretation under s.3 of the HRA 1998 reaches its limits when the statute is incompatible with the Convention in expressed terms[108] or by 'necessary implication'.[109]

The threshold of 'possible' interpretation under s.3(1) achieved its culmination in the case of *Ghaidan v Godin-Mendoza*.[110] In this case the House of Lords unanimously held that denying a surviving same-sex partner the right to succeed to a statutory tenancy under the Rent Act 1977 would be incompatible with Article 14 of the ECHR. Furthermore, their Lordships found that under s.3(1) of the HRA 1998 it is possible to interpret the words 'as his or her wife or husband' to include also a same-sex partner.[111] Lord Nicholls, on behalf of the majority, stated that it was already firmly established that interpretative obligation under s.3 'is of an unusual and far-reaching character', which, in contrast to ordinary interpretation of legislation, may even require departing 'from the intention of the Parliament which enacted the legislation'.[112] Therefore, the critical issue was to determine the limit of departing from the intention of Parliament required by s.3 which again 'depends upon the intention reasonably to be attributed to Parliament in enacting section 3'.[113] In deciding this question Lord Nicholls argued that the intention of Parliament should be determined not from the

104 John Bell and Georg Engle (eds), *Cross on Statutory Interpretation* (3rd edn, Butterworths 1995) 165.

105 ibid 165–166.

106 Jan Van Zyl Smit, 'The New Purposive Interpretation of Statutes: HRA Section 3 after Ghaidan v Godin-Mendoza' (2007) 70(2) *Modern Law Review* 294, 295.

107 *R v A (No 2)* [2001] UKHL 25; *R v Lambert* [2001] UKHL 37; *R (P&Q) v Home Secretary.*

108 *R v A (No 2)* (n.107) 45.

109 *R (Anderson) v Secretary of State for the Home Department* [2002] UKHL 46, 59.

110 *Ghaidan v Godin-Mendoza* [2004] UKHL 30.

111 ibid.

112 ibid 30.

113 ibid.

language of the legislative provision under consideration, but rather from 'the fundamental feature of legislation'.[114]

This was, indeed, a far-reaching approach to the interpretation of legislation under s.3. However, this position of their Lordships was short-lived. Not long after delivering this remarkable judgment, the House of Lords in *R (Wilkinson) v IRC* limited the application of the far-reaching decision in *Ghaidan.*[115] Lord Hoffmann argued that:[116]

> It is ... sometimes possible ... to construe a statutory provision as referring to, or qualified by, some general concept implied rather than expressly mentioned in the language used by Parliament. Thus in the Ghaidan case, the words 'as his or her wife or husband' were interpreted to refer to a relationship of social and sexual intimacy exemplified by, but not limited to, the heterosexual relationship of husband and wife.

This statement, indeed, means that the interpretative approach developed in *Ghaidan* could only sometimes be used to read general and evaluative words of a statutory provision that is incompatible with the Convention in a Convention-compatible manner.[117]

Despite this setback, s.3 of HRA 1998 offers an unprecedented power to interpret domestic legislation to uphold fundamental rights protected under the ECHR. Even Lord Millet in his dissenting opinion in *Ghaidan* recognised that interpretation under s.3 could require judges to divert from meanings of otherwise unambiguous statutes by 'reading down statutory words or reading other words in a statute'.[118]

The Court of Appeal has on numerous occasions stated that it is possible to interpret the compassionate release provision under s.30 of the Criminal Justice Act 1997 to comply with the Article 3 requirement of reducibility of *de jure* whole life orders.[119] In *Bieber* the Court particularly stated:[120]

> At present it is the practice of the Secretary of State to use this power sparingly, in circumstances where, for instance, a prisoner is suffering from a terminal illness or is bedridden or similarly incapacitated. If, however, the position is reached where the continued imprisonment of a prisoner is held to amount to inhuman or degrading treatment, we can see no reason why, having particular regard to the requirement to comply with the Convention, the Secretary of State should not use his statutory power to release the prisoner.

114 ibid 33.

115 *R (Wilkinson) v IRC* [2005] UKHL 30.

116 ibid 18.

117 Van Zyl Smit (n.106), 305.

118 *Ghaidan v Godin-Mendoza* (n.110) 67.

119 *R v Bieber* (n.8) para.48; *R v Oakes* [2013] 3 WLR 137 (Court of Appeal) para.15; *Attorney General's Reference (No.69 of 2013)* [2014] 2 Cr App R (S) 40 (Court of Appeal).

120 *R v Bieber* (n.8) para.48.

As with the ground of whole life sentences, likelihood of dying in prison as a result of a normal ageing process is not included in the policy as a ground for compassionate release. It has been argued in this book that this is also a ground for review required by Article 3 of the ECHR. Therefore, based on the above-described approach of the Court of Appeal, it could be stated that it is possible to interpret this provision to require review of continued imprisonment of elderly indeterminate prisoners who meet the age threshold. The method of interpretation articulated by the Court of Appeal can be similarly extended to the compassionate release provision which relates to determinate prisoners, because both provisions are formulated in identical terms.[121]

By contrast, terminal illness with three months of life expectancy and being bedridden or similarly incapacitated are regarded as exceptional circumstances in the respective PSO and PSI. In these situations the Secretary of State may release a prisoner on compassionate grounds. However, to comply with the Article 3 right to review on the ground of serious illness, the Secretary of State would be obliged to interpret the exceptional circumstances meriting compassionate release more broadly than is set out in the current policy. Thus, he will be obliged to review continued imprisonment not only when the prisoner is terminally ill and has a life expectancy of three months or is severely incapacitated, but also in cases of other serious medical conditions. This is clearly possible in view of the discussion of the scope of the obligation of interpretation outlined above.

It follows that, irrespective of the restrictive policy, it would be unlawful for the Secretary of State not to review the lawfulness of continued imprisonment both on the ground of likelihood of dying in prison as a result of the normal ageing process and serious physical illness. In the case of old age/likelihood of dying in custody, the scope of the review should allow for an evaluation of whether in view of the likelihood of dying in custody the sentence that is not *de jure* whole life would constitute *de facto* whole life. It should also allow evaluation of whether, in view of the above factor, the time already served and the progress towards rehabilitation, the balance between the aims of punishment has changed to a degree that would justify releasing the prisoner early. Whereas, in the case of serious illness, the scope of the review should be wide enough to allow assessment of whether an appropriate arrangement in custody could reconcile the legitimate aims of the punishment with the health and wellbeing of the prisoner or whether detention is absolutely incompatible with the state of the health of the prisoner.

In such cases it would be the Secretary of State's responsibility to assess the situation and determine whether continued imprisonment in view of old age/likelihood of dying in custody and a serious medical condition reaches the threshold in Article 3. As with cases where the Secretary of State exercises her/his statutory power on the ground of compassion and in line with the written policy, the exercise of this statutory power in line with the above provisions of the HRA 1998 would be susceptible to judicial review. This course is prescribed

121 Crime (Sentence) Act (n.40) s.30; Criminal Justice Act (n.36) s.248.

by s.7 of the HRA 1998.[122] The Grand Chamber of the ECtHR regarded judicial review as a mechanism capable of acting as a check on the Secretary of State's power of compassionate release and a guarantee of execution of this power in compliance with the Article 3 right to review in *de jure* whole life cases. The Grand Chamber also took note of the Government's statement that judicial review would not be confined to formal grounds, but would also include examination of the merits. Moreover, the Grand Chamber was convinced that the domestic court would have power to order release of a prisoner based on the results of judicial review if it finds that continued imprisonment violates Article 3.[123] The Grand Chamber was not provided with any examples of domestic practice that would support the existence of this possibility not only in theory but also in practice. However, it was satisfied that the necessary safeguards were in place to protect the right to review under Article 3.[124] If the scope of the judicial review would allow the course envisaged by the ECtHR, this would also affect the issue of the compatibility of the power of compassionate release with the Article 3 right to review on the ground of old age/likelihood of dying and serious illness. In order to see whether this course is in fact possible, it is necessary to carry out a detailed review of the remedy of judicial review in English law.

The scope of judicial review before the Human Rights Act 1998

Before coming to the approach of the courts in judicial reviews of Secretary of State decisions to refuse release on compassionate grounds, it is useful to start with a discussion of the nature of judicial review and its relationship to the judicial protection of rights under the HRA 1998. This is necessary in order better to understand the various issues arising in this context and to clarify whether and to what extent this is an appropriate legal mechanism to ensure the compliance of compassionate release with the Article 3 right to review.

In this regard it should be stressed that judicial review is not exclusively a mechanism for the judicial protection of human rights. It is a procedure in administrative law which serves as a check on the administrative decisions of public bodies, including government ministers and inferior courts. This procedure aims to ensure that these officials do not act outside the boundaries of the powers granted to them by law (*ultra vires*) 'and to observe the elements of fair procedure' preventing the abuse of discretionary powers.[125] To fulfil this task, the courts have developed the doctrine of *ultra vires* which serves as the underlying legal rationale for judicial review and is considered to be the central principle of English administrative law.[126]

122 Human Rights Act (n.92).
123 *Hutchinson v United Kingdom* [GC] (n.31) para.52.
124 ibid para.53.
125 Wade and Forsyth (n.80) 21, 596.
126 ibid 35.

While reviewing decisions where the executive has very wide discretion, the jurisdiction of the courts is limited to checking whether the decision-maker has acted against the law, i.e. exercised the discretion in bad faith, dishonestly, giving attention to extraneous circumstances while ignoring any relevant factors, in disregard of public policy or unreasonably.[127] Although such powers are highly discretionary, the decision-maker also has a duty to give reasons for her/his decisions.[128]

The judicial interpretation of the above grounds demonstrates that four out of five relate to the decision-making process and only 'unreasonableness' relates to the substance of the decision.[129] Thus, the subject of review based on the first four grounds is the quality of the decision-making process without questioning the factual basis of the decision.[130] Only under the last ground is the substance of the decision reviewed in terms of 'unreasonableness'. However, the Court of Appeal had established a very high threshold for invalidating a decision on the ground of unreasonableness; courts cannot intervene when in their opinion the decision is unreasonable. The decision can be invalidated on this ground only in cases where no rational decision-maker could have come to such decision.[131] However, as the Court of Appeal put it, 'to prove a case of that kind would require something overwhelming'.[132] This test, which has become known as the *Wednesbury* reasonableness test, has been traditionally regarded as the only test under which a decision can be invalidated on a substantive ground at judicial review.[133]

It therefore follows that at judicial reviews of the Secretary of State's decisions to refuse compassionate release, courts could not examine the merits of the decision, e.g. medical documents and documents relating to the risk of reoffending, with the purpose of forming their own opinion on whether it was correct to refuse the compassionate release of a particular prisoner. The courts could not have required reconsideration of the matter even if in their opinion the prisoner met the requirements of compassionate release. This would be possible only if the decision of the Secretary of State was perverse in view of the materials before him or when it was established that the Secretary of State formed his decision without taking into account relevant materials or having taken into account irrelevant materials.[134] Indeed, the only occasion when the court required the Secretary of State to reconsider the decision to refuse compassionate release was when the

127 *Associated Provincial Picture Houses Ltd v Wednesbury Corporation* (n.80) 228.

128 Hugh Southey and Adrian Fulford, *Judicial review: A practical guide* (Jordans 2004) 31.

129 *Associated Provincial Picture Houses Ltd v Wednesbury Corporation* (n.80)

130 Richard JF Gordon, *Judicial review: Law and procedure* (2nd edn, Sweet & Maxwell 1996) 19.

131 *Associated Provincial Picture Houses Ltd v Wednesbury Corporation* (n.80) 230.

132 ibid 231.

133 Lord Sumption, 'Anxious Scrutiny' (The Administrative Law Bar Association Annual Lecture, London, 4 November 2014) accessed 9 April 2016.

134 *R. (on the application of Spinks) v Secretary of State for the Home Department* (n.81) 42; *R. (Spinks) v Secretary of State for the Home Department* (n.70) 24; *Queen (on the application of A.S.) v Secretary of State for Justice* (n.81) 44.

Secretary of State failed to take into account the latest medical report regarding the condition of the prisoner and to consider whether the latest developments of his illness rendered the prisoner incapable of reoffending.[135]

The rationale of this approach is that appropriate bodies which are entrusted by Parliament with discretionary powers in a particular area have the necessary expertise in that field to enable them to judge facts and make decisions. The courts which lack expertise in a particular field should not attempt to substitute themselves for appropriate bodies in judging facts, which means that, save in exceptional cases, the court would not make a *de novo* decision.[136] However, courts have gradually developed the review standards which allow decision-makers less freedom of action and require more in the way of justification for making a particular decision. In recent cases the courts have used phrases such as 'heightened or anxious scrutiny' to describe the test which they used for substantive review in cases claiming violation of common law fundamental rights.[137] In essence, anxious review is not substantially different from *Wednesbury* reasonableness. As the Court of Appeal explicitly mentioned, this standard keeps the substantive review within the boundaries of *Wednesbury* reasonableness.[138] It only limits the range of choices available to a rational decision-maker, requiring more justifications for a particular conclusion.[139]

More significantly, anxious scrutiny shifted the burden of proof from the claimant to the defendant. Under *Wednesbury* reasonableness the claimant was required to substantiate the unreasonableness claim, whereas under the anxious scrutiny standard the court firmly places the burden of justifying the decision on the decision-maker. This standard requires more in the way of justification to convince the court that the decision is justified in the sense of the *Wednesbury* test.[140] The decision-making body must now demonstrate that it carried out a comprehensive review before making the decision. This is required in order to satisfy the court that the decision-maker has not contravened the law.[141] According to Lord Sumption, anxious scrutiny only entitled the court to assess whether the balance between the right and competing interests was within the range of rational possibilities. It did not allow a court to go into an assessment of the relative weight accorded by a decision-maker to each of the competing factors. Finally, this standard does not allow a consideration of whether the interference was greater than necessary in a democratic society.[142]

Following the introduction of anxious scrutiny as a test for substantive review in judicial reviews of claims involving fundamental rights, the courts have also developed the principle of legality applicable in the same class of cases. This

135 *Queen (on the application of A.S) v Secretary of State for Justice* (n.81) 48–49.
136 Richard JF Gordon (n.130) 18.
137 *Bugdaycay v Secretary of State for the Home Department* [1987] 1 AC 514 (House of Lords).
138 *R v Ministry of Defence ex p. Smith* [1996] QB 517 (Court of Appeal).
139 Lord Sumption (n.133), 3.
140 *R v Ministry of Defence ex p. Smith* (n.138) 554.
141 Lord Sumption (n.133).
142 ibid.

principle suggests that unjustified restrictions on fundamental rights are not permitted, unless authorised by Parliament in express terms. It recognises that there are no legal constraints on the power of Parliament to legislate contrary to fundamental human rights principles. However, if Parliament chooses to legislate in this way, it shall do this in express terms; fundamental rights cannot be overridden by 'general or ambiguous words'. According to the principle of legality, in the absence of express language or necessary implication to the contrary, it is presumed that Parliament legislates in line with fundamental human rights principles and even the most general words were intended to be in line with fundamental rights.[143]

Indeed, the application of the legality standard can be observed in cases related to limitations of prisoners' fundamental rights.[144] However, the courts have highlighted that the intensity of review will depend on the degree of interference with fundamental rights and the standard of justification must vary depending on the significance of the right at stake.[145] In the *R v Ministry of Defence ex parte Smith* the Court of Appeal specified that 'the more substantial the interference with human rights, the more the court will require in the way of justification before it is satisfied that the decision is reasonable'.[146]

The scope of judicial review after adoption of the Human Rights Act 1998

Since the adoption of the Human Rights Act 1998, public authorities, including government ministers and the courts, are required to act in line with Convention rights unless the authority is required to act otherwise by a provision of primary legislation. The same is true in the case of secondary legislation if it cannot be read or given effect in line with the Convention owing to the requirement of primary legislation.[147] According to s.7 of the HRA 1998, individuals who have been the victims of acts or omissions by public authorities can bring claims under existing proceedings such as judicial review, criminal or civil procedures. However, where no such procedure exists, it is possible to bring a complaint to the 'appropriate court or tribunal' on the ground of violation of ECHR rights alone.[148] As discussed above, judicial review is an established proceedure for reviewing decisions of the Secretary of State, including her/his decisions on compassionate release.[149] Therefore, even if a prisoner claims that the decision of the Secretary of State not

143 *R v Secretary of State for the Home Department, Ex p. Pierson* [1998] AC 539 (House of Lords) 575; *R v Secretary of State for the Home Department, Ex p. Simms* [2000] 2 AC 115 (House of Lords) 341.

144 See e.g. *Raymond v Honey* [1983] 1 AC 1 (House of Lords); *R v Secretary of State for the Home Department, Ex parte Leech (2)* [1994] QB 198 (Court of Appeal).

145 *R v Secretary of State for the Home Department ex p. McQuillan* [1995] 4 All ER 400 (High Court of Justice) 422–423.

146 *R v Ministry of Defence ex parte Smith* (n.138) 554.

147 Human Rights Act (n.92) s.6.

148 ibid.

149 Wade and Forsyth (n.80) 22.

to release her/him in view of her/his old age/likelihood of dying in prison or serious medical condition violates Article 3 of the ECHR, such a claim can be brought only under judicial review proceedings.

The introduction of a claim of violation of ECHR rights as an independent ground for judicial review made possible the adoption of proportionality as a test for reviewing claims on this ground.[150] The scope and the specificities of this test for review were clarified by Lord Steyn in the case of *Daly*.[151] According to the test adopted in this case, in determining the proportionality of the measure (act, rule or decision) in question which is claimed to violate a Convention right, the court should ask itself whether:[152]

> (i) the legislative objective is sufficiently important to justify limiting a fundamental right;
> (ii) the measures designed to meet the legislative objective are rationally connected to it; and
> (iii) the means used to impair the right or freedom are no more than is necessary to accomplish the objective.

In his *obiter dictum* Lord Steyn usefully clarified the specificities of the proportionality test, emphasising how it differs from the traditional grounds for review. He described proportionality as a more precise and more sophisticated test under which 'the intensity of review is somewhat greater'.[153]

Lord Steyn set out the differences between proportionality and traditional grounds for review which affect the intensity of the review. These are the requirements to assess the balance struck by the decision-maker between available courses of action, including looking at the relative weight accorded to interests and considerations. Furthermore, he emphasised that even the heightened scrutiny test developed in the case of *Smith*[154] is not necessarily appropriate for the protection of human rights, because, as stressed by the ECtHR,[155] it placed the threshold at which the policy could be found irrational so high that it effectively excluded any consideration of whether the interference with the applicant's rights answered a pressing social need or was proportionate to the aims pursued.[156] In summary, the intensity of review in Convention rights cases 'is guaranteed by twin requirements that the limitation of the right was necessary in a democratic society, in the sense of meeting a pressing social need, and the question whether the interference was really proportionate to the legitimate aim being pursued'.[157] However, Lord Steyn also warned that the adoption of proportionality does not

150 *R (Daly) v Secretary of State for the Home Department* [2001] 2 AC 532 (House of Lords) 548.
151 ibid 547.
152 ibid.
153 ibid.
154 *R v Ministry of Defence ex parte Smith* (n.138).
155 *Smith and Grady v United Kingdom* ECHR 1999-VI 45.
156 *Regina (Daly) v Secretary of State for the Home Department* (n.150) 541.
157 ibid.

mean a shift to a *merits review*, and even in Convention rights cases the intensity of review will depend on the subject matter at hand.[158]

It could be stated that proportionality has been formally commonly recognised as the appropriate standard of review in judicial review proceedings of human rights claims.[159] In comparison with the other standards of review discussed above, proportionality apparently offers the possibility of more intensive review of claims of human rights violations. It allows the following three questions to be answered: whether the objective of limiting a human right is sufficiently important; whether the measure used to limit the right is rationally connected to the objective; and whether it is no more than necessary to achieve that objective.

Adoption of the HRA 1998 and the introduction of the proportionality test in human rights adjudication was celebrated by human rights advocates, because it provided an opportunity for enhancing human rights protection. As Lord Steyn acknowledged in *Daly*, the proportionality test provides for more intensive review of right-limiting measures than all review tests previously at the disposal of courts.[160] However, it seems that, even after the adoption of proportionality, the courts either openly relied on the 'anxious scrutiny' standard or used different approaches to side-step a proportionality analysis. This was done in order to avoid conducting a merits review, which would have been the ultimate consequence of the application of the proportionality test approved in *Daly*.[161] This approach can also be clearly observed in judicial review decisions regarding the Secretary of State's refusal to release prisoners on compassionate grounds.

Judicial review of Article 3 claims concerning continued imprisonment of prisoners with serious medical conditions

In three out of the six applications for judicial review of the Secretary of State's decisions to refuse compassionate release, applicants' request for judicial review was based both on traditional grounds and on Article 3 of the ECHR.[162] In *Spinks*[163] the claimant, who was serving a life sentence with a minimum term of 12 years, imposed in 1996 for murder, was diagnosed with terminal cancer of the colon in October 2003. He applied for compassionate release in January 2004 when his life expectancy was estimated to be between three and six months. The Secretary of State refused the application in June 2004. The Secretary of State informed the claimant that he did not meet the criteria for compassionate release;

158 ibid 548.

159 See e.g. *Begum v Denbigh High School Governors* [2006] UKHL 15, 116; *Huang v Secretary of State for the Home Department* [2007] UKHL 11, 13.

160 *R (Daly) v Secretary of State for the Home Department* (n.150) 547.

161 Tom Hickman, *Public law after the Human Rights Act* (Hart 2010) 182; Cora Chan, 'Proportionality and invariable baseline intensity of review' (2013) 33(1) *Legal Studies* 1.

162 *R. (on the application of Spinks) v Secretary of State for the Home Department* (n.81) 4; *R. (Spinks) v Secretary of State for the Home Department* (n.70) 12; *,Queen (on the application of A.S) v Secretary of State for Justice* (n.81) 4.

163 *R. (on the application of Spinks) v Secretary of State for the Home Department* (n.81).

it could be granted only if 'there were the most exceptional circumstances and life expectancy was very short'.[164]

Spinks applied for judicial review of this decision, alleging that his continued imprisonment raised the issue of a violation of Article 3 of the ECHR. The claim was based on a number of incidents that occurred in relation to his cancer treatment. First, he claimed that the prison failed to produce him for two chemotherapy sessions, which could have affected the efficacy of his treatment. Second, while attending the hospital and during the treatment the claimant was handcuffed, including during his three-week hospital stay for an operation. Third, on occasions he was not allowed access to colostomy bags and necessary medicine because of the deliberately obstructive attitude of prison staff.[165]

Based on these facts the claimant submitted that Article 3 of the ECHR obliged the State to investigate whether in these circumstances his continued imprisonment attained the threshold necessary to establish a breach of Article 3. The High Court rejected the claim that the procedural obligation under Article 3 was relevant in the material case. According to the Court: [166]

> the procedural obligation needs to be complied with, in circumstances where there is something out of the normal run of things which has occurred which needs explanation or justification and which arguably involves a breach of Art.3.

Whereas, in this case, complaints were related to the application of established prison policies in a particular case which allegedly breached the claimant's human rights.[167]

Furthermore, the Court stated that even if it were established that the applicant's Article 3 rights were breached, this would not in itself have secured the release of the applicant. To secure release one would have to demonstrate that 'one can infer that the breach will continue'.[168]

In coming to its decision, the Court rejected the claimant's request to obtain and examine up-to-date medical reports and hear evidence in this regard. It argued that save in the case of an obvious breach of Article 3, the Secretary of State should have an opportunity to consider new materials first, because he is the person authorised by Parliament to make decisions on whether to release the prisoner on compassionate grounds. However, the Court accepted that, given the nature of the human right at stake, it was required to adopt a 'heightened scrutiny' test in reviewing the Secretary of State's decision and 'assessing whether he has acted lawfully in the way he has struck the balance between competing considerations'.[169]

164 ibid 1.
165 ibid 12–16.
166 ibid 34.
167 ibid 35.
168 ibid 38.
169 ibid 40.

After assessing the situation of the claimant under the specified review standard, the Court came to the conclusion that in the present case the treatment of the applicant did not reach the threshold of severity set by the ECtHR with regard to Article 3: regardless of the terminal illness, the prisoner remained mobile and fully self-carrying with no evidence that his condition inflicted on him any kind of psychological harm.[170]

Similarly, the Court of Appeal rejected the claim that continued imprisonment of the claimant breached Article 3 of the ECHR. In this decision Lord Buxton also considered the issue of whether the alleged continued violation of Article 3 in this case triggered the procedural obligation to investigate the alleged breaches, which, as the claimant suggested, should be carried out by the Parole Board. According to his Lordship, in this case it was claimed that the breach of the human right was in place or continuing, for which the appropriate remedy would be terminating the continuing breach by releasing the prisoner.[171] In such circumstances the Parole Board has no role; rather, the role of overseeing the lawfulness of the actions of the executive branch in domestic legal order is reserved for courts. Therefore:[172]

> the court's role is to determine whether an actual breach of Article 3 is in progress and, if it is, to require its termination. If, in such circumstances, termination would only be possible by release of a prisoner, then the court can either rule that under Section 30 circumstances exist which require the Secretary of State to act, that is to say that he cannot lawfully exercise his power under Section 30 (1) except by exercising the terms of release; or, more simply, the court could itself straightforwardly order the release of the prisoner under its powers under Section 8 (1) of the Human Rights Act 1998.

According to the Court, while making a judgment whether the violation of Article 3 is in progress the court should adopt:[173]

> an intense review of the sort referred to by Lord Walker of Gestingsthorpe in a case mentioned to us by Mr Southey – Pro-life Alliance [2004] 1 AC 185 at paragraph 139. The review will be of the decision made by the Secretary of State, but it will be a review which looks again at the evidence and in certain circumstances may have itself de novo to look at further evidence.

Lord Justice May has further explained the specificity of this approach. According to his Lordship, when the Secretary of State exercises his discretionary power to release a prisoner on compassionate grounds, he needs to balance

170 ibid 52.
171 *R.(Spinks) v Secretary of State for the Home Department* (n.70) 30.
172 ibid 32.
173 ibid 33.

various relevant considerations against one another and it is for the Secretary of State to evaluate that balance. When the Secretary of State has properly carried out this evaluation, as in the material case, the Court cannot intervene unless it concludes that the Secretary of State's balance evaluation is 'plainly wrong'.[174] As in the case of exercising the power of compassionate release, the issue of whether there has been a breach of Article 3 is also a matter of evaluation. Although the issue of Article 3 needs to be considered in addition to whether exceptional circumstances justify compassionate release, it does not 'alter or add to the quality of the evaluation the Secretary of State has to make'.[175] This means that:[176]

> the injection of Article 3 considerations into the evaluation does not alter or add to the task of the court in a case such as the present. The court would not require the Secretary of State, by whatever particular order, to take the matter further unless the court concluded that the Secretary of State's balance evaluation, taking account of Article 3, was plainly wrong. In reaching this decision, the court will review the Secretary of State's decision "with an intensity appropriate to all the circumstances of the case" (see for example R (Bloggs 61) v Home Secretary [2003] 1 WLR 2724 at 2746 paragraph 64 citing R (ProLife Alliance) v British Broadcasting Corporation [2003] 2 WLR 1403, at 1439 paragraph 139).

This decision demonstrates that, regardless of the fact that a judicial review of the Secretary of State's decision to refuse compassionate release was requested on the basis that it violated Article 3 of the ECHR, the scope of the review remained the same as in the cases when the application for judicial review was made on traditional grounds such as *Wednesbury* unreasonableness.[177] The only difference was that in cases claiming violation of the ECHR rights, courts reviewed the decision of the Secretary of State more carefully to see whether, based on the material before the executive decision-maker, she/he exercised discretion within the powers granted by Parliament. The courts are not authorised to overturn the decision of the Secretary of State when, contrary to the decision, they find that based on the material before them there has been a violation of Article 3. The decision can be overturned only when the Court comes to the conclusion that the judgment of the Secretary of State is perverse, i.e. no reasonable decision-maker would come to such judgment based on the available material. The same approach was followed in a more recent case where a similar claim was made.[178]

Indeed, the Court of Appeal decisions in cases which alleged that the decision of the Secretary of State to refuse asylum violated Article 3 of the ECHR reveal that the Court applied the same standard of judicial review as in cases concerning

174 ibid 51.
175 ibid 52.
176 ibid.
177 *Associated Provincial Picture Houses Ltd v Wednesbury Corporation* (n.80) 230.
178 *Queen (on the application of A.S) v The Secretary of State for Justice* (n.81) 51.

decisions of compassionate release.[179] In the case of *Turgut*, the Court of Appeal seemed to make a strong statement that in cases concerning Article 3 it is not constrained by the judgment of the Secretary of State on the facts of the case and the assessment of the situation in the light of Article 3.[180] However, the reasoning used by the Court to support its finding in this case demonstrates that the statements about independent assessment are not put into practice. This is made clear by the following statement of Lord Brown:[181]

> Despite the great wealth of material available to show that grave human rights abuses still regrettably occur in Turkey, and despite the lingering sense of unease which one must inevitably feel at the return of those like this applicant to Turkey, I am unable to hold that the Secretary of State was bound to find the risk of this particular applicant being ill-treated to be a real one. Clearly, there exists a conflict of opinion as to the degree of risk faced generally by returnees to Turkey. I cannot say that the Secretary of State has not conscientiously appraised the question. Whether I myself would necessarily have made the same judgment is immaterial. His judgment, I conclude, was reasonable. It is, therefore, unassailable. I would dismiss the application.

In this case the Court of Appeal carefully examined the material before it. However, as the conclusion demonstrates, the purpose of the careful examination was not to find out whether, based on the materials, the decision of the Secretary of State to deport the applicant to Turkey was a violation of Article 3, but to assess whether this was a decision which a 'reasonable' Secretary of State could make.

It is clear that when the Court of Appeal speaks about the obligation of the domestic courts to subject a decision to rigorous examination by considering underlying facts for themselves to find out 'whether or not it compels a different conclusion', it means not a different conclusion in the view of the court itself, but in the view of a reasonable decision-maker. Apart from much evidence supporting this conclusion, it is supported by the Court of Appeal assessment of the facts in *Turgut*. Moreover, this fact is supported by the conclusive statement of Lord Brown which underscores that, regardless of the view which the Court has formed based on the examination of the materials before it, if the decision is not one which no 'reasonable' decision maker could come to, the Court is not authorised to intervene.

It appears that, regardless of the adoption of HRA and recognition of proportionality as the appropriate standard for review in human rights cases, the courts

179 See e.g. *R. (Turgut) v Secretary of State for the Home Department* [2000] HRLR 337 (Court of Appeal).

180 ibid 350–351.

181 ibid 355.

still tend to use traditional judicial review tests or do not follow the test approved in *Daly*[182] correctly. Lord Sumption, speaking extrajudicially, observed:[183]

> A search on Westlaw, admittedly a rather crude measure, suggests that in the last ten years the concept [anxious scrutiny] has been deployed by judges in 598 cases. An examination of a largish sample of these decisions suggests that the great majority of them fall into two categories. Most are about immigration or asylum and turn on common law principles rather than Convention rights. In those cases where the decision was quashed, it was commonly because the decision-maker's fact finding process were found to be deficient. These cases fit comfortably within the traditional grounds of review, without the need to invoke some special standard of scrutiny. The rest are cases like A v Secretary of State for the Home Department [2005] 2 AC 68, in which a heightened level of scrutiny was simply treated as part of the court's assessment of proportionality. When the courts say, as they often do, that the intensity of review varies with the context, they are usually saying no more than that the more significant the right interfered with, the more cogent will be the justification required for the interference.

It is clear that in judicial review proceedings 'anxious scrutiny' means that the court carefully reviews the materials before it to ensure that even minor defects in the decision-making process are not overlooked, or to adopt a particularly benevolent view of a minister's evidence. As Lord Sumption usefully illustrated, 'anxious scrutiny' is no more than a slogan meaning 'we try as hard as the context warrants', which has little or no legal content.[184] Furthermore, it has been well documented by researchers that often in cases where courts state that they adopt proportionality as the standard of review, the proportionality test approved in *Daly*[185] is not followed correctly. Courts have used different approaches to short-cut proportionality analysis in order to avoid conducting a merits review which would have been the ultimate consequence of the application of proportionality test approved in *Daly*.[186]

It should be acknowledged that the case of *Turgut*[187] and the cases mentioned by Lord Sumption concern situations which are different from continued imprisonment in the light of old age and serious illness. Most of them relate to deportation decisions where applicants claimed that they faced a risk of treatment prohibited by Article 3 in the country of destination.[188] These cases involve a situation which requires a different type of assessment of the threshold of Article 3 of the ECHR. However, in both types of case, the standard of review which was

182 *R (Daly) v Secretary of State for the Home Department* (n.150).
183 Lord Sumption (n.133).
184 ibid.
185 *R. (Daly) v Secretary of State for the Home Department* (n.150).
186 Hickman (n.161) 182; Chan (n.161).
187 *R. (Turgut) v Secretary of State for the Home Department* (n.179).
188 See e.g. ibid.

adopted by the courts does not allow them to substitute their own assessment for the Secretary of State's evaluation of the situation in the light of Article 3.

The adoption of the HRA 1998 has put an obligation on the Secretary of State to regard the power of compassionate release not only as an area of the State's policy of compassion, but also to interpret and apply this power in compliance with ECHR rights, including the Article 3 right to review of the lawfulness of continued imprisonment. The Grand Chamber of the ECtHR put faith in judicial review as a remedy capable of protecting the Article 3 right to review if the Secretary of State does not act in a manner compatible with Convention rights.[189] Thus, the compatibility of compassionate release with the Article 3 right to review, among other factors, is dependent on the scope of judicial review. However, as the foregoing analysis has demonstrated, courts have stopped short of adopting a scope of review allowing for assessment of the correctness of a decision in terms of compliance with human rights. In this regard the adoption of the HRA 1998 and the development of judicial review as a remedy for the judicial protection of human rights did not change the situation much. The courts were reluctant to intervene unless it could be demonstrated that the Secretary of State's judgment that respective facts disclosed no violation of Article 3 was one that no reasonable decision-maker would make. This standard was adopted even in cases where claims of Article 3 violation were based on the ground of terminal illness of the prisoner, which is included as a ground of release in the published policy of compassionate release.[190] Therefore, in cases where compassionate release would be rejected on grounds which are not included in the published policy of the Secretary of State but require review of continued imprisonment under Article 3 of the ECHR, the scope of judicial review would preclude determination of whether or not the Secretary of State acted in compliance with Article 3. This is contrary to what was envisaged by the Grand Chamber in *Hutchinson*, when the Court concluded that the power of compassionate release in light of the HRA 1998 and in conjunction with judicial review met the requirements of Article 3 right to review.[191]

Furthermore, apart from substantive requirements Article 3 right to review of continued deprivation of liberty has also procedural requirements. The Grand Chamber on several occasions declared inadmissible the complaint that the lack of procedure to review continued imprisonment of whole life prisoners is contrary to Article 5(4).[192] However, it has been argued in this book that Article 5(4) is indeed applicable when Article 3 requires review of the lawfulness of continued imprisonment. Therefore, in order to assess whether the power of compassionate release together with judicial review would meet procedural requirements of Article 5(4) it is necessary also to assess this aggregate remedy in the light of Article 5(4) of the ECHR.

189 *Hutchinson v United Kingdom* [GC] (n.31) para.52.

190 *R.(Spinks) v Secretary of State for the Home Department* (n.70) 52.

191 *Hutchinson v United Kingdom* [GC] (n.31).

192 See e.g. *Vinter v United Kingdom* [GC] (n.7) para.132.

Assessing the power of compassionate release in conjunction with judicial review proceedings in light of Article 5(4) ECHR

As discussed earlier, in cases on reducibility of whole life sentences the ECtHR has not so far delivered a judgment assessing the compatibility of the ministerial power of compassionate release in England, or similar executive powers in other countries, with the procedural requirements of Article 5(4). Therefore, no direct analogy can be made as to whether the statutory power of compassionate release in conjunction with judicial review would comply with the procedural requirements of Article 5(4) in cases where the right to review under Article 3 arises on the ground of serious illness or likelihood of dying in detention because of advanced age or terminal illness.

On the other hand, the ECtHR has a rich jurisprudence as to compatibility of executive powers in England with Article 5(4) of the ECHR. This issue has come before the Court in numerous cases relating to prisoners serving life-sentences who could be released after serving a minimum term set at sentencing. Therefore, a conclusion on compatibility of the ministerial power of compassionate release in England, or similar executive powers in other countries, with the procedural requirements of Article 5(4) could be drawn based on the ECtHR approach in such cases. These judgments of the ECtHR have had a profound effect on the development of domestic law in this area.[193] As a result of a number of ECtHR judgments relating to the applicability of Article 5(4) to the post-tariff part of indeterminate sentences in England and Wales, such sentences moved from being wholly administered by the executive to being controlled by the Parole Board, which is recognised as an independent judicial body.[194]

The former system for the release of prisoners sentenced to life imprisonment to whom tariff periods (minimum terms) applied was first successfully challenged before the ECtHR in *Weeks v the United Kingdom*.[195] The issue under consideration in this case was *inter alia* whether procedures relating to recall to prison of lifers released on licence and reviews of continued detention thereafter met the requirements of Article 5(4).[196] Under the applicable law at the time, for this category of prisoners the decisions of the Parole Board regarding release, recall and re-release after confirming the revocation were purely advisory; the Secretary of State was not bound to follow the recommendations. Therefore, the ECtHR found that there was a violation of Article 5(4) because the Parole Board lacked 'the power of decision required by Article 5(4)'.[197]

193 Nicola Padfield, *Beyond the tariff: Human rights and the release of life sentence prisoners* (Willan 2002) 58–59.

194 *Weeks v United Kingdom* Series A no 114; *Thynne, Wilson and Gunnell v United Kingdom* App no 11787/84; 11978/86; 12009/86 (ECtHR, 25 October 1990); *Hussain v United Kingdom* App no 21928/93 (ECtHR, 21 February 1996); *Stafford v United Kingdom* [2002] 35 EHRR 32.

195 *Weeks v United Kingdom* (n.194).

196 ibid para.54.

197 ibid para.64.

Irrespective of finding a violation on this ground, the ECtHR also considered the question whether other guarantees required by Article 5(4) were secured by the available release mechanism. The Court considered this issue, because there was a single case where the Parole Board had the power to make a binding decision: immediate release of prisoners following recall by the Secretary of State.[198] In relation to this case, the Court observed that according to the law the Parole Board makes decisions in cases referred to it on the basis of information supplied by the Secretary of State, representations made by the prisoner, any other reports it has requested, and any other information oral or written that it has obtained, including information obtained through interviewing the prisoner.[199]

Furthermore, the prisoner must be sufficiently informed about the reasons for the recall in order to enable her/him to challenge the recall and take legal advice in relation to making submissions challenging the recall. However, the ECtHR stressed that the Court of Appeal held that the common law principle of fairness in these cases does not oblige the Parole Board to fully disclose the adverse materials which it has in its possession. Therefore the ECtHR found that the procedure did not allow 'proper participation of the individual adversely affected by the contested decision' which is one of the 'principle guarantees' of the judicial procedure in the meaning of the Convention. According to the Court, this procedure cannot be regarded as having a 'judicial character'.[200]

Although the ECtHR concluded that the Parole Board's procedure, as such, did not meet the requirements of Article 5(4),[201] it went on to consider whether the procedural defects of the Parole Board review might be set right by safeguards offered by judicial review. In line with English administrative law, a prisoner could challenge the decisions of both the Parole Board and the Secretary of State before the High Court.[202] The ECtHR, relying on domestic case law, concluded that under judicial review the decision could be reviewed only on the ground of 'illegality', 'irrationality' or 'procedural impropriety'. It could be quashed only on the following grounds: if the law in the particular case was incorrectly applied; if it was so irrational that no rational decision-maker would have arrived at it; or if it was made through a process which failed to respect either the procedural rules expressly laid down in an appropriate instrument or rules of natural justice. The Court concluded that the scope of the judicial review would not allow for consideration as to whether in the case of the applicant 'it [detention] was consistent with and therefore justified by the objectives of the indeterminate sentence'. [203] The ECtHR found that Article 5(4) was violated in this case because:[204]

198 ibid.
199 ibid paras 26, 29.
200 ibid para.66.
201 ibid para.68.
202 ibid para.69.
203 ibid.
204 ibid.

> having regard to the nature of the control it allows, the remedy of judicial review can neither itself provide the proceedings required by Article 5 para. 4 (art. 5-4) nor serve to remedy the inadequacy, for the purposes of that provision, of the procedure before the Parole Board.

It can be observed that the finding of a violation of Article 5(4) was based on the lack of binding decision-making power on the part of the Parole Board and the deficiencies of its procedure. The ECtHR pointed in particular to the lack of one of the principle attributes of the judicial character of the procedure, the obligation for full disclosure of the materials before the Parole Board. Although it stated that in principle the apparent shortcomings of one procedure may be remedied by safeguards available in other procedures within the domestic legal system, in this particular case it found that this deficiency cannot be remedied by the judicial review procedure. In this case the Court did not consider whether Article 5(4) required an oral hearing in this category of cases or whether the 'proceedings before the Board were speedy'.[205]

In the judgments following *Weeks*, the ECtHR extended application of Article 5(4) first to initial release of discretionary life prisoners after expiry of the tariff period,[206] and subsequently to mandatory life sentences imposed on juveniles[207] and adults[208] convicted of murder. In *Thynne, Gunnar and Wilson*,[209] a case concerning initial release of discretionary life prisoners, the ECtHR – without mentioning which specific attributes of the procedural requirements of Article 5(4) the Parole Board's procedure did not meet – simply confirmed its judgment in *Weeks*,[210] finding a violation of Article 5(4).

The ECtHR also found a violation of Article 5(4) in cases of *Singh*[211] and *Hussain*[212] which concerned the issue of release from mandatory life sentences imposed on juveniles. It should be noted that since the ECtHR's decision in the case of *Weeks*, legislative changes were made allowing full disclosure of materials before the Parole Board. However, the ECtHR found that the procedural requirements of Article 5(4) were still not met, because the lack of adversarial procedure – an oral hearing involving legal representation and the possibility to call and question witnesses – prevented the Parole Board from being regarded as a court-like body within the meaning of Article 5(4). According to the Court, this is required by Article 5(4) in cases 'where a substantial term of imprisonment may be at stake and where characteristics pertaining to [the

205 ibid para.67.
206 *Thynne, Wilson and Gunnell v United Kingdom* (n.194).
207 *Singh v United Kingdom* App no 23389/94 (ECtHR, 21 February 1996); *Hussain v United Kingdom* (n.194).
208 *Stafford v United Kingdom* (n.194).
209 *Thynne, Wilson and Gunnell v United Kingdom* (n.194).
210 *Weeks v United Kingdom* (n.194).
211 *Singh v United Kingdom* (n.207).
212 *Hussain v United Kingdom* (n.194).

prisoner's] personality and level of maturity are of importance in deciding on his dangerousness'.[213]

More importantly, in contrast to its findings in *Weeks* that in principle the requirements of Article 5(4) can be met by aggregate remedies,[214] in both *Singh* and *Hussain* the Court changed its position, stating that this was no longer the case. According to the ECtHR, Article 5(4) presupposes the existence of a review which meets its requirements 'without the necessity of instituting separate legal proceedings in order to bring it about'. Furthermore, it reaffirmed that even were it possible to meet the requirements of Article 5(4) through separate legal procedures, the remedy of judicial review as it exists in English administrative law could not meet the requirements of Article 5(4) given the nature and the safeguards offered by this remedy.[215]

The ECtHR confirmed its approach, rejecting the possibility of complying with the requirements of Article 5(4) through the provision of more than one separate remedy in the case of *Benjamin and Wilson v United Kingdom*.[216] Despite the fact that by the time of this decision the HRA 1998 had already entered into force, affecting the intensity and the scope of judicial review,[217] the ECtHR stated that:[218]

> In this case, the power to order release lay with the Secretary of State, even though he may have been under some constraints of administrative law as regarded the situations in which he could or could not depart from a policy that had created legitimate expectations. The ability of an applicant to challenge a refusal by the Secretary of State to follow his previous policy in the courts would not remedy the lack of power of decision in the Tribunal. Article 5 § 4 presupposes the existence of a procedure in conformity with its provisions without the necessity to institute separate legal proceedings in order to bring it about. Similarly, although both parties appear to agree that the Secretary of State, following entry into force of the Human Rights Act 1998, would not be able lawfully to depart from the Tribunal's recommendation, this does not alter the fact that the decision to release would be taken by a member of the executive and not by the Tribunal. This is not a matter of form but impinges on the fundamental principle of separation of powers and detracts from a necessary guarantee against the possibility of abuse.

As the foregoing analysis has demonstrated, the former system of discretionary release of lifers after they have served the tariff part of their sentence failed to meet the procedural requirements of Article 5(4) for the following reasons.

213 *Singh v United Kingdom* (n.207) para.68; *Hussain v United Kingdom* (n 194) para.60.
214 *Weeks v United Kingdom* (n.194) para.69.
215 *Singh v United Kingdom* (n.207) para.69; *Hussain v United Kingdom* (n.194) para.61.
216 *Benjamin and Wilson v United Kingdom* App no 28212/95 (ECtHR, 26 September 2002).
217 *R (Daly) v Secretary of State for the Home Department* (n.150) 547.
218 *Benjamin and Wilson v .United Kingdom* (n.216) para.36.

First, the procedure before the Parole Board did not allow full disclosure of documents based on which the Parole Board made its advisory decisions, and therefore the procedure failed to be judicial in character. Second, the procedure was not adversarial because it did not provide for an oral hearing, including the possibility to call and examine witnesses, which was essential in cases where the determination of the lawfulness of further detention depended on characteristics pertaining to the personality and level of maturity of the prisoner. Third, despite the Secretary of State's obligation under the HRA 1998 to act in compliance with the Convention rights by releasing a prisoner whose continued imprisonment is unlawful, such procedure violates the fundamental principle of separation of powers, detracting 'from a necessary guarantee against the possibility of abuse'.[219] And finally, the requirements shall be met by a review which does not require initiation of an additional procedure to set right the deficiencies of the first review. Even if it were accepted that the requirements of Article 5(4) could be met through aggregate remedies, the judicial review procedure in English law is not capable of remedying the deficiencies of the procedure of review conducted by the Secretary of State.

Conclusion

The question remains whether the Secretary of State's power of compassionate release will meet the requirements of Article 5(4). As demonstrated earlier, the procedure of compassionate release does not allow for any possibility of an oral hearing or independent assessment of factors which are of utmost importance for deciding whether continued imprisonment is compatible with Article 3. Moreover, in judicial review procedure domestic courts could not even oblige the Secretary of State to order an independent assessment of risk before deciding whether or not to release a prisoner. It is true that section 36 of Criminal Justice Act 1991 and section 30 of the Crime (Sentence) Act 1997 require the Secretary of State to consult the Parole Board unless the circumstances render such consultation impractical.[220] However, the Court of Appeal has interpreted this procedure in such a way as to put no obligation on the Secretary of State to consult the Parole Board if he decides that no exceptional circumstances for compassionate release exist.[221]

More importantly, the power of compassionate release, even interpreted in the light of the HRA 1998, does not meet the procedural requirements of Article 5(4) because the decision rests with a member of the executive, abusing the fundamental principle of separation of powers which derives 'from a necessary guarantee against the possibility of abuse'.[222] Furthermore, as demonstrated, the remedy of judicial review could not put right the failings of the power of compas-

219 ibid.

220 Criminal Justice Act (n.37); Crime (Sentences) Act (n.40).

221 *R.(Spinks) v Secretary of State for the Home Department* (n.70) paras 28, 50, 51.

222 *Benjamin and Wilson v United Kingdom* (n.216) para.36.

sionate release in terms of meeting the requirements of Article 5(4). However, even if this had been possible in theory, the ECtHR has explicitly stated that the requirements of Article 5(4) could not be met through aggregate remedies, because these requirements should be met without the need to initiate additional legal proceedings in order to set right the deficiencies of the initial remedy.[223]

223 *Singh v United Kingdom* (n.207) para.69; *Hussain v United Kingdom* (n.194) para.61; *Benjamin and Wilson v United Kingdom* (n.216) para.36.

Conclusion

Abstract
The number of prisoners aged 50 and over has risen and will continue to rise in many countries. Among elderly prisoners there are many who are seriously or terminally ill. Moreover, there are prisoners whose mandatory custodial term is longer than their actuarial life expectancy, meaning that they will not be released or considered for release within their actuarial life expectancy. Prisons are poorly equipped to deal with the problems of the rising population of elderly prisoners. Moreover, they are not the places to treat the seriously ill or to provide comfort for the dying; continued detention of these prisoners comes at enormous human and financial cost. Imprisonment after conviction by a court of law is a lawful deprivation of the right to liberty. However, in order to remain lawful, imprisonment should not undermine human dignity. This chapter draws together the core arguments of the book in order to emphasise that respect for a human being sufficiently affected by a decision, and the respect for the rule of law, require giving a fair chance to seriously ill and dying prisoners to regain their freedom by demonstrating that they have atoned for their crimes and can be safely released from prison.

This book aims to demonstrate that the number of prisoners aged 50 and over has risen and will continue to rise in many countries. These prisoners are a diverse group in terms of types of crime committed and the types of prison sentence they are serving. There are both prisoners who have grown old in prisons owing to serving long terms, life or indeterminate sentences, and those who are sent to prison in old age. Among elderly prisoners there are fixed-term and indeterminate prisoners whose mandatory custodial term is longer than their actuarial life expectancy.

Moreover, elderly prisoners are also diverse in terms of their capabilities and needs. There are many prisoners in this age group who are relatively healthy and active and are coping well even in the harsh environment of prison. However, there are also those who are seriously or terminally ill, requiring intensive medical treatment and social care. Given the fact that chronic diseases are progressive, many elderly prisoners experience increasing levels of functional impairment and a number of older inmates with chronic diseases reach a terminal stage and die in prison. With the rise of the elderly prison population, the number of natural deaths in prisons has been also rising. Even those elderly prisoners who are healthy and active will experience decline and most probably will die in prison if the mandatory custodial part of their sentences runs longer than their natural life.

Prisons are poorly equipped to deal with the problems this brings. However, even if they were able to meet the needs of elderly prisoners, prisons are not the places to treat the seriously ill or to provide comfort for dying; continued imprisonment of these prisoners comes at enormous human and financial cost. Many elderly prisoners have been sentenced for their crimes to fixed prison terms, meaning that based on the circumstances of the case it was appropriate to deprive them of their liberty only for a fixed term rather than for life or indeterminately. However, given their advanced age, a fixed term could become a *de facto* natural life sentence for them. There are also indeterminate prisoners, including all types of lifers whose sentence review point is beyond their natural life expectancy. On the other hand, there are also terminally ill prisoners with short-term life expectancies and those who are experiencing increasing levels of functional impairment and requiring extensive medical and social care.

Imprisonment after conviction by a court of law is a lawful deprivation of the right to liberty. However, in order to remain lawful, imprisonment should not undermine human dignity. The review of human rights limits on imprisonment demonstrates that among the reviewed tribunals the ECtHR has the most progressive jurisprudence on the matter. Therefore, this book takes as the point of departure and reference the jurisprudence of the ECtHR in order to articulate the right to review of continued imprisonment of seriously ill prisoners and those who are serving sentences with custodial terms running longer than their actuarial or clinical life expectancy.

The ECtHR has already recognised that protection of human dignity may in exceptional cases require release of seriously ill prisoners, if their health is absolutely incompatible with detention. However, in order to determine whether a prisoner's health is absolutely incompatible with detention, there is a need for a review of the situation, involving medical and other experts. The review process should exclude arbitrariness and ensure fairness, in order to avoid a sense of injustice, to demonstrate respect for the human being significantly affected by the decision and to uphold the rule of law. Although the situation when the health of the prisoner is absolutely incompatible with imprisonment comes within the scope of Article 3 ECHR, the process of determination of the issue is left outside of the scope of the Convention. This leaves many elderly and seriously ill prisoners with a sense of injustice.

Moreover, in relation to prisoners whose mandatory custodial term is longer than their actuarial life expectancy, the ECtHR has remained very vague. In the most general terms it has stated that imprisonment of elderly persons over a lengthy time in certain circumstances may raise an issue under Article 3. A prisoner who is not deprived of liberty for his natural life by a court, but is not given a chance to regain her/his right to liberty and is left to die in prison appears to suffer injustice by being punished more than was considered an appropriate punishment by a competent court at the time of sentencing.

In a whole life imprisonment case the ECtHR stated that 'all prisoners, including those serving life sentences, should be offered the possibility of rehabilitation and the prospect of release if that rehabilitation is achieved'.[1] The rationale of this requirement is the human being's capacity for change, which means that even those who committed the worst crimes can be rehabilitated. Therefore, even if the legitimate aims of punishment justify the imposition of a whole life sentence, after a passage of years the balance between these aims may change, making imprisonment unjustified. It follows that Article 3 requires a mechanism for review of continued imprisonment of lifers at some point of their sentences in order to see whether their continued imprisonment is still justified. The release of a whole lifer will be required if the aims of punishment do not justify continued imprisonment.

The protection offered to lifers has a broader scope than that available to prisoners whose health is absolutely incompatible with continued detention. If in the latter situation Article 3 comes into effect requiring release of the prisoner when further detention is incompatible with health, the former is set up to prevent a violation requiring review to determine whether or not continued imprisonment is still justified. If the review mechanism must be available to whole lifers, it must also be available to terminally and seriously ill prisoners and those whose mandatory custodial part of the sentence is more than their actuarial life expectancy: it will be unjust to offer parole to those convicted of the most serious crimes and deny it to others. Moreover, the rationale of the requirement of review is also applicable to these prisoners.

In the case of prisoners who have been sentenced to whole life imprisonment, Article 3 requires a possibility of review and a prospect of release, because irrespective of the seriousness of the crime committed human beings are capable of change. This means that even if at the time of sentencing the aims of punishment and deterrence justify imprisoning an offender for the rest of her/his life, respect for human beings requires that she/he be given the hope of regaining her/his freedom by rehabilitation. Depriving human beings of this hope is to deny a fundamental aspect of their humanity and is degrading.

It follows that the aims of punishment that justified its imposition would not necessarily remain static; after a passage of time the balance between the aims of punishment may shift, so that there is a possibility that the continued imprisonment may no longer be justified. To continue depriving a person of liberty without legitimate aims would be grossly disproportionate and unlawful. Therefore, a review is required in order not to deprive a human being of hope and to prevent grossly disproportionate punishment. The Court believed that if as a result of rehabilitation the offender no longer posed a danger to the public, she/he should not be denied the possibility of regaining her/his freedom. In summary, it is the change in the circumstances of the offender since the imposition of the life imprisonment, namely her/his rehabilitation, which may at some

1 *Vinter and others v United Kingdom* [GC] ECHR 2013-III 317 para.114.

point during the administration of the sentence make continuation of a lawfully imposed prison sentence unlawful.

The situation of elderly and seriously ill prisoners who serve other than whole life sentences is different from that of whole lifers. The hopelessness as it exists in whole life sentences is absent even in cases where a mandatory custodial term of a fixed or indeterminate sentence is longer than actuarial or clinical life expectancy. Moreover, it is not applicable to the situation of seriously ill prisoners. However, there are similarities in these cases which make the underlying rationale of the requirement of review of continued imprisonment applicable in the cases of elderly and seriously ill prisoners. As with whole life sentences, in the cases of those elderly prisoners who are likely to die in prison or are seriously ill, a possible shift of balance between the aims of punishment may occur earlier than presumed, making the continued punishment disproportionately more severe. Elderly and seriously ill prisoners may cease to pose a danger to society because of the age and serious illness. Moreover, these prisoners may not have to serve the term required to achieve the aims of punishment and deterrence. The impact of old age and serious medical conditions on the severity of prison sentences may compensate for the length of time necessary to achieve the aims of punishment and deterrence. The impact of these characteristics is taken into account in law and practice in many jurisdictions.

Review of a whole life sentence is required to ensure that the deprivation of liberty has not become an affront to human dignity. It is due to the fundamental nature of human dignity that the review is required by Article 3. Similarly, in the cases of seriously ill prisoners and those who are likely to die in prison because of age or illness, owing to the change of circumstances the imprisonment may become grossly more severe than was considered to be appropriate at the time of its imposition. It would fly in the face of justice if a review which pursued the same aim and was based on the same rationale in the cases of whole life sentences were to be protected by Article 3 and all other cases were left outside its scope.

Despite some differences in terms of time and the substance of the review of lawfulness of continued imprisonment among cases of whole life prisoners, prisoners whose custodial terms are longer than their actuarial or clinical life expectancy and seriously ill prisoners, the value which the review aims to protect is the same in all these cases. Therefore, there should be no difference in terms of safeguards against arbitrariness of the process and the decision.

In this regard, the ECtHR rejected the view that guarantees against arbitrariness in the review of life imprisonment prescribed by Article 5(4) are applicable to the review of whole life imprisonment. The court articulated some guarantees which should be applicable to this type of review. However, review of the case law demonstrates that these guarantees offer less protection against arbitrariness than those provided under Article 5(4).

The analysis demonstrates that the reasons for rejecting the applicability of Article 5(4) cannot hold ground. Review of continued imprisonment required by Article 3 aims to determine whether the purposes which justified imposition of a particular term of imprisonment continues to justify it in view of the change of circumstances of the prisoner. The release of the prisoner must be ordered if these purposes no longer justify continued imprisonment, because detention which is not justified by legitimate aims is arbitrary. Thus, review aims to prevent unlawful deprivation of liberty. Although in essence arbitrary deprivation of liberty is a violation of the right to liberty, an aggravated violation of the right to liberty may raise an issue under Article 3. Therefore, contrary to the finding of the ECtHR, in the review required by Article 3, fundamental guarantees against arbitrariness prescribed by Article 5(4) should apply.

Furthermore, a detailed review of the law and practice of English compassionate release, a type of procedure which according to the ECtHR is able to meet the requirements articulated specifically for the review required by Article 3, demonstrated that this is not the case. The ECtHR put great weight on availability of judicial review in accepting the compatibility of executive mechanisms such as English compassionate release with the review required by Article 3. The Court assumed that judicial review can conduct independent assessment of facts and correct the decision of an executive, if the independent assessment of facts demonstrates that continued imprisonment is no longer justified by legitimate purposes of punishment. Contrary to this theoretical possibility, the English judicial review procedure does not allow independent assessment of factors which are of utmost importance for deciding whether continued imprisonment is compatible with Article 3. The courts cannot correct the decision of the executive based on their own assessment of facts.

More importantly, executive powers such as compassionate release, even if they are susceptible to judicial review, would not meet the procedural requirements of Article 5(4) because the decision rests with a member of the executive, abusing the fundamental principle of the separation of powers. This defect cannot be put right by availability of judicial review, because the requirements of Article 5(4) should be met without the need to initiate additional legal proceedings.

To meet both the substantive and procedural requirements of review of continued imprisonment on the ground of old age/likelihood of dying and serious physical illness will require major legislative amendments in Council of Europe jurisdictions which, like England and Wales, rely on loose executive powers in order to fulfil their ECHR obligations in this regard. In England and Wales in particular, it will require the introduction of new legislation. Without any reservations such legislation should prescribe a requirement of review of the continued imprisonment of prisoners who have not yet achieved their automatic or discretionary release dates (if any), on the ground of the likelihood of dying in prison, because of fatal illness or as a result of the normal aging process, and on the ground of a serious illness.

Furthermore, the legislation should ascribe the review of continued imprisonment in such cases to an independent judicial body with powers meeting the requirements of Article 5(4) of the ECHR. In England and Wales the only body involved in administration of sentences that in general meets the procedural requirements of Article 5(4) is the Parole Board. However, notwithstanding decades of reforms to ensure that the Parole Board meets the requirements of

Article 5(4),[2] concerns over its independence have not yet been resolved.[3] There have been calls for the Parole Board to be replaced by fully independent specialised tribunals with full powers over decisions on discretionary release, prisoner transfers to open conditions and the recall of conditionally released prisoners.[4] Therefore, the part of the reforms, specifically those required to meet the procedural guarantees of the review of continued imprisonment on the ground of old age/likelihood of dying in prison and serious illness, should be seen in the context of wider reforms in this area.

Such a proposal is also supported by the example of other countries. As stated earlier, in the ECtHR cases dealing with claims that the continued imprisonment of persons with serious medical conditions violates Article 3 of the ECHR, the issue of the effectiveness of national remedies has not been raised. However, most of these cases demonstrate that there was a judicial mechanism in place to review the appropriateness of the further imprisonment in the light of the serious medical conditions of prisoners who have not yet reached their discretionary or automatic release date. For instance, in the case of *Mouisel v France*, the ECtHR noted the various remedies in French law which afford the authorities means of dealing with seriously ill prisoners. In particular, the ECtHR pointed out that new legislative developments allow judges responsible for the execution of sentences to take into account the health condition of the prisoner in parole decisions, particularly when the prisoner needs 'to undergo treatment'.[5] Moreover, under the French Law No 2002–303 of 4 March 2002 on patient rights, prisoners are able to apply for release if they suffer from a life-threatening illness or 'if their condition is incompatible in the long term with their continued detention'.[6]

According to the ECtHR, these judicial remedies 'may provide sufficient guarantees to ensure the protection of prisoners' health and wellbeing, which States must reconcile with the legitimate requirements of a custodial sentence'.[7] The Court emphasised that these judicial remedies were not available to the applicant during the period of detention considered by the Court. The only remedy available to the applicant at the time was a presidential pardon on medical grounds. Such pardons are granted by the President alone and on a highly discretionary

2 Nicola Padfield, 'England and Wales' in Nicola Padfield (ed.), *Release from prison: European policy and practice* (Willan 2010); Nicola Padfield, 'The Parole Board in transition' [2006] *Criminal Law Review* 3; Nicola Padfield, 'Parole and early release: the Criminal Justice and Immigration Act 2008 changes in context' (2009) 3 *Criminal Law Review* 166 accessed 17 March 2016.

3 See e.g. *R (Brooke and another) v Parole Board* [2008] EWCA Civ 29; Simon Creighton, 'The Parole Board as a court' in Nicola Padfield (ed), *Who to release?: Parole, fairness and criminal justice* (Willan 2007).

4 Justice, 'A New Parole System for England and Wales' (London 2009) available at https://justice.org.uk/new-parole-system-england-wales/, accessed 23 November 2017; Nicola Padfield, Rod Morgan and Mike Maguire, 'Out of Court, Out of Site? Criminal Sanctions and Non-Judicial Decision Making' in Mike Maguire, Rod Morgan and Reiner Robert (eds), *Oxford Handbook of Criminology* (5th edn, Open University Press 2012).

5 *Mouisel v France* ECHR 2002-IX 219 para.43.

6 ibid.

7 ibid para.44.

basis. In this case, the appeal for a presidential pardon had been rejected without reasons being specified.[8]

Similarly, judicial mechanisms for suspension of a prison sentence or the possibility of replacing it with house arrest, based on the incompatibility of the health conditions of the prisoner with continued detention, were available in jurisdictions such as Italy and Latvia.[9] Indeed, as many cases demonstrate, some prisoners made good use of these remedies and were eventually released, because domestic courts for the execution of sentences found that continued detention was incompatible with the health condition of the prisoner.[10] As some of the ECtHR cases on the subject demonstrate,[11] the availability of judicial remedies allowing for an order of stay of imprisonment or release of prisoners whose health conditions are incompatible with further detention do not always guarantee the correct human rights adjudication. However, they provide strong checks on the obligation of the State to ensure that the legitimate deprivation of liberty of seriously ill prisoners does not turn into degrading/inhuman punishment in violation of Article 3 of the ECHR.

Even if the major legislative reforms mentioned above were to be carried out, establishing a right to review of continued imprisonment on the grounds of old age and serious illness, it could not be guaranteed that a significant number of very old prisoners and those who are seriously ill would be released as a result of a review. Although the decision-making body would be independent of the executive, the decision to release would be discretionary. This appears to cast a shadow over the practical impact of such a right on the fate of those who die in prison or, as a result of serious illness, suffer greater deprivations than was intended by the prison sentence imposed. However, as the UK Supreme Court in the case of *Osborn*[12] stated, there are at least two major reasons (which are also relevant for the situations under discussion in this book) which demonstrate why the fairness of the process matters irrespective of the outcome achieved. First is respect for the human being significantly affected by the decision, and the avoidance of a sense of injustice. Second is respect for the rule of law which requires that a fair procedure be employed for determining the lawfulness of continued imprisonment, irrespective of whether or not such a process results in the release of prisoners.

8 ibid.

9 See e.g. *Farbtuhs v Latvia* no. 4672/02 (ECtHR, 2 December 2004) paras 31–33; *Scoppola v Italy* no. 50550/06 (ECtHR, 10 June 2008); *Enea v Italy* [GC] ECHR 2009-IV 163; *Cara-Damiani v Italy* no 2447/05 (ECtHR, 7 February 2012); *Contrada v Italy (no.2)* 7509/08 (ECtHR, 11 February 2014).

10 See e.g. *Enea v Italy* [GC] ECHR 2009-IV 163 para.62; *Cara-Damiani v Italy* (n.9) para.44.

11 *Contrada v Italy (no.2)* (n.9) paras 80–85; *Farbtuhs v Latvia* (n.9) paras 22–27; *Scoppola v Italy* (n.9) paras 47–51

12 *Osborn v Parole Board* [2014] AC 1115.

Index

D

E

F

G